iOS 11
by Tutorials

By the raywenderlich.com Tutorial Team

Jeff Rames, Andy Pereira, Michael Katz, Richard Critz
Jawwad Ahmad, Michael Ciurus, Mic Pringle & Jerry Beers

iOS 11 by Tutorials

Jeff Rames, Andy Pereira, Michael Katz, Richard Critz, Jawwad Ahmad, Michael Ciurus, Mic Pringle & Jerry Beers

ISBN: 978-1-942878-38-4

About the authors

Jawwad Ahmad is a freelance iOS Developer that dove into Swift head first and has not looked back. He enjoys mentoring and teaching and was the original founder of the NYC iOS Study Group Meetup and later on the Atlanta iOS Study Group Meetup. He's worked for companies as large as The New York Times, and as small as GateGuru, a 6 person startup.

Jerry Beers is a co-founder of Five Pack Creative, a mobile development company specializing in iOS development. He's worked on client projects, like American Airlines and Match.com, but lately he's been pouring his focus into Hours, a time tracking app. He is passionate about creating well-crafted code and teaching others. In partnership with Ray Wenderlich, he recently launched Alt-U, a live remote and in-person iOS training program. Jerry enjoys spending time on the beach with his wife and kids, SCUBA diving, and watching movies.

Michael Ciurus is an iOS developer at Jodel. He likes to blog about his Swift adventures. His love of computer games has led to him to look what's under the hood. He started with C++ at a young age and his first game was a memory leak simulator. He's also addicted to discovering new technologies and learning iOS software architecture.

Richard Critz is on career number three as a professional photographer (after first being a software engineer doing mainframe O/S development for 20+ years and then a stint as a corporate pilot) doing contract iOS development on the side. Some would say he just can't make up his mind. Actually, he just likes diversity! When he's not working on either of those, he's probably playing League of Legends (with or without the rest of his family). On Twitter, while being mainly read-only, he can be found at @rcritz. The rest of his professional life can be found at www.rwcfoto.com.

Michael Katz envisions a world where mobile apps always work, respect users' privacy, and integrate well with their users' life. When not coding, he can be found with his family playing board games, brewing, gardening, and watching the Yankees. Say hi to Michael on Twitter: @TheMikeKatz.

Andy Pereira is a senior iOS developer with Delta Air Lines. When he's not coding, he's spending time traveling the world with his wife, and playing guitar.

Mic Pringle is an iOS developer by trade, but he's recently found himself dabbling in Ruby, PHP, and JavaScript. An F1 nut at heart, Mic enjoys spending time with his wife Lucy and their daughter Evie, watching his beloved Fulham F.C. and, weather permitting, tearing up the English countryside on his motorbike.

Jeff Rames is an enterprise iOS developer in San Antonio, TX. When not working, he's spending time with his wife and daughters, watching rocket launches, or cooking wood fired pizza. Say hi to Jeff on Twitter: @jefframes .

About the editors

Soheil Azarpour (Technical Editor): Soheil is an engineer, developer, author, creator, husband and father. He enjoys bicycling, boating and playing the piano. He lives in Merrimack, NH, and creates iOS apps both professionally and independently.

Chris Belanger (Editor): Chris is the Book Team Lead and Lead Editor for raywenderlich.com. He was a developer for nearly 20 years in various fields from e-health to aerial surveillance to industrial controls. If there are words to wrangle or a paragraph to ponder, he's on the case. When he kicks back, you can usually find Chris with guitar in hand, looking for the nearest beach. Twitter: @crispytwit

Antonio Bello (Technical Editor): After 5 years spent writing Objective C and Swift, Antonio is still in love with iOS development. Before that, he was used to do a bit of everything. Tomorrow he sees himself still freelancing and writing Swift code. Say hi to Antonio on Twitter: @ant_bello

Tammy Coron (Technical Editor): Tammy is an independent creative professional and the host of Roundabout: Creative Chaos. She's also the co-founder of Day Of The Indie and the founder of Just Write Code. For more information visit TammyCoron.com.

Richard Critz (Final Pass Editor): Richard is on career number three as a professional photographer (after first being a software engineer doing mainframe O/S development for 20+ years and then a stint as a corporate pilot) doing contract iOS development on the side. Some would say he just can't make up his mind. Actually, he just likes diversity! When he's not working on either of those, he's probably playing League of Legends (with or without the rest of his family). On Twitter, while being mainly read-only, he can be found @rcritz. The rest of his professional life can be found at www.rwcfoto.com.

Morten Faarkrog (Technical Editor): Morten is a twenty-something Software Development student and iOS developer from Copenhagen, Denmark. He was first introduced to iOS development around the launch of Swift and has been in love with it ever since. He strives to learn something new about iOS development every single day and he has at least one side project running at all times. When Morten isn't developing apps and studying, and his adorable cat isn't riding on his shoulders, he spends his time working out, reading interesting books, and diving into the world of biohacking. You can find Morten on Facebook, LinkedIn and Twitter: @mfaarkrog.

Kyle Gorlick (Technical Editor): Kyle creates mobile apps and games. He likes to play volleyball and watch basketball. More info at kylegorlick.com.

Felipe Laso (Technical Editor): Felipe Laso is a Senior Systems Engineer working at Lextech Global Services. He likes sports, video games, cooking, and music. You can follow him on Twitter as @iFeliLM, or on his blog at iFeli.me

Lea Marolt Sonnenschein (Technical Editor): Lea is an iOS developer turned Product Manager at Rent the Runway. She loves running experiments and evaluating hypothesis (in the office and in life), and will eagerly engage in any UX-related discussion. In her free time, she enjoys playing with Arduinos and making LEDs blink. Say hi to Lea on Twitter: @hellosunschein

Adrian Strahan (Technical Editor): Adrian is a freelance iOS developer, Product Owner and Scrum Master. He's worked with iOS since 2010 and specializes in mobile- and web-based application development. He lives in the South West of England and spends what little spare time he has building with Lego.

Table of Contents:

Introduction

Each year at WWDC, Apple introduces brand new tools and APIs for iOS developers. WWDC 2017 was no different, as iOS 11 and Xcode 9 introduced a pile of amazing new technologies and features for developers of all backgrounds!

The most exciting feature in iOS 11 by far is ARKit, which opens up the world of augmented reality to iPhone developers everywhere. Sure, it was possible to do some basic AR on the iPhone before iOS 11, but ARKit does the heavy lifting of plane detection and camera placement for you, so you can focus on building amazing experiences instead. ARKit makes it easier than ever to create incredibly immersive experiences, including portals to virtual worlds, 3D games and art, and compelling ecommerce apps. What new worlds will you create with ARKit?

The new Vision and Core ML frameworks bring the power of machine learning models into your apps. Whether you're building a sentiment analysis app, creating advanced face and scene detection algorithms, or just trying to figure out whether something is a hot dog or not, Core ML makes it easy to plug pre-trained machine learning models into your app, and Vision provides a host of advanced detection technologies for text, images, faces, and more.

Xcode 9 sports a completely rewritten editor, helpers for code refactoring, improved responsiveness, support for Markdown, and (finally!) wireless debugging. Add in the other new features in iOS 11, such as the new drag-and-drop, PDFKit, MusicKit, Swift 4 updates and more, and you have one of the most exciting iOS releases to date.

Gone are the days when every third-party developer knew everything there is to know about iOS. The sheer size of iOS can make new releases seem daunting. That's why the Tutorial Team has been working really hard to extract the important parts of the new APIs, and to present this information in an easy-to-understand tutorial format. This means you can focus on what you want to be doing — building amazing apps!

Get ready for your own private tour through the amazing new features of iOS 11. By the time you're done, your iOS knowledge will be completely up-to-date and you'll be able to benefit from the amazing new opportunities in iOS 11.

What you need

To follow along with the tutorials in this book, you'll need the following:

- **A Mac running macOS Sierra or later.** You'll need this to be able to install the latest version of Xcode.

- **Xcode 9.0 or later.** Xcode is the main development tool for iOS. You'll need Xcode 9.0 or later for all tasks in this book. You can download the latest version of Xcode 9 from Apple's developer site here: apple.co/2asi58y

- **One or more devices (iPhone, iPad) running iOS 11 or later.** Most of the chapters in the book let you run your code on the iOS 11 Simulator that comes with Xcode. However, a few chapters later in the book require one or more physical iOS devices for testing. For ARKit chapters, you'll need a device with an A9 processor or better.

Once you have these items in place, you'll be able to follow along with every chapter in this book.

Who this book is for

This book is for intermediate or advanced iOS developers who already know the basics of iOS and Swift development but want to learn about the new APIs, frameworks, and changes in Xcode 9 and iOS 11.

- **If you are a complete beginner to iOS development**, we recommend you read through *The iOS Apprentice, Fifth Edition* first. Otherwise this book may be a bit too advanced for you.

- **If you are a beginner to Swift**, we recommend you read through either *The iOS Apprentice, Fifth Edition* (if you are a complete beginner to programming), or *The Swift Apprentice, Second Edition* (if you already have some programming experience) first.

If you need one of these prerequisite books, you can find them on our store here:

- store.raywenderlich.com

As with raywenderlich.com, all the tutorials in this book are in Swift.

What's in store

Here's a quick summary of what you'll find in each chapter:

Chapter 1, What's New in Swift 4: Swift 4 shows a maturing of the Swift language, and brings new functionality to Strings, improvements to Dictionaries and Sets, the new Codable protocol, multi-line string literals, one-sided ranges and more. Read this chapter for a quick overview of what's new!

Chapter 2, What's New in Foundation: Learn about all the best updates under the hood, including updates to keypath, KVO, encoding and decoding, and more.

Chapter 3, What's New in Xcode 9: From editor improvements, to Markdown support, to refactoring, to wireless debugging, Xcode 9 makes your life as a developer easier than ever before. Learn what's new and improved in the latest release of Apple's IDE.

Chapter 4, What's New in UIKit: This chapter covers the best new UI features of iOS 11, such as Drag and Drop, the Document Browser, table view changes, and changes to Auto Layout.

Chapter 5, What's New in Layout: Expanding upon the previous chapter, you'll explore the way Auto Layout works in iOS 11, including changes to navigation controllers, large titles, safe areas, table views, stack views, and more.

Chapter 6, Beginning Drag and Drop: Take advantage of the new drag-and-drop features to select one or more files from within your application, drag them around, and drop them on target locations within your app.

Chapter 7, Advanced Drag and Drop: Building on the previous chapter, you'll explore how to drag and drop files between different applications, how NSItemProvider and UIDragItem work, and how to animate your drag-and-drop in intelligent, meaningful ways.

Chapter 8, Document-Based Apps: Learn how the Document Provider works, how it stands apart from the Document Picker, how to create new files, import existing files, and even add custom actions.

Chapter 9, Core ML & Vision: Get started with the exciting Core ML and Vision frameworks as you build a face-detection and text-recognition app, complete with filters and object classification.

Chapter 10, Natural Language Processing: Learn how to detect the language of a body of text, how to work with named entities, how sentiment analysis works, how to perform searches with NSLinguisticTagger, and more!

Chapter 11, ARKit: Build your own augmented reality app as you learn how to set up ARKit, detect feature points and draw planes, how to create and locate 3D models in your scene, handle low lighting conditions and manage session interruptions. With all the amazing things happening in AR lately, you won't want to miss this chapter!

Chapter 12, PDFKit: Finally — you can easily create and annotate PDFs using native Apple libraries on the iPhone with PDFKit. Learn how to create thumbnails, add text, UI controls and watermarks to your documents, and even create custom actions for the UI controls in your PDF documents.

Chapter 13, MusicKit: Enjoy your vast collection of songs in Apple Music — directly in your own apps! You'll create a fun song-guessing game to play with your friends as you learn how to select, share and play music from your library, manage access permissions and even detect when a user isn't a member of Apple Music and encourage them to sign up.

Chapter 14, Password Autofill: A vast improvement on iOS 8's Safari Autofill, the new password autofilling option in iOS 11 makes it easier for your users to log in to your app, while maintaining user confidentiality at all times. Learn how to auto-recognize username and password fields, set up associated domains, and create a seamless login experience for your users.

Chapter 15, Dynamic Type: Dynamic type is even better in iOS 11 — less truncation and clipping, improved titles on tab bars, and more intelligent scaling make using text onscreen a breeze. Learn how to think about Dynamic Type as you architect your app, and how to accommodate large typefaces in your app's layout.

Book source code and forums

You can get the source code for the book here:

www.raywenderlich.com/store/ios-11-by-tutorials/source-code

You'll find all source code from the chapters, as well as solutions to any challenges for your reference.

We've also set up an official forum for the book at www.raywenderlich.com/forums. This is a great place to ask any questions you have about the book, or to submit any errors you might find.

PDF version

We also have a PDF version of this book available, which can be handy if you want a soft copy to take with you, or you want to quickly search for a specific term within the book.

Buying the PDF version of the book also has a few extra benefits: free PDF updates each time we update the book, access to older PDF versions of the book, and you can download the PDF from anywhere, at anytime.

Visit our iOS 11 by Tutorials store page here:

• https://store.raywenderlich.com/products/ios-11-by-tutorials.

And since you purchased the print version of this book, you're eligible to upgrade to the PDF at a significant discount! Simply email support@razeware.com with your receipt for the physical copy and we'll get you set up with the discounted PDF version of the book.

License

By purchasing *iOS 11 by Tutorials*, you have the following license:

• You are allowed to use and/or modify the source code in *iOS 11 by Tutorials* in as many apps as you want, with no attribution required.

• You are allowed to use and/or modify all art, images, or designs that are included in *iOS 11 by Tutorials* in as many apps as you want, but must include this attribution line somewhere inside your app: "Artwork/images/designs: from the *iOS 11 by Tutorials* book, available at www.raywenderlich.com".

• The source code included in *iOS 11 by Tutorials* is for your own personal use only. You are NOT allowed to distribute or sell the source code in *iOS 11 by Tutorials* without prior authorization.

• This book is for your own personal use only. You are NOT allowed to sell this book without prior authorization, or distribute it to friends, co-workers, or students; they must to purchase their own copy instead.

Acknowledgments

We would like to thank many people for their assistance in making this possible:

- **Our families:** For bearing with us in this crazy time as we worked all hours of the night to get this book ready for publication!

- **Everyone at Apple:** For developing an amazing operating system and set of APIs, for constantly inspiring us to improve our apps and skills, and for making it possible for many developers to have their dream jobs!

- **And most importantly, the readers of raywenderlich.com — especially you!** Thank you so much for reading our site and purchasing this book. Your continued readership and support is what makes all of this possible!

About the cover

The blue sugeonfish, also known as the regal blue tang, hippo tang, doctorfish and letter six fish, sports bright yellow tails and pectoral fins, in contrast to the vivid blue of their bodies. The black markings on their side form a rough "6" — hence the "six" name.

Surgeonfish get their name from the sharp, venomous scalpel-like spines on their body that they use to fight off predators, and sometimes, each other. Although they can defend themselves, surgeonfish often float motionless on their side and "play dead" to avoid being detected by larger, passing predators.

However, we *don't* recommend that same approach to avoid being detected by your boss, when you're spending all your work hours building cool ARKit apps!

Chapter 1: What's New in Swift 4

By Richard Critz

If last year's changes for Swift 3 still cause you uncontrollable night terrors, you're in for a pleasant surprise with Swift 4. By comparison, the changes in Swift 4 are much more modest and even bring back some old capabilities, in new and improved form. Even better, you don't have to update right away!

The Swift 4 compiler integrated into Xcode 9 has a "Swift 3.2" mode. This is not a separate compiler, but a mode that allows you to continue building your Swift 3 sources so you can update to Swift 4 on your schedule. Your favorite CocoaPod has not yet been updated? No problem. You can select your Swift language version on a per-target basis in your project, so you can mix Swift 3 and Swift 4 targets in the same project.

> **Note:** Since Swift is an open source project, each change must go through the "Swift Evolution" process. This process involves the Swift Community working together to propose, discuss and review new ideas to help improve the language. Each proposal is numbered and made publicly available at https://github.com/apple/swift-evolution/tree/master/proposals.
>
> At the the beginning of each section in this chapter is the number(s) of the proposal(s) that instigated the changes — just in case you're interested in the gory details.

One-sided ranges

[SE-0172]

Swift 4 introduces `RangeExpression`, a new protocol to simplify how ranges can be described. It's adopted by a number of other protocols to enable the creation of new prefix and postfix operators. As a result, you can omit the upper or lower bound of a range specification to create a one-sided range.

This can be really useful when you want to extract the beginning or ending of a collection.

```swift
let esports = ["Hearthstone", "CS:GO", "League of Legends",
               "Super Smash Bros", "Overwatch", "Gigantic"]

esports[3...]
// returns ["Super Smash Bros", "Overwatch", "Gigantic"]

// In Swift 3, you had to write
esports[3..<esports.endIndex]

esports[...2]
// returns ["Hearthstone", "CS:GO", "League of Legends"]

esports[..<2]
// returns ["Hearthstone", "CS:GO"]
```

Infinite sequences

A one-sided range can be used to create an infinite sequence, one where only the beginning is defined. For example, you can build an array of tuples matching the decimal ASCII code of a character with the character itself.

```swift
let uppercase = ["A", "B", "C", "D"]
let asciiCodes = zip(65..., uppercase)
print(Array(asciiCodes))
// prints [(65, "A"), (66, "B"), (67, "C"), (68, "D")]
```

Pattern matching

A one-sided range can greatly simplify the patterns for a `switch` statement.

```swift
func gameRank(_ index: Int) -> String {
  switch index {
  case ...1:
    return "Oldie but goodie"
  case 3...:
```

```
      return "Meh"
    default:
      return "Awesome-sauce!"
    }
  }

gameRank(2)
// prints "Awesome-sauce!"
```

The switch expression need not be an `Int`.

```
/// Produce an emoji based on a numeric value
/// - parameter rating: a value between 0 and 1
func sentiment(_ rating: Double) -> String {
  switch rating {
  case ..<0.33:
    return "😞"
  case ..<0.66:
    return "😐"
  default:
    return "😄"
  }
}

sentiment(0.5)

// returns 😐
```

Strings

[SE-0162, SE-0168, SE-0178, SE-0182, SE-0183]

Strings received a lot of love in Swift 4, and all of that attention made them more powerful and easier to use. The most significant change is that `String`s are now `Collection`s, like they were in Swift 1. This means that all the fancy things that a `Collection` can do, a `String` can do too!

```
let text = "Hakuna Matata"
let unicodeText = "👇👏🐢🌭🎴🎢🎑📷"

text.count      // 13
text.isEmpty    // false
"".isEmpty      // true

// `reversed()` returns a `ReversedCollection<String>` so
// it must be converted back to `String`
```

```
String(text.reversed())
// "atataM anukaH"
```

It's easy to iterate through each character in a string, and it works properly for Unicode characters as well.

```
for c in unicodeText {
  print(c) // prints each of 8 characters, one to a line
}
```

String subscripts are not primitive types such as `Int`. Instead, they must be either a `String.Index` or `Range<String.Index>`.

```
var index = text.index(text.startIndex, offsetBy: 7)
text[index]
// "M"

// You can use prefix(upTo:) and suffix(from:)
// but why not use one-sided ranges instead

let lastWord = text[index...]
// lastWord is "Matata"

index = text.index(text.endIndex, offsetBy: -7)
let firstWord = text[..<index]
// firstWord is "Hakuna"
```

Introducing Substring

Swift tries to be efficient when managing the buffers associated with strings. As such, subscripting operations return a view of portion of the original string's buffer, incrementing that buffer's reference count. Depending on the application and its data, this has the potential to keep large, unused portions of strings in memory. While this technically isn't a memory leak, it will look, smell and quack a lot like one.

The Swift standard library solves this by introducing a new type: `Substring`, returned by string subscripting operations. Most APIs will continue to use `String` parameters and you must explicitly create a new `String` from the `Substring` to use them. This allows the original, larger string to go out-of-scope naturally and be deallocated.

This is not as unpleasant as it first may seem, because the standard library also introduces a new protocol: `StringProtocol`. Most of the String API is moved into `StringProtocol`, and both `String` and `Substring` conform to this new protocol.

```
type(of: lastWord)
// Substring.Type
```

```
lastWord.uppercased()
// "MATATA"

let lastWordAsString = String(lastWord)
type(of: lastWordAsString)
// String.Type
```

> **Note:** Option-clicking a variable name such as `lastWord` in Xcode to see its type will get the answer `String.Subsequence`. This is simply a `typealias` for `Substring`. `type(of: lastWord)` does, in fact, return `Substring.Type`.

Unicode magic

If you wanted to access the individual Unicode values of a `Character` in Swift 3, you first had to convert it to `String`. Now, `Character` has a `unicodeScalars` property.

```
let c: Character = "🇨🇭"
Array(c.unicodeScalars)
// [127464, 127469]
```

Swift 3 didn't like any of the following expressions, giving the wrong answer in each case. Swift 4, on the other hand, handles them correctly, giving the expected length based on what you see rather than what's required to encode it.

```
"🇨🇭🇮🇴".count    // 3
"👇".count         // 1
"👋".count         // 1
"🏳️".count         // 1
```

And, as you saw earlier, iterating through a string shows each Unicode character correctly.

Converting between Range<String.Index> and NSRange

The range of a Swift string is described by `Range<String.Index>`. Many Foundation APIs (e.g., `NSRegularExpression`, `NSAttributedString`, `NSLinguisticTagger`) require `NSRange` instead.

Foundation now includes new initializers on both `NSRange` and `Range<String.Index>`, which makes converting between the two a breeze. It's no longer necessary to muck around with UTF-16 offsets and views.

```
let population = "1🤠2🐔3👭"
population.count
// 6

var nsRange = NSRange(population.startIndex...,
                      in: population)
// population.startIndex... is a Range<String.Index>
// (0, 29)

population.utf16.count
// 29

let display = NSMutableAttributedString(
      string: population,
      attributes: [.font: UIFont.systemFont(ofSize: 20)])
```

As expected, the length of the NSRange matches the length of the UTF-16 view.
display looks like this:

```
let oneIndex = population.index(of: "1")!
let twoIndex = population.index(of: "2")!
let threeIndex = population.index(of: "3")!
var range = oneIndex..<twoIndex
nsRange = NSRange(range, in: population)
display.addAttribute(.font,
                     value: UIFont.systemFont(ofSize: 40),
                     range: nsRange)
```

The above finds the indices of each of the number badges, creates a range
(Range<String.Index>) for the first part of the string and converts it to an NSRange.
Then, it applies a new font attribute and now display looks like this:

```
range = twoIndex..<threeIndex
nsRange = NSRange(range, in: population)
display.addAttribute(.font,
                     value: UIFont.systemFont(ofSize: 30),
                     range: nsRange)
```

Next, this code makes the range represent the middle section of the string, converts it to `NSRange` and applies another new font attribute. Now `display` looks like this:

It's just as easy to go the other way and create a `Range<String.Index>` from an `NSRange`. Note that this initializer is failable, so the result is an optional.

```
let textInput = "You have traveled 483.2 miles."
let pattern = "[0-9]+(\\.([0-9])?)?"
let regex = try! NSRegularExpression(pattern: pattern,
                                     options: [])
nsRange = NSRange(textInput.startIndex..., in: textInput)
let mileage = regex.rangeOfFirstMatch(in: textInput,
                                      range: nsRange)
range = Range(mileage, in: textInput)!
textInput[range]
// "483.2"
```

Note: These new initializers also make things like `UITextFieldDelegate`'s `textField(_:shouldChangeCharactersIn:replacementString:)` easier to write without the ugly cast to `NSString` that is so common in pre-iOS 11 code.

Multi-line string literals

You can now create multi-line string literals, making it easy to produce precisely formatted output or to paste "pretty" inputs (e.g., JSON or HTML) directly into your source. String interpolation still works, and you can even escape newlines so that they're not included in the resulting literal!

The literal is delimited by `"""` and the indentation of the closing delimiter determines how much whitespace is stripped from the beginning of each line. You can use quotes in the literal without escaping them.

```
let firstVerse = """
  Half a league, half a league,
    Half a league onward,
  All in the valley of Death
    Rode the six hundred.
  "Forward, the Light Brigade!
  "Charge for the guns!" he said:
  Into the valley of Death
```

```
      Rode the six hundred.
    """
```

`print(firstVerse)` results in:

```
Half a league, half a league,
   Half a league onward,
All in the valley of Death
   Rode the six hundred.
"Forward, the Light Brigade!
"Charge for the guns!" he said:
Into the valley of Death
   Rode the six hundred.
```

```
let details = """
  Note that the indentation of the
     closing delimiter determines
     the amount of whitespace removed.
  You can insert \(firstWord) and \
  \(lastWord) and escape newlines too!
  """
```

`print(details)` looks like this:

```
Note that the indentation of the
   closing delimiter determines
   the amount of whitespace removed.
You can insert Hakuna and Matata and escape newlines too!
```

Dictionary enhancements

[SE-0165]

As a Swift programmer, you know how important Dictionary is to your daily life. Swift 4 brings a number of improvements to make it even more powerful, useful and usable.

Sequence-based initializer

You can now create dictionaries from a sequence of key-value pairs. For example, you can create a numbered list of items.

```
let groceries = Dictionary(uniqueKeysWithValues: zip(
  1...,
  ["Prosciutto", "Heavy Cream", "Butter", "Parmesan",
  "Small shells"])
)
// [5: "Small shells", 2: "Heavy Cream", 3: "Butter",
```

```
//  1: "Prosciutto", 4: "Parmesan"]
```

Or, if you already have a stream of tuples:

```
let housePointTotals = [("Slytherin", 472),
                        ("Ravenclaw", 426),
                        ("Hufflepuff", 352),
                        ("Gryffindor", 312)]
let banquetBegins = Dictionary(
    uniqueKeysWithValues: housePointTotals)
// ["Ravenclaw": 426, "Hufflepuff": 352, "Gryffindor": 312,
//  "Slytherin": 472]
```

Merging

`Dictionary` now includes an initializer that allows you to merge two dictionaries together. If you want to merge one dictionary into another, Swift also provides a `merge` method. Both allow you to specify a closure to resolve merge conflicts caused by duplicate keys.

```
let duplicates = [("a", 1), ("b", 2), ("a", 3), ("b", 4)]
let oldest = Dictionary(duplicates) { (current, _) in
  current
}
// ["b": 2, "a": 1]
```

You can take advantage of the closure to transform your input. Here's a more powerful example that takes an array of key-value pairs and turns them into a dictionary of arrays:

```
let sortingHat = [
  ("Gryffindor", "Harry Potter"), ("Slytherin", "Draco Malfoy"),
  ("Gryffindor", "Ron Weasley"),
  ("Slytherin", "Pansy Parkinson"),
  ("Gryffindor", "Hermione Granger"),
  ("Hufflepuff", "Hannah Abbott"),
  ("Ravenclaw", "Terry Boot"), ("Hufflepuff", "Susan Bones"),
  ("Ravenclaw", "Lisa Turpin"),
  ("Gryffindor", "Neville Longbottom")
]
let houses = Dictionary(
  sortingHat.map { ($0.0, [$0.1]) },
  uniquingKeysWith: { (current, new) in
    return current + new
})
// ["Ravenclaw": ["Terry Boot", "Lisa Turpin"],
//  "Hufflepuff": ["Hannah Abbott", "Susan Bones"],
//  "Slytherin": ["Draco Malfoy", "Pansy Parkinson"],
//  "Gryffindor": ["Harry Potter", "Ron Weasley",
//                 "Hermione Granger", "Neville Longbottom"]]
```

As you can see, you can do far more than just create a dictionary. Suppose you want to know how often each letter occurs in a string? Dictionary merging is on the case!

```
let spell = "I solemnly swear I am up to no good"
var frequencies: [Character: Int] = [:]
let baseCounts = zip(
  spell.filter { $0 != " " }.map { $0 },
  repeatElement(1, count: Int.max))
frequencies = Dictionary(baseCounts, uniquingKeysWith: +)
// ["w": 1, "p": 1, "n": 2, "o": 5, "I": 2, "u": 1, "t": 1,
//  "d": 1, "a": 2, "r": 1, "m": 2, "s": 2, "e": 2, "l": 2,
//  "g": 1, "y": 1]
```

If you have a set of defaults and wish to combine them with user settings, this is a perfect use for the merge method.

```
let defaultStyling: [String: UIColor] = [
  "body": .black, "title": .blue, "byline": .green
]
var userStyling: [String: UIColor] = [
  "body": .purple, "title": .blue
]
userStyling.merge(defaultStyling) { (user, _) -> UIColor in
  user
}
// ["body": .purple, "title": .blue, "byline": .green]
```

Default value for subscript

Dictionary values are returned as optionals. While this is necessary, it requires you to take what might otherwise be straightforward code and wrap it up with optional bindings, forced unwraps or optional chaining. In the past, a common way to address this was to use the nil coalescing operator (??) to provide a default value and make the result non-optional.

This is a sufficiently common practice that Swift 4 adds the ability to specify the default value right in the subscript.

```
let swift3 = banquetBegins["House elves"] ?? 0
let swift4 = banquetBegins["House elves", default: 0]
// both are 0; both are Int and not Int?
let housePoints = banquetBegins["Hufflepuff", default: 0]
// value is 352 with or without the default.
// Without, type is Int?; with, Int.
```

The default subscript provides another way to implement the frequency counter you saw earlier.

```
frequencies.removeAll()
spell.filter { $0 != " " }.map {
  frequencies[$0, default: 0] += 1
}
// produces the same results as before
```

Filtering and mapping

In Swift 4, filtering a dictionary preserves its structure and type in the result.

```
let oddGroceries = groceries.filter { $0.key % 2 == 1 }
// [5: "Small shells", 3: "Butter", 1: "Prosciutto"]
```

This is also now true for `Set`:

```
let set: Set = ["a", "b", "c", "d", "e"]
let filteredSet = set.filter { $0.hashValue % 2 == 0 }
// ["b", "d"]
```

The `map` function always returns an `Array`. Frequently, when working with a dictionary, this is precisely *not* what you want! Swift 4 adds `mapValue` to allow you to retain the dictionary's structure and type.

```
let mirroredGroceries = oddGroceries.mapValues {
  String($0.reversed())
}
// [5: "sllehs llamS", 3: "rettuB", 1: "ottuicsorP"]
```

Grouping

One of `Dictionary`'s most powerful new features is the ability is partition your data based on an arbitrary predicate, creating groups or buckets of similar data.

The simplest example is grouping a list of names by their first letter.

```
let names = ["Harry", "ron", "Hermione", "Hannah",
             "neville", "pansy", "Padma"].map { $0.capitalized }
let nameList = Dictionary(grouping: names) { $0.prefix(1) }
// ["H": ["Harry", "Hermione", "Hannah"], "R": ["Ron"],
// "N": ["Neville"], "P": ["Pansy", "Padma"]]
```

The fact that you can specify an arbitrary predicate lets you get more creative.

```
enum Multiples {
  case threes, notThrees
}
let numbers = 1...18
```

```
let predicate: (Int) -> Multiples =
  { $0 % 3 == 0 ? .threes : .notThrees }
let multiplesOfThree = Dictionary(grouping: numbers,
                                    by: predicate)
// [.threes: [3, 6, 9, 12, 15, 18],
// [.notThrees: [1, 2, 4, 5, 7, 8, 10, 11, 13, 14, 16, 17]]
type(of: multiplesOfThree)
// [Multiples: [Int]]
```

In a more realistic example, you may want to form your groups based on a value buried inside a structure. Combining grouping with Swift 4's new keyPath feature makes this a breeze.

```
// 1
struct Student {
  let firstName: String
  let lastName: String
}
// 2
let classRoll = sortingHat.map { $0.1.split(separator: " ") }
  .map { Student(firstName: String($0[0]),
                 lastName: String($0[1])) }
// 3
let lastNameKeypath = \Student.lastName
// 4
let contactList = Dictionary(grouping: classRoll) {
  $0[keyPath: lastNameKeypath].prefix(1)
}
```

Here's what you're doing in the code above:

1. Define your structure to describe a student.

2. Use the list of students from before to create an array of Student values.

3. Use the new keyPath syntax to reference the lastName field of Student. You'll learn more about keypaths in Chapter 2, "What's New in Foundation".

4. Use the first letter of the last name to group your students.

Generic subscripts and associated type constraints

[SE-0142, SE-0148]

Working with mixed data type dictionaries in Swift 3 is rather painful due to the need to typecast each value before you can use it. Swift 4 allows subscripts to return a generic type.

```swift
struct Grade {
  private var data: [String: Any]

  init(data: [String: Any]) {
    self.data = data
  }

  subscript<T>(key: String) -> T? {
    return data[key] as? T
  }
}

let gradebook = Grade(data: ["name": "Neil Armstrong",
                             "exam": "LEM Landing",
                             "grade": 97])
let who: String? = gradebook["name"]
let grade: Int?  = gradebook["grade"]
// No need to coerce the type with "as?"
```

This is definitely *not* the best way to implement a structure. However, if you're using the new `Decodable` facility, this concept might simplify your custom `init(from:)`. See Chapter 2, "What's New in Foundation" for more on `Decodable`.

The subscript itself can now be generic as well. For example, you can implement a way to use a sequence to retrieve an array of values from a collection.

```swift
extension Grade {
  subscript<Keys: Sequence>(keys: Keys) -> [Any]
    where Keys.Element == String {
    var values: [Any] = []
    for key in keys {
      if let value = data[key] {
        values.append(value)
      }
    }
    return values
  }
}
```

```
gradebook[["name", "grade"]]
gradebook[Set(["name", "grade"])]
// both return ["Neil Armstrong", 97]
```

You can also use this feature to add new capabilities to standard library types.

```
extension Collection {
  subscript<Indices: Sequence>(indices: Indices) -> [Element]
    where Indices.Element == Index {
    var result: [Element] = []
    for index in indices {
      result.append(self[index])
    }
    return result
  }
}
let words = "It was the best of times it was the worst of times"
  .split(separator: " ")
words[[3, 9, 11]]
// ["best", "worst", "times"]
```

Both of the previous examples took advantage of another new feature: associated type constraints. An associated type can now be constrained with a where clause. This can vastly simplify working with generics.

For example, in the extension to Grade, Swift 3 requires you to specify where Keys.Iterator.Element == String.

Allowing constraints on associated types can also make it easier to extend standard library types.

```
extension Sequence where Element: Numeric {
  var product: Element {
    return self.reduce(1, *)
  }
}
[2,4,6,8].product
// 384
[1.5, 3.0, -2.0].product
// -9 (a Double)
```

Limiting @objc inference

[SE-0160]

To make Swift code accessible from Objective-C, the Swift compiler must generate something known as a "thunk" method to convert between the Objective-C and Swift calling conventions. These thunks are only used for calls from Objective-C, not Swift. To ease the burden of interoperating with existing Objective-C code, Swift 3 (and earlier) inferred the need for these thunks in a number of cases.

Unfortunately, experience has shown that many of these inferred thunks are unneeded, resulting in app binaries that are larger than necessary. In many cases, 6-8% of an app's total size is comprised of this "glue" code. To eliminate this waste, Swift 4 does far less automatic inference.

For example, classes derived from `NSObject` are no longer automatically accessible to Objective-C. You must explicitly use the `@objc` annotation to make a Swift method visible to Objective-C.

```
class MyClass: NSObject {
    func print() { Swift.print("hello") } // not visible to Obj-C
    @objc func show() { print() } // visible to Obj-C
}
```

Apple recommends that you group all of your methods that need to be visible to Objective-C in an extension. If you add the `@objc` annotation to the extension itself, everything it contains will be accessible. If you need to exclude a single method because it can't be represented in Objective-C, use the `@nonobjc` annotation.

```
@objc extension MyClass {
    func f(_ foo: String?) {}
    @nonobjc func g(_ goo: Int?) {}
}
```

Without the `@nonobjc` above, the compiler generates an error message for g(_:):

```
error: method cannot be in an @objc extension of a class
(without @nonobjc) because the type of the parameter cannot be
represented in Objective-C
```

If you need a class, along with all of its extensions, subclasses and their extensions, to be accessible to Objective-C, use the `@objcMembers` annotation on the class.

```
@objcMembers
class MySecondClass: NSObject {
    func f() {}
    // can't be called from ObjC but no error
    func g() -> (Int, Int) {
        return (1, 1)
    }
}
```

Hide your exceptions in an extension using `@nonobjc`:

```
@nonobjc extension MySecondClass {
  func h() -> Int? { return nil }
  func j(_ value: Double?) {}
}
```

Swift 4 inference

The rules for when Swift 4 will automatically infer `@objc` are well-defined. It will infer `@objc` if a declaration is an override of an `@objc` method declaration:

```
class Super {
  @objc func foo() {}
}

class Sub: Super {
  // inferred @objc
  override func foo() {}
}
```

It will infer `@objc` if a declaration satisfies a requirement of an `@objc` protocol:

```
@objc protocol MyDelegate {
  func bar()
}

class MyThirdClass: MyDelegate {
  // inferred @objc
  func bar() {}
}
```

In this case, this inference is required because calling `MyDelegate.bar()`, whether from Objective-C or Swift, will be via an Objective-C message send, so conforming to the protocol requires an Objective-C entry point. For the same reason, Swift 4 will also infer `@objc` for any declaration having one or more of the following attributes:

- `@IBAction`

- `@IBOutlet`

- `@IBInspectable`

- `@GKInspectable`

- `@NSManaged`

Finally, while `dynamic` is currently implemented using Objective-C messaging, it no longer causes an `@objc` inference. You must add the annotation explicitly.

Other changes

There a number of other smaller changes worthy of note.

Private access in extensions

[SE-0169]

Swift 3 introduced the awful `fileprivate` and broke a ton of code that had been properly partitioned into extensions. Swift 4 makes it better. Now, methods and variables declared `private` are accessible to extensions in the same source file. `fileprivate` is still there with its "single file scope" meaning, but its use should be much more rare.

```swift
struct Person {
  private let firstName: String
  private let lastName: String

  init(firstName: String, lastName: String) {
    self.firstName = firstName
    self.lastName = lastName
  }

  var name: String {
    return "\(firstName) \(lastName)"
  }
}

extension Person {
  func greeting(with message: String) -> String {
    return "\(message), \(firstName)!"
  }
}


let dumbledore = Person(firstName: "Albus",
                        lastName: "Dumbledore")
dumbledore.greeting(with: "Good mornafterevening")
```

swapAt(_:_:)

[SE-0173, SE-0176]

In preparation for the future, Swift 4 introduces a new concept of exclusive access to memory such that only one actor can write to the memory occupied by a single object at a time. This breaks the use of swap(_:_:) for exchanging two items in a collection. Now, instead, you use swapAt(_:_:).

```
var numbers = Array(1...5)
//swap(&numbers[1], &numbers[3]) // Illegal in Swift 4
numbers.swapAt(1, 3)
// [1, 4, 3, 2, 5]
```

NSNumber bridging

[SE-0170]

Swift 3 didn't check whether an integer value stored in an NSNumber could be expressed in the Swift scalar type to which it was cast. For example:

```
let n = NSNumber(value: 603)
let v = n as? Int8
```

...would give the value 91. This is clearly wrong and unsafe. In Swift 4, v will be nil. To quote from the Swift Evolution proposal, "as? for NSNumber should mean 'Can I safely express the value stored in this opaque box called a NSNumber as the value I want?'." This is equally true for is.

```
if n is Int8 {
  print("n must be pretty small")
} else {
  print("nope, doesn't fit. Get a bigger bucket!")
}
```

Composing classes and protocols

[SE-0156]

Prior to Swift 4, there was no way to specify that an object had to be both a particular type *and* conform to a protocol. Now there is!

```
protocol MySpecialDelegateProtocol {}
class MySpecialView: UIView {}
class MyController {
  var delegate: (UIView & MySpecialDelegateProtocol)?
}
```

This is also used in interesting ways in the Swift standard library. The Codable protocol, which you'll learn about in Chapter 2, "What's New in Foundation", is actually simply a typealias:

```
public typealias Codable = Decodable & Encodable
```

Migrating to Swift 4

Now that you know about all of the cool changes, you're ready to migrate your project to Swift 4, right? Don't sweat it — it's an easy process. In Xcode 9, select **Edit\Convert\To Current Swift Syntax...** to fire off the migrator. With one exception, it's all straightforward and simple. The migrator will ask you what style of @objc inference you want. The recommended choice, **Minimize Inference**, will be pre-selected in the dialog.

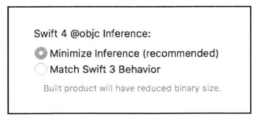

If you stick with **Minimize Inference**, your builds will include a warning:

```
The use of Swift 3 @objc inference in Swift 4 mode is
deprecated. Please address deprecated @objc inference warnings,
test your code with "Use of deprecated Swift 3 @objc inference"
logging enabled, and then disable inference by changing the
"Swift 3 @objc Inference" build setting to "Default" for the
"<your project>" target.
```

This is expected as you test your program. Once you are satisfied that you made all of the necessary annotations in your source, open your **Target**'s build settings and change **Swift 3 @objc Inference** to **Default**, as instructed in the warning message.

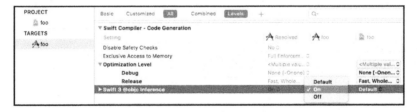

Where to go from here?

As I mentioned at the beginning, Swift is an open source language. You can see all of the proposed, implemented and rejected changes, and even submit your own ideas (though it's gotten much harder for Swift 5), by visiting https://github.com/apple/swift-evolution.

You can find even more details about these changes and the motivations behind them by watching the WWDC 2017 video for session 402, "What's New in Swift". You can find it at https://developer.apple.com/videos/play/wwdc2017/402/.

Most importantly, **turn the page** and continue on to Chapter 2, "What's New in Foundation" to learn about the new features for data serialization and key-value observing!

Chapter 2: What's New In Foundation

By Mic Pringle

Each year at WWDC, when Apple announces the latest version of the iOS SDK, developers and the tech media have a tendency to focus on the shiny new big-ticket items and often overlook credible changes to iOS stalwarts such as `Foundation`.

This year was no different, and while everyone was purring over `ARKit` and `CoreML`, the `Foundation` team delivered two big-ticket items of their own, and that's what you'll explore throughout this chapter.

The first is `Codable` — a composition of protocols that allow for easy encoding and decoding of data, and two concrete implementations for handling JSON and plist formats. The charm of `Codable` is the fact that you can adopt it without writing a single-line of code. Simply declare conformance on your class or struct and the compiler will take care of the rest. And if the defaults don't work for you, you can customize it *all the way down!*

Next up are some pretty big changes to Key-Value Observing (KVO). Not only can you declare keypaths with a wonderful new syntax, but you can now pass a closure as an observer instead of being forced to rely on the hideous `observeValue(forKeyPath:of:change:context:)` and a bunch of switches to figure out which object and what keypath you are being notified about!

You'll be introduced to both these new features in `Foundation` as you work through this chapter, but not independently — oh no! Instead, you shall use both in the same sample project, providing you with a good understanding of how each one works, and how they can be used together.

So read on; I think you'll be pleasantly surprised just how easy it is to work with these new features.

Getting started

Throughout this chapter, you'll be working with JSON data provided by newsapi.org. But before you can start, you'll need to grab yourself an API key. Don't worry though, it's a quick and painless process that you'll have done in a jiffy!

First, open your browser and head on over to newsapi.org. Once the page had loaded, click the big green **GET API KEY** button located on the far right of the navigation bar:

On the registration page that follows, provide your email address, a password, agree to the terms and conditions, and hit **Submit**. If all goes well you'll be taken to your account page where you can find your API key:

Go ahead and copy your API key. You're gonna need it shortly!

Headlines — a newsworthy app

Everyone loves news, right? There are newspapers, TV channels broadcasting news 24 hours a day, and you even have access to news on-demand using your mobile phone. But news can be overwhelming, and sometimes all you want are the headlines — snippets of information that provide just enough context to satisfy your hunger.

That's where **Headlines** comes in. It's an iOS app that displays the latest headlines from over 70 news sources. Consider it the ultimate drug for the news junkie!

There is a small problem though. The app isn't quite finished. Would you believe the previous developer left to take up a role as an anchorman? Oh, the irony.

It's fallen on your shoulders to complete the app. Are you up for the challenge?

Locate and open **Headlines.xcodeproj** with Xcode 9. Once Xcode has finished launching, open **Services/NewsAPI.swift** and locate the `key` property of the private `API` enum. Replace the value of the string with the API key you copied earlier, so it looks something like this:

```
private static let key = "7ff55d453a844be8b7aca4fd4792ca09"
```

With that done, you can now build and run.

Granted, it's a little sparse, but there's more going on here than first meets the eye. When this view controller is initially loaded, the app requests a list of news sources from NewsAPI, and for the time being dumps the response to the console. You *did* notice all that gobbledygook in the console, right?

So the first order of the day is to decode that JSON into the relevant model objects, and then display them using this view controller. It's time to get cracking!

Decoding Sources

As there is a lack of formatting in the API response, it's unlikely you're able to make heads or tails of the JSON dumped to the console. The following is a pretty-printed snippet from the JSON response, showing just enough for you to understand the structure, and how the keys map to the properties in the `Source` model object.

```
{
  "status": "ok",
  "sources": [
    {
      "id": "abc-news-au",
      "name": "ABC News (AU)",
      "description": "...",
      "url": "http://www.abc.net.au/news",
      "category": "general",
      "language": "en",
      "country": "au",
      "urlsToLogos": {
        "small": "",
        "medium": "",
        "large": ""
      },
      "sortBysAvailable": [
        "top"
      ]
    },
    ...
  ]
}
```

You can see that the top-level object is a dictionary, and there's a nested array of dictionaries named `sources`. Each source has a number of keys, but you're only interested in a handful of them. In this section you'll get your hands dirty learning how to decode this JSON into instances of `Source`.

Open **Source.swift** and update the class definition to include the `Codable` protocol:

```
class Source: Codable
```

`Codable` is a protocol composition of both `Encodable` and `Decodable`. If your stored properties are themselves `Encodable` and `Decodable`, and your JSON keys match your property names 1:1, then this is all you need to do, as the compiler will generate the necessary methods required by the two protocols for you at compile time. Seriously, how cool is that!?

However, since `Source` has a property named `overview` that maps to the JSON key `description` — and there's a very good reason for this you'll learn about later in this chapter — you can explicitly provide the key mappings using an enum that conforms to the `CodingKey` protocol.

Add the following to the top of `Source`, just below the property definitions:

```
enum CodingKeys: String, CodingKey {
  case id
  case name
  case overview = "description"
  case category
}
```

Here you define an enum of type `String`, which conforms to `CodingKey`. If you didn't provide this enum, the compiler would generate an enumeration named `CodingKeys` for you automatically. By naming this enum identically, the compiler will acknowledge you've provided your own implemention and look to use that instead.

As the type of the enum is `String`, you can provide each case with a value, and that value will be used as the corresponding JSON key when encoding and decoding. In this instance, you set the value of the case `overview` (*the property*) to `description` (*the JSON key*).

The thinking behind this is to provide static type checking for your JSON keys, as opposed to simply using strings everywhere. And we all know that to be a bad idea, right?

Finally, open **Article.swift**. You will come back to this class later in the chapter, but for now update the class definition to include the `Codable` protocol as well.

```
class Article: Codable
```

Nested elements and container objects

When consuming data from an external API, you'll often find inconsistencies between the structure of the types you're modelling locally and those modelled by the provider of the API. In many cases, a logical group of data within your app is shared out among several nested objects or arrays within the JSON responses.

One way to plug this structural discrepancy is to create one or more container types that can be used as an intermediate step in the decoding process. Depending on how it's modelled, you can either query this container for its child types, or use the container as the data source of an initializer for the type that is then used throughout the rest of the app.

You'll create an ephemeral container type matching the structure of the top-level dictionary of the sources JSON, which can then be queried for the sources themselves.

Open **NewsAPI.swift** and add the following just above the private `API` enum declaration:

```
private struct Response: Codable {
  let sources: [Source]?
  let articles: [Article]?
}
```

Here you create a struct that can be used to handle the response from both API requests: sources and articles. If you remember from the JSON snippet shown earlier, the top-level dictionary includes some metadata and an array of dictionaries keyed as `sources`.

The metadata is irrelevant within the scope of this chapter so you don't declare any properties. If the decoding process finds a key in the JSON for which there's no matching property it's simply discarded.

Luckily, the articles JSON is almost identical to sources, except the array is keyed as `articles`. Since both properties are optionals within `Response` the decoding process will only look to set them if they're present in the JSON. This means you can reuse the `Response` struct across requests that return sources, articles or both, and only the property matching the current request will be set. Nice!

Still within **NewsAPI.swift**, locate `fetchSources()` and replace the contents of the fetch-closure with:

```
if let sources = try! JSONDecoder().decode(
    Response.self, from: data).sources {
  self.sources = sources
}
```

Here you create a `JSONDecoder` and ask it to decode the data from the API response into an instance of `Response`. You place it within an `if-let` statement, since `sources` is an optional so it needs unwrapping. If that's successful, you then set `self.sources` to the array of sources from the response.

> **Note:** You're using `try!` here since `decode` throws, but in production you'd definitely want to use `try` and handle any errors. See https://developer.apple.com/videos/play/wwdc2017/212 for examples on how to handle errors thrown by `Codable`.

If you were to build and run now, nothing would have changed other than the JSON response is no longer dumped to the console. You've decoded the JSON array into instances of `Source`, but you haven't notified the consumer — the sources view controller — that its data is ready to be consumed.

You'll tackle this now using Key-Value Observing.

May I make an observation?

You could use the delegate pattern, or update `NewsAPI` so its methods accept a completion handler, but both of those options tightly couple the API service to the view controller. Instead, you're going to use KVO to observe when the `sources` array changes and then respond accordingly. This allows you to loosely couple the `NewsAPI` and the view controllers consuming its data.

As KVO is a technology built around the Objective-C runtime, you do have to jump through a few hoops to get everything working. But by the end of this section you'll agree that the extra effort is worth it!

Open **Source.swift** and update the class definition so it inherits from `NSObject`:

```
class Source: NSObject, Codable
```

Next, open **NewsAPI.swift** and make the same change:

```
class NewsAPI: NSObject
```

In order to use key-value observing with a Swift class, it needs to inherit from `NSObject`, hence why you've made these two changes. This is due to the KVO APIs being declared on `NSObject` and not natively part of Swift.

The final part to making a class KVO-compliant is to mark any observable properties as requiring dynamic dispatch. Update the `sources` property declaration inside **NewsAPI.swift** so it matches the following:

```
@objc dynamic private(set) var sources: [Source] = []
```

Here you add the `objc` attribute to let the compiler know this property is available to use from within Objective-C, along with the `dynamic` modifier to inform the compiler that no optimizations should take place, as the property needs to be dynamically dispatched through the Objective-C runtime so the getter and setter can be replaced at runtime. This is a fundamental building block of KVO.

> **Note:** If you're interested in learning more about how KVO works and KVO-Swift interoperability, or if any of the above sentence makes no sense, then I highly recommend reading through apple.co/2w5dUsA, apple.co/2uT8InZ,

apple.co/2x7jI1F, and apple.co/2vFWxOc.

Next, open **SourceListController.swift** and add the following property declaration to the top of the class:

```
private var token: NSKeyValueObservation?
```

Here you declare a property to store the token returned when calling `observe(_:changeHandler:)` on a class derived from `NSObject`. It's important to retain this token as long as you want to observe the keypath, otherwise the observer is released immediately and will never be called. Having a reference to the token also allows you to invalidate the observer when you're finished with it.

Still in **SourceListController.swift**, add the following to `viewDidLoad()` right between the call to `super` and the call to `fetchSources()` on `NewsAPI`:

```
// 1
token = NewsAPI.service.observe(\.sources) { _, _ in
  // 2
  DispatchQueue.main.async {
    // 3
    self.tableView.reloadData()
  }
}
```

Here's the play-by-play of what's happening above:

1. Call `observe(_:changeHandler:)` on the `service` singleton of `NewsAPI`, passing `\.sources` as the keypath. Note the sexy new syntax! This will call the closure passed as the change handler whenever the value of `sources` changes — that's the value, not the contents of the array! You store the returned token in the property you set up in the previous step since you want the observer to be around as long as the view controller.

2. The observer is called on a background queue, but since you're going to update the UI, you use GCD to dispatch back to the main queue.

3. Ask the table view to reload its data. As the table view is already wired up to use `sources` as its data source, it will re-query the array and update accordingly.

And that's all there is to configuring KVO on the `sources` array of `NewsAPI`, and having the table view refresh automatically whenever it changes.

Build and run. You should now see a list of news sources displayed once the API call has succeeded and the returned JSON decoded into instances of `Source`.

If you tap a source you'll see... *another empty view controller!* Well, that just won't do. This view controller is supposed to display the most recent articles from the selected source. Roll up those sleeves, grab yourself a fresh mug of Yorkshire tea and let's do this!

Decoding articles

Here is a pretty-printed snippet from the articles JSON response so you can get an understanding of the structure and how its keys map to the properties of the `Article` model object:

```
{
  "status": "ok",
  "source": "the-next-web",
  "sortBy": "latest",
  "articles": [
    {
      "author": "Neil C. Hughes",
      "title": "...",
      "description": "...",
      "url": "...",
      "urlToImage": "...",
      "publishedAt": "2017-08-16T13:46:53Z"
    },
    ...
  ]
}
```

Just as with the previous JSON response, there is a top-level dictionary and a nested array of dictionaries named `articles`. Luckily, the `Response` container type you created earlier is already set up to handle this JSON and can be reused once `Article` is completely `Codable` ready.

You need the `Article` class to conform to `Codable` as it's the model class representing an article, and you want the articles in the JSON response to be decoded into instances of this class. You need to have it descend from `NSObject` so that the class can be represented in Objective-C, and that's important because, later, you'll once again use KVO to observe changes to an array storing instances of this class. Open **Article.swift** and update the class definition:

```
class Article: NSObject, Codable
```

Looking at the JSON snippet and the class definition, you may have already noticed that there isn't a 1:1 relationship between the property names and the JSON keys, so just like before you'll need to override the `CodingKeys` enumeration to provide the custom mappings.

Still in **Article.swift**, add the following just below the property declarations:

```
enum CodingKeys: String, CodingKey {
  case author
  case title
  case snippet = "description"
  case sourceURL = "url"
  case imageURL = "urlToImage"
  case published = "publishedAt"
}
```

I mentioned earlier that there was a good reason why you remapped `description` to `overview` in `Source`, and the same applies here. As both model classes now descend from `NSObject` due to the KVO requirements, having a property named `description` creates a conflict with a method of the same name already defined on `NSObject`. Luckily you can use the custom key mapping feature of `Codable` to work around this conflict and keep the compiler happy — happy compiler, happy developer! :]

Now that `Article` is both KVO- and `Codable`-ready, you need to update the `articles` member of `NewsAPI` to use dynamic dispatch since this is what you'll be observing to keep the articles table view up-to-date.

Open `NewsAPI.swift` and update the `articles` property declaration so it matches the following:

```
@objc dynamic private(set) var articles: [Article] = []
```

Remember that @objc tells the compiler to make this property available to Objective-C code, and dynamic tells the compiler *not* to make any optimizations such as inlining the implementation, and instead to dynamically dispatch the property through the Objective-C runtime so the getter and setter can be replaced at runtime.

While you're working in NewsAPI, add the following to the closure in fetchArticles(for:):

```
let decoder = JSONDecoder()
decoder.dateDecodingStrategy = .iso8601
if let articles = try! decoder.decode(
    Response.self, from: data).articles {
  self.articles = articles
}
```

Here you create an instance of JSONDecoder, set its date decoding strategy to interpret dates using the ISO 8601 standard, ask it to decode the articles API JSON response into an instance of Response, and then attempt to unwrap the articles optional. If this succeeds, you set self.articles to the unwrapped value, which in turn will trigger any observers of this property. There aren't any at the moment, so you'll add one now!

Open **ArticleListController.swift** and add the following property declaration to the top of the class:

```
private var token: NSKeyValueObservation?
```

You'll use this property to store the token provided by the observer. Remember it's important to retain a reference to the token as long you need to keep observing, otherwise the observer will be released and never called. As ArticleListController is a detail view controller and will be reused, you'll also use this token to invalidate the observer each time the user navigates back to the master view controller to choose a different news source.

Add the following just below the call to super in viewDidAppear(animated:):

```
// 1
guard let source = source else { return }
// 2
token = NewsAPI.service.observe(\.articles) { _, _ in
  // 3
  DispatchQueue.main.async {
    // 4
    self.tableView.reloadData()
  }
}
// 5
NewsAPI.service.fetchArticles(for: source)
```

Here's the breakdown of what's happening above:

1. Use `guard` to make sure a `source` has been passed from the sources view controller, otherwise exit early. A valid `source` is required by `fetchArticles(for:)`, so without one, execution can't continue.

2. Call `observe(_:changeHandler:)` on the `service` singleton of `NewsAPI`, this time passing `\.articles` as the keypath, and store the returned token in `token`. This will cause the closure passed as the change handler to be called whenever the value of `articles` changes.

3. The observer is called on a background queue, but since you're going to update the UI, you use GCD to dispatch back to the main queue.

4. Ask the table view to reload its data. The table view is already set up to use `articles` as its data source so will re-query the array and update itself accordingly.

5. Finally, call `fetchArticles(for:)` on the `NewsAPI` singleton, which will hit the NewsAPI articles API, decode the returned JSON, and then update `articles` causing the observer to be called and the table view to update. Magic!

When a user has finished perusing the news articles from the current and navigates back to the sources view controller, you'll need to do a little housekeeping.

Inside **ArticleListController.swift**, add the following to `viewDidDisappear(animated:)`, just below the call to `super`:

```
// 1
token?.invalidate()
// 2
NewsAPI.service.resetArticles()
```

Here's what's happening above:

1. You invalidate the observation token and as a result release the observer. It's important to invalidate any observers that are no longer required to avoid them being called unexpectedly, since a single keypath can have many observers, and you create a new one each time the view is shown.

2. You reset `articles` to an empty array. This is needed since there is a delay between submitting the API request, receiving the response, decoding it, and updating the table view. If you didn't reset the array, then articles from the previously chosen source would be displayed temporarily, leading to a poor user experience.

Build and run. Scroll through the list of sources until you find **BBC News** and tap it. You should now see a list of articles displayed.

NewsAPI is an aggregator and as such, despite their best efforts, there are some inconsistencies in their data. The reason I asked you to select **BBC News** is because I know they provide values for each of the keys in the JSON, but if you continue to select different news sources — **ABC News (AU)** is a good choice — the app will eventually crash and you'll see the following printed in the console:

```
fatal error: 'try!' expression unexpectedly raised an error:
Swift.DecodingError.valueNotFound(Foundation.Date,
Swift.DecodingError.Context(codingPath: [Headlines.NewsAPI.
(Response in
_0829A67BC5D743BCE8668E6276E9747D).CodingKeys.articles,
Foundation.(_JSONKey in _12768CA107A31EF2DCE034FD75B541C9)
(stringValue: "Index 5", intValue: Optional(5)),
Headlines.Article.CodingKeys.published], debugDescription:
"Expected Date value but found null instead."...
```

The errors `Codable` throws are extremely helpful, and you can see from the above exactly what the issue is: `Expected Date value but found null instead`, and which key caused the error: `Headlines.Article.CodingKeys.published`.

Not all news sources consistently provide publication dates or authors, and you've not yet configured `Article` to handle `null` values when being decoded, so you'll look at that in the next section.

> **Note:** As you select different sources, you may run into another crash where the error printed to the console mentions `"Expected to decode Double but found a string/data instead"` or `"Expected date string to be ISO8601-formatted."`. Don't worry, this is yet another issue of aggregating various news sources into a single output and is one that you'll fix later in this section.

Much ado about null

Open **Article.swift** and add a `?` to both `author` and `published` to turn them into optionals:

```
let author: String?
...
let published: Date?
```

Surprisingly, this is all you need to do to handle `null` values with `Codable`. The compiler is smart enough when generating the default implementations of the protocol methods to only try and set an optional property if the corresponding value is present, since you've explicitly stated it *could* be `null` by using optionals.

But before you can build and run, there is another change you need to make. Since `published` is now an optional you need to update `ArticleCell` to account for the change. `ArticleCell` is the custom `UITableViewCell` class used to display articles in the table view.

Open **ArticleCell.swift** and locate the following line in `render(article:using:)`:

```
publishedLabel.text = formatter.string(from: article.published)
```

Replace it with this snippet:

```
if let published = article.published {
  publishedLabel.text = formatter.string(from: published)
} else {
  publishedLabel.text = nil
}
```

Here you attempt to unwrap `published`, and if it's successful you set the text of the label to a textual representation of the date, formatted using an instance of `DateFormatter` that's passed to the enclosing method. If the unwrapping fail you set the text of the label to `nil`. You use `nil` instead of an empty string because the table view cells are self-sizing, and you want the label to collapse its height and not affect the size of the cell, which won't happen with an empty string.

Build and run, this time choosing **ABC News (AU)** as the source. Scroll through the articles and you should see some with dates and some without:

Notice how the cells without dates have collapsed the space where the date should be, preserving the overall look of the cell. Nice work!

> **Note:** Don't worry if all your headlines include dates when selecting **ABC News (AU)**. This simply means it was a `null` author that caused the crash earlier, and in this section, you've addressed both cases. This new source frequently excluded dates when the chapter was written, but as these feeds change hourly it's not guaranteed to be that way now. Such is the risk when working with live APIs. Feel free to select a few other news sources, and I'm confident you'll quickly come across a cell without a date.

If it wasn't for those pesky newlines

Another issue you'll come across when working with the data from NewsAPI is that some publishers put extraneous newline characters in their article descriptions. I can only assume these serve some sort of formatting purpose, but they have no place in the Headlines app and therefore need to be removed.

You could do this clean-up retrospectively, once the decoding has taken place, but since part of the charm of `Codable` is that you can provide your own implementation for any of the methods generated by the compiler, you can actually do it *as part* of the decoding process!

Open **Article.swift** and add the following initializer to the bottom of the class:

```
required init(from decoder: Decoder) throws {

}
```

This is the single method declared by the `Decodable` protocol. Remember that `Codable` is a protocol composition of both `Decodable` and `Encodable`. As you're providing the implementation and not relying on the compiler-generated one, you assume responsibility for decoding the entire object and therefore need to implement the initializer in its entirety.

You're passed an instance of `Decoder`, but you don't use this directly to decode the JSON objects. Instead, you ask the decoder for containers that, surprisingly, contain those objects. There are three types of container: a *keyed container* for dictionaries, an *unkeyed container* for arrays, and a *single value container*. In this instance, since you're dealing with a JSON dictionary, you're only interested in the keyed container type.

Add the following to the top of the initializer:

```
let container = try decoder.container(keyedBy: CodingKeys.self)
```

Here you ask the decoder for a container, keyed by the `CodingKeys` enumeration. It's worth remembering that encoding and decoding is a recursive process, so as long as your model layer mirrors the structure of the JSON, the container returned here should be the one you're expecting. Therefore the JSON keys should match those in `CodingKeys`.

You can now begin using the container to decode the values it contains into their corresponding types.

Add the following just below the statement you added in the previous step:

```
title = try container.decode(String.self, forKey: .title)
sourceURL = try container.decode(URL.self, forKey: .sourceURL)
imageURL = try container.decode(URL.self, forKey: .imageURL)
```

Containers can decode a variety of types including `String`, `Float`, `Int`, and `Bool`, but can also decode any type that is itself `Decodable`. You see this in action here because while `KeyedDecodingContainer` — the type of container you're using — provides a method to decode strings, it also provides a generic implementation for anything conforming to `Decodable`, which you're using to decode URLs. This is how `Codable` provides support for both native Swift types and your own custom types.

That takes care of the values you know are *always* present, but what about `author` and `published` that can be `null`? The process is the same, except you use `decodeIfPresent(_:forKey:)` instead.

Add the following to the bottom of the initializer:

```
author = try container.decodeIfPresent(String.self,
    forKey: .author)
published = try container.decodeIfPresent(Date.self,
    forKey: .published)
```

Decoding this way means these properties will only be set if their corresponding value is present in the container, otherwise they'll be `nil`.

Finally, you can now remove those pesky newline characters from the articles description.

Add the following just below the code you added in the prior step:

```
let rawSnippet = try container.decode(
    String.self, forKey: .snippet)
snippet = rawSnippet.deletingCharacters(
    in: CharacterSet.newlines)
```

Here you decode `description` from the container into a temporary `String` variable, using the `snippet` key to handle the mapping between JSON key and property name. You then delete any newline characters from the temporary string and use that to set `snippet`.

Build and run. Everything should appear just as it did before, but you can rest safe in the knowledge that there are no extraneous newline characters in Headlines data. See if there's anything interesting going on in the world by tapping **Bloomberg**...

Uh oh! So much for that short rest.

Damned dirty dates

When you selected **Bloomberg** and the app crashed, you'll have seen the following printed to the console:

```
fatal error: 'try!' expression unexpectedly raised an error:
Swift.DecodingError.dataCorrupted(Swift.DecodingError.Context(co
dingPath: [Headlines.NewsAPI.(Response in
_0829A67BC5D743BCE8668E6276E9747D).CodingKeys.articles,
Foundation.(_JSONKey in _12768CA107A31EF2DCE034FD75B541C9)
(stringValue: "Index 0", intValue: Optional(0)),
Headlines.Article.CodingKeys.published], debugDescription:
"Expected date string to be ISO8601-formatted."...
```

This error message is once again incredibly useful. It provides the source of the crash: the failed decoding of `Headlines.Article.CodingKeys.published`, and the reason: the date is expected to be ISO8601-formatted. This is because you explicitly told the decoder that dates would be in the ISO 8601, but in this case it's come across one that isn't.

For most news sources this works just fine; the date is interpreted as ISO 8601 and the decoding process uses `ISO8601DateFormatter` to decode it. What's different about Bloomberg is their dates include milliseconds — `2017-08-19T21:22:30.028Z` instead of `2017-08-19T21:22:30Z` — and Apple's `ISO8601DateFormatter` can't handle them, despite milliseconds being a perfectly valid part of the ISO 8601 specification.

You can see this for yourself by visiting the following URL, making sure to append your API key:

- `https://newsapi.org/v1/articles?source=bloomberg&apiKey=`

The easiest way to fix this is to provide the decoder with a custom date handler, and delete the milliseconds before converting the string to a date.

Open **NewsAPI.swift** and add the following to the top of `fetchArticles(for:)`:

```
let formatter = ISO8601DateFormatter()
let customDateHandler: (Decoder) throws -> Date = { decoder in

}
```

Here you've created an instance of `ISO8601DateFormatter` that you'll use within the following closure to decode dates. As the closure will be called multiple times, once for each date the decoder finds, it's far more efficient to create one formatter and reuse it. The closure is passed an instance of `Decoder` and expects in return an instance of `Date`.

Add the following to the closure:

```
// 1
var string = try decoder.singleValueContainer()
    .decode(String.self)
// 2
string.deleteMillisecondsIfPresent()
// 3
guard let date = formatter.date(from: string)
    else { return Date() }
// 4
return date
```

Here's the play-by-play of what's happening above:

1. Remember that encoding and decoding is recursive, so the decoder that's passed to the closure doesn't represent the entire JSON object, but only the value that contains the date. Calling `singleValueContainer()` returns an instance of `SingleValueDecodingContainer`, which you use to decode the date into a string.

2. `deleteMillisecondsIfPresent()` is provided by an extension on `String`. It looks at the length of the string and if it equals 24, which is the length of an ISO8601-formatted date, including milliseconds, it removes characters 20-23.

3. Use the date formatter from the previous step to create a date from the string. If it can't, fail gracefully by simply returning today's date.

4. Return the date to the decoding process.

With your custom date handler implemented, you simply need to tell the decoding process to use it.

Replace the contents of the closure passed to `API.articles(source).fetch(_:)` with the following:

```
// 1
let decoder = JSONDecoder()
// 2
decoder.dateDecodingStrategy = .custom(customDateHandler)
// 3
if let articles = try! decoder.decode(
    Response.self, from: data).articles {
  self.articles = articles
}
```

Here's what's happening above:

1. Just like you did earlier, you create an instance of `JSONDecoder` so that you can configure its date handling manually.

2. This time you set the date decoding strategy to `.custom` and pass your custom date handler.

3. Ask the decode to decode the article's API JSON response into an instance of `Response`, and then attempt to unwrap the `articles` optional. If this succeeds you set `self.articles` to the unwrapped value.

Build and run, and choose **Bloomberg** as the news source:

The app should no longer crash, and you'll now see a properly formatted date displayed on each cell.

Where to go from here?

With very little effort, you've been able to decode two separate streams of JSON into the app's data layer using just a few lines of code and the magic of `Codable`. You've learned how to create custom mappings between your JSON keys and type properties, how to handle `null` values, how to massage data as part of the decoding process, and finally how to handle inconsistent dates.

On top of that you've also learned how you can use Key-Value Observing to decouple the data layer from the user interface, and observe changes in that data layer and have the interface update automatically.

I highly recommend you watch **What's New in Foundation**: http://apple.co/2v3RjsV, for more information on these and other changes to `Foundation`, as well as read these two articles by Greg Heo on the inner workings of `Encodable` and `Decodable`: http://bit.ly/2vUAJgd, http://bit.ly/2weXPke.

Your `Codable`-fu is strong. Go forth and decode!

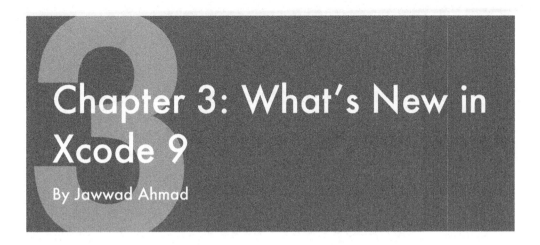

Chapter 3: What's New in Xcode 9

By Jawwad Ahmad

Xcode 9 brings with it a few major updates to Xcode, one of the most significant being refactoring support for Swift. Xcode's source editor has been completely rewritten in Swift, and because of this, scrolling, search and refactoring are extremely fast. Xcode now also has support for editing Markdown files as well. You can now build wirelessly to your device, and you can also open multiple simulators at the same time.

And if *that* wasn't enough, there is also GitHub account integration, a new source code navigator, much smarter fix-its, improvements to breakpoints, and the ability to run Xcode bots without the need to run a separate instance of Xcode Server.

In the first section of this chapter, you'll learn about all of the improvements to Xcode's source editor. In the second section, you'll learn about GitHub integration and the new Source Code navigator. The remaining sections will be shorter and will quickly cover a variety of topics.

There is a lot to explore, so let's dive right in!

Getting started

You'll explore the new features of Xcode with the ApplesToOranges app. It's an app that lets you compare fruits by calories. Say you wanted to know how many oranges it would take to equal the same amount of calories in five apples? With this app you can find out!

Open **ApplesToOranges.xcodeproj** from the starter folder of this chapter, and build and run the app. There are three tabs in the app. The first lets you convert from fruits to fruits, the second tab lets you specify the input in calories instead of fruits and the third tab is a basic settings tab that lets you edit the number of calories in each fruit.

Delicious!

You'll start off by learning all of the cool new things you can do with Xcode's brand new source editor.

Source editor improvements

Knowing and taking advantage of the various features of your editor is a key skill of a productive developer. This year, there have been a lot of improvements — not only in features, but also in performance, since the source editor has been completely rewritten in Swift.

Code structure

Start off by expanding all of the groups in the project navigator, and select **CaloriesInputViewController.swift** under the **Controllers** group.

Hold down the **Command** key and move your mouse over various parts of the code; for example, hover over the `class`, `func` and `var` keywords. Notice how different parts of the code structure highlight as you move over them:

```
private func reloadData() {
    let totalCalories = Double(caloriesTextField.text ?? "") ?? 0
    fruitsTableViewController.configure(calories: totalCalories)
}
```

This can be pretty useful if you want to quickly see where a corresponding closing brace or closing parenthesis is.

Command-hover over `Double` in the first line of `reloadData()`, which will allow you to more easily see where its closing parenthesis is:

```
private func reloadData() {
    let totalCalories = Double(caloriesTextField.text ?? "") ?? 0
    fruitsTableViewController.configure(calories: totalCalories)
}
```

Find the following `if` statement towards the end of the file:

```
if let calories = Double(updatedText) {
```

With nested if-statements, it may be a bit difficult to tell at first glance where the closing brace is. If you hold down **Command** and hover over the `if` keyword or over the opening brace, Xcode will visually select the structure for you.

Actions menu

Now if you **Command-click** on the same `if` keyword, you'll see a context menu pop up with various actions you can take:

```
                                    82    Tunc textField(_ textField: UITextField, sh
                                          let currentText = textField.text ?? ""
   Q Actions                              let updatedText = (currentText as NSStrin

  {∞}  Fold                            if let calories = Double(updatedText) {
                                          if calories <= maxCalories {
  }∘{  Add "else if" Statement             return true
                                          } else {
  ⌘()  Extract Method                       flashBackground(of: textField, with:
                                    90
```

You don't need to add an `else-if` statement right now, but click on the **Add "else if" Statement** option anyway, just to see what Xcode does. Then press **Command-Z** to undo.

For another example, locate the following method:

```
private func flashBackground(of view: UIView,
                            withColor color: UIColor) {
```

You'll get different options depending whether you click the `func` keyword instead of the method name itself.

Command-click on `func`.

```
                            }

Q Actions                   private func reloadData() {
                                let textFieldCalories = Double(caloriesTextField.text ?? "") ?? 0
 Jump to Definition    ^⌘       fruitsTableViewController.configure(calories: textFieldCalories)
                            }
 Show Quick Help       ⌥
                            private func flashBackground(of view: UIView, with color: UIColor) {
 Edit All in Scope              UIView.animate(withDuration: 0.2, animations: {
                                    view.backgroundColor = color
 Fold                           }, completion: { _ in
                                    UIView.animate(withDuration: 0.2) {
 Add Parameter                      view.backgroundColor = nil
                                    }
 Add Return Type                })
                            })
 Rename...
```

Now **Command-click** on the `flashBackground` method name and note that you don't see the **Fold**, **Add Parameter** or **Add Return Type** options.

And if you **Command-click** on `private`, the actions menu won't appear at all.

If you like keyboard shortcuts, you can use **Command-Shift-A** to bring up the actions menu based on the position of your text cursor. Click on `func` to position your cursor on it and press **Command-Shift-A** to try it out.

Where's my "jump to definition" shortcut?

Over the years you've become used to **Command-clicking** to jump to the declaration of a variable or method, but now the new actions menu has hijacked that shortcut! Of course, you can choose **Jump to Definition** from the menu, but you'd still prefer to do it without the extra step.

You can jump directly if you hold down Control while Command-clicking: **Control-Command-click**. And since Control-clicking is the same as right-clicking, you can also use **Command-right-click**. And while we're on the topic, the keyboard shortcut is **Control-Command-J**. The J is for "Just Jump already!"

I want my Command-click shortcut back!

If you're still not satisfied with the above options, there is a preference that you can set to go back to the previous behavior of just Command-clicking.

In the Preferences dialog on the **Navigation** tab, you'll see a dropdown for **Command-click on Code**. From there, you can select the **Jumps to Definition** option.

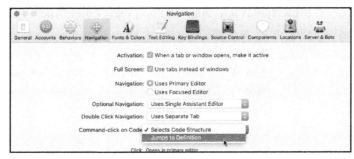

If you select this option, you can use **Command-right-click** for the actions menu.

Refactoring is back

Refactoring is back, and it's better than ever! It's been a long wait, but you'll love how smooth and fast refactoring is now.

You'll use this shiny new functionality to rename a class. Towards the top of `CaloriesInputViewController`, locate the following line:

```
private var fruitsTableViewController:
    FruitsDisplayTableViewController!
```

The word "Display" in `FruitsDisplayTableViewController` feels superfluous, so you'll remove it. **Command-click** on `FruitsDisplayTableViewController` and select **Rename**. Xcode will then show anywhere the class is used including in `Main.storyboard`:

Rename the class to **FruitsTableViewController** and press **Enter**. And with that, you're done! Even the filename has been renamed.

If you just want to rename a local variable you can use the same steps, but it's faster to use the **Edit All in Scope** option. The shortcut for **Edit All in Scope** is **Command-Control-E**. There isn't a shortcut for **Rename**, but you can set a custom one in Preferences.

New fix-its

When implementing a protocol, wouldn't it be nice if Xcode could insert the required methods for you? Now it can!

Open **SettingsTableViewController.swift** and locate the following line in `textFieldEditingDidEnd`:

```
if let index = FruitStore.fruits.index(
  where: { $0.name == fruit.name }) {
```

Wouldn't it be nice if you could write it in the following way?

```
if let index = FruitStore.fruits.index(of: fruit) {
```

Replace it with the shorter version and note the compiler error:

```
Cannot invoke 'index' with an argument list of type '(of:
Fruit)'
```

This is because `Fruit` does not yet implement `Equatable`. No problem, you'll go ahead and add it.

Open **Fruit.swift**, and at the very bottom of the file add the following extension:

```
extension Fruit: Equatable {

}
```

You'll now see the following compile error:

```
Type 'Fruit' does not conform to protocol 'Equatable'
```

Note that there is a small dot to the left of the error. That's an indication that this includes a fix-it, otherwise, it would have been a tiny exclamation point.

Click on the red dot and you'll see Xcode's offer to add the protocol stub for you.

```
50
51  extension Fruit: Equatable {
52
53  }
54
55
```

    ⊘ Type 'Fruit' does not conform to protocol 'Equatable'   ⊗
       Do you want to add protocol stubs?   Fix

Click on **Fix** and Xcode will enter the method signature for you.

```
extension Fruit: Equatable {
  static func ==(lhs: Fruit, rhs: Fruit) -> Bool {
    [code]
  }
}
```

Replace the **code** placeholder with the following:

```
return lhs.name == rhs.name
```

You should end up with the following:

```
extension Fruit: Equatable {
  static func ==(lhs: Fruit, rhs: Fruit) -> Bool {
    return lhs.name == rhs.name
  }
}
```

And you're done! The code will now compile successfully.

There are many other new fix-its as well, such as adding missing overrides, adding remaining case statements and many more.

Parentheses and quoting around selection

Sometimes you'd like to enclose a boolean condition in parentheses for readability.

Open **FruitsInputViewController** and locate the following line:

```
let containWord = countTextField.text == "1" ?
  "Contains" : "Contain"
```

Select `countTextField.text == "1"` with your mouse and type an opening parenthesis (on the keyboard. In previous versions of Xcode, this would have replaced the highlighted text with an open parenthesis, but now it encloses the selected text within a pair of parentheses for you. This behavior also works with square brackets and quotes, such as [and ".

Command +/-

The ⌘+ and ⌘- shortcuts are almost universal in macOS applications to either Zoom in or out, or to increase or decrease the font size. However, support for this has been lacking in Xcode... until now! No longer do you have to go into preferences to change your font size.

Try it out! When you're done being mesmerized, use **Control-Command-0** to reset.

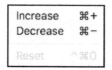

Code folding

Did you miss being able to fold methods and comments in Swift? The wait is over! Position your cursor within a method and press **Command-Option-Left** to collapse it.

You can also collapse comments. Press **Command-Up** to move your cursor to the top of the file, then press **Command-Option-Left** to collapse the copyright text.

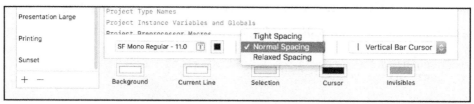

New editor options

You can now adjust the line spacing in the **Fonts & Colors** tab of preferences:

Choose between Tight, Normal and Relaxed

The Tight Spacing option in Xcode 9 is still more relaxed than the default spacing in Xcode 8. With the Tight Spacing option, you're able to see approximately 96 lines in the editor, whereas in Xcode 8 you would have seen 104 in the same amount of space. Since you're wondering, it's 84 lines with Normal Spacing, and 75 with Relaxed.

You can also update the cursor to an **Underline Cursor** or a **Block Cursor** in case you're an eccentric:

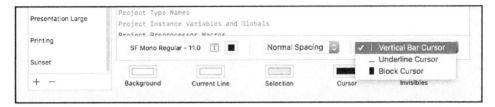

Trailing newlines by default

You'll never again forget to include the trailing newline, as Xcode now adds one by default. In fact, you can't even delete the last newline. Try it!

You can close the ApplesToOranges project for now, but leave Xcode open. Next, you'll learn about GitHub integration and the new source control navigator.

Source control improvements

Xcode 9 brings GitHub account integration and a new source control navigator. You can search for and clone GitHub projects without leaving Xcode. You can also create branches, merge branches and push code to GitHub all from within Xcode.

GitHub account integration

If you haven't yet added your GitHub account to Xcode, do this now since you'll be using it to clone a GitHub repository from within Xcode.

Open Preferences and go to the **Accounts** tab. Click on the + button at the bottom left, then select **GitHub** and click on **Continue**. Enter your login credentials and click **Sign In**. Close Preferences once you're done.

Clone a repository

In Xcode's menu bar, click on **Source Control** and select **Clone....** In the search bar, enter **alamofire** and select the first result that comes up:

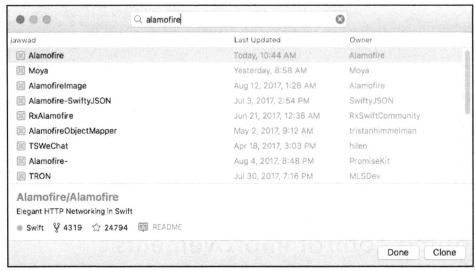

From this view, you can also star a repository, as well as view the README file.

With the first result selected, click **Clone**. Select a directory to save it to and click **Clone**. Now press **Command-2** to open up the new **source control navigator**. Select the **master** branch and you'll see the commits for the master branch in the main editor.

While you can **Double-click** on any commit to view the changes for that commit, it's nicer to view the changes in the assistant editor. Hold down **Option** and **Double-click** on a commit to open it up in the assistant editor:

You can select different commits in the main editor and the details will show up in the assistant editor. If the assistant editor doesn't automatically update, you might have to change the mode of the assistant editor from **Manual** to **Commit**:

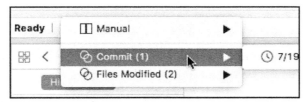

When you're done browsing, use **Command-Enter** to close the assistant editor.

Searching and filtering

You can search for and filter commits in various ways such as **Last 24 Hours**, **Last 7 Days** or **Last 30 Days**. You can also filter by author, commit message or revision.

Type **changelog** in the search field. As you type, you'll see that you can select the **Message:** or **Author:** prefix to limit the scope of the search.

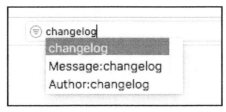

For now, simply press **Enter**, which will search both. You can modify the scope later by clicking on the **ALL** dropdown and selecting **Message**, **Author** or **Revision**:

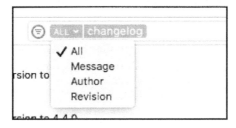

Next, you'll search by a SHA. Right-click on any commit and select **Copy Identifier**:

Clear the existing search text and paste the copied SHA into the search field. In the search results, you'll only see the commit with that revision.

Note that when searching by revision, Xcode will only search from the beginning of the SHA. This isn't the case with message and author search where you can start from the middle, so if you type **"angelog"** you'll still see results for **changelog**. However, fuzzy search won't work in this case, so typing **chalog** won't yield any results.

One handy option to note in the right-click context menu is the **View on GitHub...** option, which will open that specific commit on github.com in your default browser.

Branching and merging

You'll now make a minor "throwaway" update to **README.md** on a branch, and then you'll merge that branch into master — right from within Xcode.

Right-click on **master** and select **Branch from "master"...**:

Enter **readme-update** for the name and click **Create**. Xcode will also check out the newly created branch for you. Use **Command-Shift-O** to open the **Open Quickly** search, and type in **readme**. Hit **Enter** to open up README.md.

Anywhere in the file, type in # **Test Heading** on a line by itself:

Select **Source Control\Commit...**. Type **Test commit** for the message.

Next, select the **readme-update** branch in the Source Control navigator and you should see your latest commit at the top.

Now you'll merge this branch into **master**. Right-click on the **master** branch and select **Merge "readme-update" into "master"**...:

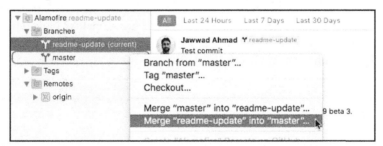

Click on **Merge** on the confirmation prompt, and click on **Merge** on the next view as well. Xcode has also switched you back to the **master** branch, so now you can **Right-click** on the **readme-update** branch and select **Delete**.

That's all for the new GitHub integration and source control features. For more on using Xcode's integrated Git support, check out our "How To Use Git Source Control with Xcode 9" tutorial at raywenderlich.com. Close the cloned Xcode project, and re-open the **ApplesToOranges** project.

Breakpoint improvements

Xcode 9 makes it much easier to use edited breakpoints. Edited breakpoints show a modified breakpoint symbol, code completion works in breakpoint text fields and you can search for breakpoints based on the text of the conditions you've set.

Editing breakpoints

First, you'll introduce a bug. Instead of using the local `fruits` variable, which contains alphabetically sorted fruits, you'll use `FruitStore.fruits`. Open **FruitsInputViewController.swift** and change the following line in `reloadData()`:

```
let selectedFruit = fruits[selectedRow]
```

To the following:

```
let selectedFruit = FruitStore.fruits[selectedRow]
```

Build and run **ApplesToOranges**. Coincidentally, Bananas are at the same index in both arrays so the initial view is correct. In the picker view, select apples. Note that it shows 5 apples as equal to 24.4 apples in the table view, which seems fishy.

You'd like to diagnose the issue without building and running the app again. In `reloadData()`, add a breakpoint on the `let totalCalories` line since you want to inspect `selectedFruit` after it's been set.

Right-click on the breakpoint, and select **Edit Breakpoint**. Leave **Condition** blank, and click on **Add Action**. In the dropdown, select **Debugger Command** and type po `selectedFruit`. Did you note the new autocomplete functionality? Now type a single period, and select **name** in the autocomplete dropdown. Finally, add a checkmark to **Automatically continue after evaluating actions**:

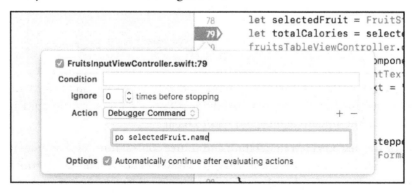

Click outside the window to exit the breakpoint editor, and note that the breakpoint now has a small white triangle within in, indicating that it has been edited.

Hover your mouse over the breakpoint, and you'll see that it says **This breakpoint has an action and will automatically continue**:

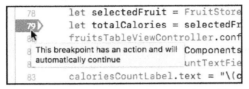

Back in the simulator, select Bananas from the picker and you'll see "Banana" printed to the console. But when you select Apples, you'll see "Pineapple" printed!

Fixing this bug is left as an exercise for the reader. :]

Searching breakpoints

You can now filter breakpoints by the text you've entered into any of its text fields. Add a breakpoint on the line above the existing breakpoint, just so that you have another breakpoint to filter against.

Select the breakpoint navigator (⌘8) and click in the **Filter** field at the bottom. Type in **selected** and note that you can only see the edited breakpoint. Delete **selected** and you'll see both of them.

You can also use the tiny filter buttons at the bottom to show only modified or active breakpoints:

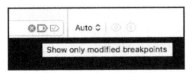

Folder and group synchrony

If you like to keep your folders and groups in sync, you're going to love this change. In Xcode 9, moving a file from one Xcode group to another Xcode group will also physically move it to that folder as well!

Open a Finder window and navigate to the **ApplesToOranges** directory. Ensure that you see the folders in list view, and expand the **Models** and **Views** folders.

Name	Date Modified	Size ⌄
▼ 🗀 ApplesToOranges	Today, 11:24 AM	132 KB
▶ 🗀 Assets.xcassets	Today, 11:24 AM	42 KB
▶ 🗀 Base.lproj	Today, 1:01 PM	29 KB
▶ 🗀 Controllers	Today, 3:56 PM	16 KB
🗎 Settings.storyboard	Today, 11:24 AM	11 KB
▼ 🗀 Models	Today, 2:10 PM	11 KB
🗎 FruitStore.swift	Today, 11:24 AM	2 KB
🗎 Fruit.swift	Today, 2:10 PM	2 KB
▼ 🗀 Views	Today, 11:24 AM	10 KB
🗎 FruitSettingsCell.swift	Today, 11:24 AM	2 KB
🗎 FruitCell.swift	Today, 11:24 AM	2 KB
▶ 🗀 Helpers	Today, 11:24 AM	2 KB

In Xcode, move **FruitStore.swift** to the **Views** group and note that the file has also moved in the Finder. Move it back and you'll see the same happen in the Finder as well.

Next, you'll create a new group. Select **AppDelegate.swift**, right-click on it, and select **New Group from Selection**. Name the group **App Delegate** and note that the directory also shows up in Finder.

On second thought, remove the space to make the group name **AppDelegate** and note that the folder is renamed in the finder window as well.

Improved view debugger

The view debugger has been greatly improved in Xcode 9. Along with the view hierarchy, it will also show View Controllers within the hierarchy. This is especially useful when getting up to speed on a new project in order to find out what view controller is being displayed.

With the app running click on the **Debug View Hierarchy** button:

Note the various view controllers within the debug navigator. You can also inspect a view controller's properties in the **Object Inspector** (⌥⌘3) pane on the right.

You can now also debug SpriteKit and SceneKit scenes with the view debugger as well.

Runtime issues checker

Xcode 8 already contained two runtime issue checkers: **Address Sanitizer** and **Thread Sanitizer**. Xcode 9 adds two more, **Undefined Behavior Sanitizer** which can check for various issues in C-based languages, and **Main Thread Checker**, which will make sure that you don't have UI-updating code on a background thread. The Main Thread Checker has negligible overhead and is therefore turned on by default.

Of course, you would *never* make this mistake yourself, but you'd still like to see the **Main Thread Checker** in action. Open **FruitSettingsCell.swift** and wrap the first line in the `configure` method in a `DispatchQueue.global().async` call so that you have the following:

```
DispatchQueue.global().async {
    self.fruitNameLabel.text = "\(fruit.emojiChar) \(fruit.name)"
}
```

Build and run the app. Note that there are no warnings when the app starts. Navigate to the Settings tab and note that the runtime warning appears:

```
38    func configure(fruit: Fruit, index: Int) {
39        DispatchQueue.global().async {
40            self.fruitNameLabel.text = "\(fruit.emojiChar) \(fruit.name)"   ⬛ UILabel.text must be used from main thread only
41        }
42        caloriesTextField.text = Formatter.string(from: fruit.calories)
```

You can also turn on the option to pause on runtime issues in the scheme editor.

Simulator improvements

Xcode 9 brings many improvements to the simulator. You've already seen the shiny new bezel, but it's not all for looks: the volume, power and ringer buttons on the bezel are functional as well. You also scale the simulator to any size by dragging any one of its corners.

You can now also have more than one iOS Simulator running. If you build and run to a new simulator, the previous simulator will remain open. This can be useful if you'd like to run the app side-by-side on two different simulators, and can also speed up testing if you'd like to run your tests on more than one simulator.

The simulator now also supports face-up and face-down orientations on supported devices.

Xcode Server

Xcode now allows you to run bots on macOS without the need for a separate Xcode server. In Preferences, there is a new **Server & Bots** tab that you can use to turn on to use various integration bots.

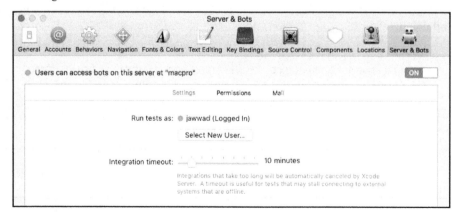

Wireless development

You can now build and run to your device wirelessly. Go to **Devices and Simulators** in the **Window** menu (⇧⌘2). Plug in your device and enable **Connect via network**.

Enable the Connect via network option

As long as you're on the same Wi-Fi network, you won't need to plug your phone in to build to it.

New build system

Xcode 9 includes a new build system written in Swift. It improves performance and catches many project configuration problems that the current build system does not catch. It's currently opt-in, but will become the default in a future version of Xcode.

To enable the build system, go to **File\Project Settings**. In the first dropdown, choose **New Build System** (**Preview**) and select **Done**.

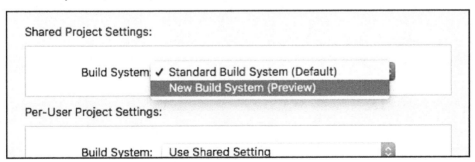

Where to go from here?

In this chapter, you've learned about the great new features in Xcode 9.

Here are a few WWDC sessions that are quite relevant to your interests as a developer in Xcode 9:

- Session 404: Debugging with Xcode 9 apple.co/2wlqhOH

- Session 401: Localizing with Xcode 9 apple.co/2uynlMw

- Session 406: Finding Bugs Using Xcode Runtime Tools apple.co/2wllzk5

- Session 405: GitHub and the New Source Control Workflows in Xcode 9

apple.co/2ufYWMk

Chapter 4: What's new in UIKit

By Jeff Rames

UIKit received a lot of love from Apple in iOS 11. Some came in the form of shiny new features like Drag and Drop and Document Browser. But as usual, incremental improvements to existing features were sprinkled throughout the framework.

This chapter is a tour of some of the most important updates to UIKit. Here's a look at what you'll be working on:

- **Paste configuration** is a new feature that allows responder objects to control paste and simple drop operations.

- **Drag and Drop** is covered in great detail in Chapters 6 and 7. Here, you'll learn the basics and configure a simple drag and drop within a table view.

- **Table view** now has a more robust swipe interaction API and closure-based batch updates. You'll get an overview of additional features covered in other chapters as well.

- **Accessibility** gains some new attributed labels, drag and drop support, and a HUD-like display for hard-to-see controls.

- **Asset catalogs** now support color sets for defining your custom colors.

Wait a minute — those large navigation titles with the integrated search bar seemed like a big deal. Password AutoFill and the new document browser were notable too! Aren't *those* important UIKit updates?

Put down the pitchforks and hear me out! iOS 11 is packed with *so* many UIKit goodies that this book has several chapters dedicated to them. Here's a quick overview of chapters covering UIKit changes you might want to check out:

- **Chapter 5, What's New in Layout** is where you'll find info on safe areas, large navigation titles, updates to scroll view's layout system, and layout changes for stack view and table view. This should be your next stop if you want a broader overview of UIKit updates.

- **Chapter 8, Document-Based Apps** introduces a feature that allows your users to view shared local and remote documents from your app.

- **Chapter 14, Password Autofill** is a new feature that allows apps to display keyboard autofill suggestions for credentials saved to iCloud Keychain.

- **Chapter 15, Dynamic Type** is a deep dive into dynamic type including iOS 11 updates.

Clearly, there's a lot to learn. You'll start by exploring an app in need of some of these features.

Getting started

You'll be working with Green Grocer, an app that lets a produce store's customers browse available products and create shopping lists. Adding products from the product to shopping list is only possible via copy and paste. Green Grocer is otherwise the pinnacle of iOS 10 technology.

You're about to make it a whole lot better with a little iOS 11 UIKit magic! Open **GreenGrocer.xcodeproj** in the starter project folder. Build and run and have a look around.

On the **Products** tab, long press a cell, then tap **Copy**. On the **List** tab, tap **+**, then paste the copied product into the text view. Tap **Add**, and you'll see the item in your shopping list.

Green Grocer has gotten its fair share of poor reviews on the app store. Many people find the process of adding items to the shopping list to be cumbersome. Some appreciate the alphabetic list sorting, but others wish they could order the items as they see fit.

You're going to tackle these requests and more in the sections ahead. Let's jump right in!

Paste configuration

The new `UIPasteConfiguration` allows UIResponders to configure what types of paste operations they can accept. Additionally, UIResponders can implement `paste(itemProviders:)` to act upon pasted data.

A key here is the use of `NSItemProvider` for conveying the pasted data. This not only enables paste operations, but simple drop operations as well.

As you saw previously, the Add Item view of Green Grocer accepts the string representation of a product. You're going to change it to accept the entire product object.

Open **ProductTableViewCell.swift** and locate `copy(_:)`. Replace the `UIPasteboard` line with the following:

```
let data = NSKeyedArchiver.archivedData(withRootObject: product)
UIPasteboard.general.setData(data,
    forPasteboardType: Product.productTypeId)
```

You call `archivedData(withRootObject:)` to encode the `product` associated with the copied cell. That data is copied to the pasteboard with `setData`, along with the custom `productTypeId` string.

In **AddItemViewController.swift** add the following below the call to super in
viewDidLoad():

```
pasteConfiguration =
  UIPasteConfiguration(acceptableTypeIdentifiers:
    [Product.productTypeId])
```

This sets the pasteConfiguration property defined in the
UIPasteConfigurationSupporting protocol, which UIResponder adopts.
acceptableTypeIdentifiers takes an array of UTI strings representing data types you
want to accept. You use the custom productTypeId to identify the Product object, just
as you did for the copy.

This was made possible by the fact that Product adopts another new protocol —
NSItemProviderReading. This allows the object to be instantiated via data provided by
an NSItemProvider. To learn more about how this works, check out Chapter 7,
"Advanced Drag and Drop".

Next, add the following method to AddItemViewController:

```
override func paste(itemProviders: [NSItemProvider]) {
  // 1
  itemProviders.forEach {
    $0.loadObject(ofClass: Product.self) { object, _ in
      guard let product = object as? Product
        else { return }
      let productImage = UIImage(named: product.photoName)
      // 2
      DispatchQueue.main.async { [weak self] in
        guard let `self` = self else { return }
        self.itemTextField.text = product.name
        self.productImageView.image = productImage
      }
    }
  }
}
```

paste(itemProviders:) is called when a paste compatible with the
UIPasteConfiguration occurs. Inside, you're doing the following:

1. The method receives an array of NSItemProvider objects, provided by the
   pasteboard. You call loadObject on each to obtain the product it has archived.
   Note that while this code can handle multiple providers, you're only expecting one
   product.

2. You dispatch to the main thread so that you can update the UI with the product
   data. This uses the product name for the text field, and displays its image in a view
   up top.

Build and run, copy an item from the **Products** table, and paste it in **Add Item**. This time, you'll see the product image load in addition to the name.

Open **Photos.app** and copy any image. Switch back to Green Grocer and attempt to paste on the **Add Item** view. The paste menu won't appear, because UIImage was not in the `pasteConfiguration`! However, because `UITextField` accepts `Strings`, attempts to paste text will be forwarded and work as before.

This code is also all you need for simple custom view drop operations. To learn about the drag side of that, check out Chapter 7, "Advanced Drag and Drop". In the meantime, you're going to explore table view drag and drop in the next section.

Drag and drop basics

Drag and drop was one of the most exciting features announced for iOS 11, and an important one to add to your toolbox. While it truly shines on the iPad when copying data between split screened apps, this is only part of the story.

Data can be copied, moved or even shared in place, allowing an app to modify strictly-controlled data living in another app. Controls can be spring-loaded, allowing drags to trigger actions or navigation events. All of this can be done between apps or within an app — even on the iPhone.

During a drag, data is serialized and then presented in a system controlled preview the user physically drags. On a drop, the serialized data is copied to the destination, deserialized and then presented to the user.

For drag and drop with custom views, you have very granular control over the animations and presentation of all phases of the interaction. Most of this happens in `UIDragInteractionDelegate` and `UIDropInteractionDelegate`, which you can learn much more about in Chapter 7.

Table and collection views get specialized support for drag and drop. You have a bit less control over the way it looks than with custom views, but the basics are the same. Let's dive right in and see how it works by adding the ability to reorder items on the shopping list.

Add the following extension to the bottom of **ShoppingListViewController.swift** and :

```
// 1
extension ShoppingListViewController: UITableViewDragDelegate {
  public func tableView(
    _ tableView: UITableView,
    itemsForBeginning session: UIDragSession,
    at indexPath: IndexPath) -> [UIDragItem]
  {
    // 2
    let listItem = shoppingList[indexPath.row]
    // 3
    let provider = NSItemProvider(object: listItem)
    let dragItem = UIDragItem(itemProvider: provider)
    return [dragItem]
  }
}
```

Here's what you're doing:

1. `UITableViewDragDelegate` is responsible for managing the drag interaction on a table view. `tableView(_:itemsForBeginning:at:)` is the sole required method. Its job is to provide a list of `UIDragItem` objects that represent the data to be dragged for the given `indexPath`.

2. You pull the current row's backing `ListItem` from `shoppingList`, the table view's data source. Note that `ListItem` already conforms to `NSItemProviderWriting`, which enables serialization. Take a look at **ListItem.swift** in the `NSItemProviderWriting` extension if you'd like to see how this is done.

3. `NSItemProvider` coordinates serializing and transferring `listItem` between the source and destination. This `provider` is wrapped in a `UIDragItem`, which represents a single object being dragged. As this method is capable of managing multi-item drags, you place the `dragItem` in an array before returning.

> **Note:** Collection views have virtually identical drag and drop APIs to those of
> table view. Naming is the main difference, with delegates named
> `UICollectionViewDragDelegate` and `UICollectionViewDropDelegate`. You
> will explore this in much more detail in Chapter 6.

In `viewDidLoad()`, add the following just below the call to `super`:

```
tableView.dragDelegate = self
tableView.dragInteractionEnabled = true
```

This sets the delegate you've just implemented. `dragInteractionEnabled` is set to
`true` to allow drags on the iPhone. For iPad, this value defaults to `true`.

Build and run, and select the **My List** tab. Long press a cell, and drag once the item lifts.
When you release, you'll see it neatly animate back to its origin, because you haven't yet
implemented the drop.

Let's implement that drop! Add the following to `ShoppingListViewController`:

```
extension ShoppingListViewController: UITableViewDropDelegate {
  func tableView(_ tableView: UITableView,
                 performDropWith
                 coordinator: UITableViewDropCoordinator) {
    // 1
    guard let destinationIndexPath
      = coordinator.destinationIndexPath
```

```
      else { return }

    // 2
    DispatchQueue.main.async { [weak self] in
      tableView.beginUpdates()
      // 3
      coordinator.items.forEach { (item) in
        guard let sourceIndexPath = item.sourceIndexPath,
          let `self` = self
          else { return }

        // 4
        let row = self.shoppingList
          .remove(at: sourceIndexPath.row)
        self.shoppingList
          .insert(row, at: destinationIndexPath.row)
        tableView.moveRow(at: sourceIndexPath,
                          to: destinationIndexPath)
      }
      tableView.endUpdates()
    }
  }
}
```

`ShoppingListViewController` now adopts `UITableViewDropDelegate` and implements the required method `tableView(_:performDropWith:)`. This is triggered when a drop is initiated. Taking a look at your implementation:

1. `destinationIndexPath` is the index path where the cell is being dropped. You obtain it from the `UITableViewDropCoordinator`, which is created by the system and manages animation of the drop.

2. You'll be moving rows here, so you dispatch to the main thread. Because the `coordinator` could contain multiple items to move, you wrap this code in `beginUpdates` and `endUpdates`.

3. The `coordinator` contains an array of `UITableViewDropItem` objects, each with a reference to a `dragItem` and its `sourceIndexPath`. For the shopping list you're only moving a single row, but this code will support dragging multiple rows.

4. You update the data source by removing the row at `sourceIndexPath` and adding it at `destinationIndexPath`. `moveRow` is then called to update the table view.

You've defined how a drop will happen, but before this happens, you have to negotiate the drop. Add the following to that same extension:

```
// 1
func tableView(
  _ tableView: UITableView,
  canHandle session: UIDropSession) -> Bool
```

```
{
  return session.canLoadObjects(ofClass: ListItem.self)
}

// 2
func tableView(
  _ tableView: UITableView,
  dropSessionDidUpdate session: UIDropSession,
  withDestinationIndexPath destinationIndexPath: IndexPath?)
  -> UITableViewDropProposal
{
  return UITableViewDropProposal(
    operation: .move,
    intent: .insertAtDestinationIndexPath)
}
```

Both of these are triggered as the `UIDragSession` and `UIDropSession` negotiate how to handle a drop. Here's a closer look:

1. `tableView(_:canHandle:)` returns a `Bool` indicating if this table view can handle data contained in the session. `canLoadObjects` checks if the `session` contains any items capable of loading a `ListItem`. This method will thus return `true` for sessions initiated by the item provider you created with `ListItem` objects.

2. `tableView(_:dropSessionDidUpdate:withDestinationIndexPath:)` is called as soon as a drag enters a droppable view, and is called continually as the drag proceeds. Its purpose is to return a `UITableViewDropProposal` that indicates what the `UIDropSession` wants to do with the incoming items. You return a proposal with the `move` operation and `insertAtDestinationIndexPath` intent, indicating you want to remove the item from the source and insert it at the destination index.

Now you just need to set the drop delegate. In `viewDidLoad()`, below the call to `super`, add the following:

```
tableView.dropDelegate = self
```

Now the delegate methods you defined will be triggered when a drop is initiated.

Build and run, and head to the **My List** tab. Drag an item from one spot on the list to another, and you'll see it drop in place. Magic!

As hinted, you can do quite a lot more with drag and drop in table views. Multiple item drags and custom drop animations would be great enhancements here.

To learn how to make those enhancements and more, check out Chapter 6, "Beginning Drag and Drop" which covers table and collection views. If you want to drag and drop with custom views, check out Chapter 7, "Advanced Drag and Drop".

What's new with table views

Drag and drop might be the most exciting addition, but table views received a few more goodies with iOS 11. You're about to use a couple of them to improve Green Grocer.

A top user complaint of the existing app is the number of manual steps required to get an item from the products table into the shopping list. You'll address this by adding a swipe action to the cell that will add an item straight to the shopping list.

This was possible prior to iOS 11 with `UITableViewRowAction`. However, iOS 11 introduced the more flexible `UISwipeActionsConfiguration`. This API allows leading and trailing actions, action button images and actions triggered by a full cell swipe.

Open **ProductTableViewController.swift** and add the following to the class:

```swift
override func tableView(
  _ tableView: UITableView,
  trailingSwipeActionsConfigurationForRowAt
  indexPath: IndexPath) -> UISwipeActionsConfiguration? {
  // 1
  guard let product = dataStore?.products[indexPath.row]
    else { return nil }

  // 2
  let addAction = UIContextualAction(style: .normal,
                                     title: "Add")
  { [weak self] (action, view, completionHandler) in // 3
    guard let `self` = self else {
      completionHandler(false)
      return
    }
    self.listController?.addItem(named: product.name)
    completionHandler(true)
  }
  addAction.backgroundColor = UIColor.ggGreen

  // 4
  let configuration =
    UISwipeActionsConfiguration(actions: [addAction])
  return configuration
}
```

Right-to-left swipe actions are enabled when you implement `tableView(_:trailingSwipeActionsConfigurationForRowAt:)` in your `UITableViewDelegate` and return a `UISwipeActionsConfiguration`. Here's a look at your implementation:

1. You obtain the `product` associated with the cell from the `dataStore`.

2. A `UIContextualAction` represents a swipe action, defining its appearance and what it does when selected. The `normal` style is used when you don't want a `destructive` action, which would delete the cell. The `title` "Add" will be shown on the button.

3. This closure will be executed when the action is selected. The `completionHandler` accepts a `Bool` indicating whether the action succeeded. `addItem`, found in **ShoppingListViewController.swift**, is passed the `product` to add to the list.

4. A `UISwipeActionsConfiguration` requires one or more actions to display for a swipe. In this case, you pass the lone `addAction`.

Next, you'll add a leading edge swipe. Add the following beneath the method you just added:

```swift
override func tableView(
  _ tableView: UITableView,
  leadingSwipeActionsConfigurationForRowAt
  indexPath: IndexPath) -> UISwipeActionsConfiguration?
{
  guard let product = dataStore?.products[indexPath.row]
    else { return nil }

  let copyAction = UIContextualAction(style: .normal,
                                      title: "Copy")
  { (action, view, completionHandler) in
    let data =
      NSKeyedArchiver.archivedData(withRootObject: product)
    UIPasteboard.general
      .setData(data, forPasteboardType: Product.productTypeId)
    completionHandler(true)
  }
  copyAction.backgroundColor = UIColor.ggDarkGreen

  let configuration =
    UISwipeActionsConfiguration(actions: [copyAction])
  return configuration
}
```

`tableView(_:leadingSwipeActionsConfigurationForRowAt:)` is just like its trailing action counterpart. You've created a `Copy` action that stores the product to the `UIPasteboard`. This will act as an alternate interaction to the currently implemented long press copy.

Build and run. Try a trailing swipe and tap the resulting **Add** button. You'll find the corresponding product added to your shopping list. Try a leading swipe, tap **Copy** and you'll be able to paste to the **Add Item** view.

Batch updates

Another small but very handy update to table view is the ability to perform batch updates in a closure with a completion handler. This may sound very familiar — because collection view has had this ability for some time! Let's give it a try by updating the batched move operations used in the drag and drop section.

Open **ShoppingListViewController.swift** and find `tableView(_:performDropWith:)`. Replace the contents of the `DispatchQueue.main.async` closure with the following:

```
tableView.performBatchUpdates(
  { coordinator.items.forEach { [weak self] (item) in
    guard let sourceIndexPath = item.sourceIndexPath,
      let `self` = self
      else { return }

    let row = self.shoppingList
      .remove(at: sourceIndexPath.row)
    self.shoppingList
      .insert(row, at: destinationIndexPath.row)
    tableView.moveRow(at: sourceIndexPath,
                      to: destinationIndexPath)
    }
}, completion: nil)
```

You deleted `beginUpdates` and `endUpdates` and wrapped the code between them in `performBatchUpdates`. This is much clearer visually, comes with the convenience of closures, and provides you a completion closure as well.

Build and run to confirm drag and drop still works properly on the shopping list.

You can learn about a few more new table view features in Chapter 5, "What's New in Layout":

- Automatic sizing for cell height is now on by default.

- `separatorInsetReference` is a new property that allows you to designate the point from where cell separator insets are measured. This works in combination with `separatorInset` to determine the horizontal start and end of separators.

- `UIRefreshControl` is now displayed within the navigation bar when added to a table view inside a navigation controller.

What's new in Accessibility

Accessibility is important to Apple, so it's no surprise there are some new features in iOS 11. In this section, you'll learn about a few notable changes.

Green Grocer already has basic support for VoiceOver with accessibility labels and hints for various controls. To work with it, you'll need a physical device running iOS 11. If you don't have one, feel free to skip ahead.

Open the **Settings** app on your device, navigate to **General\Accessibility\Accessibility Shortcut** and select **VoiceOver**. This will allow you to enable and disable VoiceOver by triple clicking your home button.

Run Green Grocer, navigate to **My List**, then tap **+** to get to the screen for adding list items. Enter an item in the text field, then triple click the home button to enable VoiceOver. Use left and right swipes to focus VoiceOver on the **Cancel** then **Add** button, and make a note of the tone used when describing them.

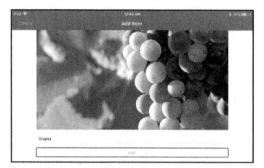

Open **AddItemViewController.swift** and look at `configureAccessibility`, where the text spoken was defined as follows:

```
addButton.accessibilityLabel = "Add"
addButton.accessibilityHint = "Add item to shopping list"

cancelButton.accessibilityLabel = "Cancel"
cancelButton.accessibilityHint = "Close without adding the item"
```

When you select the Cancel button, VoiceOver speaks the `accessibilityLabel` string, followed by the control type and then the `accessibilityHint`. The Add button also reads the text you had entered.

That's accomplished by this piece of code, also in `AddItemViewController`:

```
@objc func textFieldDidChange(_ textField: UITextField) {
  addButton.accessibilityValue = textField.text
}
```

`accessibilityValue` is read after the label. `textFieldDidChange` is set to fire every time the user modifies the text field, thus keeping the `accessibilityValue` up to date.

iOS 11 introduces attributed versions of these three attributes:

- `accessibilityAttributedLabel`

- `accessibilityAttributedHint`

- `accessibilityAttributedValue`

These use `NSAttributedStrings` to provide additional characteristics to your accessibility attributes. A particularly handy one is `UIAccessibilitySpeechAttributePitch`, which controls the pitch of the spoken text. This can be used to convey additional information about a control without slowing things down.

Apple suggests using a lower pitch to identify destructive operations, and higher pitch for creation. Let's try this with Green Grocer's Add and Cancel buttons.

Change the contents of `configureAccessibility` to the following:

```
let addLabel = NSAttributedString(string:
  "Add ", attributes: [NSAttributedStringKey(
    UIAccessibilitySpeechAttributePitch): 1.5])
addButton.accessibilityAttributedLabel = addLabel
addButton.accessibilityHint = "Add item to shopping list"

let cancelLabel = NSAttributedString(string:
  "Cancel ", attributes: [NSAttributedStringKey(
    UIAccessibilitySpeechAttributePitch): 0.5])
cancelButton.accessibilityAttributedLabel = cancelLabel
cancelButton.accessibilityHint = "Close without adding the item"
```

For both labels, you create an `NSAttributedString` with one attribute — `UIAccessibilitySpeechAttributePitch`. For `addLabel` you set the pitch to 1.5 and for `cancelLabel` you used 0.5. You use the same text as before, and add the attributed label using `accessibilityAttributedLabel`.

Build and run, enable VoiceOver, and listen to the pronunciation of the buttons you've modified in **Add Item**. As promised, the Add button's spoken text is higher pitched, and the Cancel button lower.

Accessibility also added `UIAccessibilityLocationDescriptor` to enable VoiceOver for drag and drop operations. These descriptors define names for draggable locations within a view. For a demo of this, check out the 2017 WWDC session on Accessibility here: apple.co/2uh7Tt1

A couple of interesting changes were made to `UITabBar` as well. When the phone is rotated to landscape mode, UITabBar now displays icons side by side with their titles in a shorter bar. `UIBarItem.landscapeImagePhone` can be set to display a custom image for the iPhone landscape UITabBar. For Green Grocer, the standard image is simply resized.

For users with limited eyesight, the smaller tab bar images pose an issue. To address this, Apple added the ability to display a pop up HUD containing a large version of the image upon long press. This feature exists in UITabBar, UIToolbar and UINavigationBar automatically.

When using a vector image for the tab bar icon, iOS will automatically resize it for the HUD without sacrificing quality. Green Grocer already has PDF tab bar icons, so you're going to leverage this.

Open **Assets.xcassets** and find **fruitbowl-green** in the icons folder. Select the icon and bring up the Attributes Inspector. Check **Preserve Vector Data** near the top of the image set options. Do the same for the **list-green** image set.

This option allows iOS to resize the assets as needed for different display purposes. In this case, you're adding it to better support landscape iPhone display and the large HUD.

> **Note:** If you don't have vector images, you can provide the HUD with a larger image via the `largeContentSizeImage` UIBarItem property. This property is also available in Interface Builder under **Accessibility** when viewing the tab bar item in Attribute Inspector.

Users will only see the accessibility HUD if they enable Large Text of a certain size. Open the **Settings** app, and navigate to **General\Accessibility\Larger Text**. Switch it on, and select a text size at least two notches higher than the middle of the scale.

Build and run Green Grocer. Long press on either tab bar icon, and you'll see the HUD display as a nicely scaled vector.

You've probably noticed that Green Grocer does not handle Dynamic Type. This feature also received attention in iOS 11, adding support for custom fonts and more. If you are interested in learning more, check out Chapter 15, "Dynamic Type".

UIColor in asset catalogs

The ability to add **Color Sets** to asset catalogs is another small but welcome change this year. These work similarly to image sets, meaning you can drop them in related projects with ease. To check it out, you'll convert Green Grocer's custom colors to use them.

Open **Assets.xcassets**, click the + and select **New Color Set**. Do this twice, as you'll be adding two custom colors.

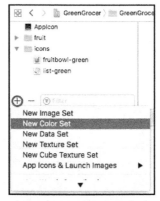

Select the color in the editor, and then open the Attributes Inspector. For the two colors, copy the **Name**, **Red**, **Green** and **Blue** values from these screenshots:

Open **AppAppearance.swift** and replace the UIColor extension at the top with:

```
let ggDarkGreen = "ggDarkGreen"
let ggGreen = "ggGreen"
```

These strings match the **name** values you set on your color sets. You'll use the names to load colors rather than the previously defined UIColor properties. In the meantime, you'll see some errors appear as the properties were being used in various places.

Find `styleNavBar` and locate the line that sets `barTintColor`. Replace it with this:

```
appearanceProxy.barTintColor = UIColor(named: ggDarkGreen)
```

`init(named:)` loads colors from asset catalogs based on name. Simple and clean!

You'll also see the deleted UIColor extensions used in `styleTabBar`, `styleTintColor` and `styleTabBarItem`. Replace these instances with `UIColor(named:)` versions. Be sure to use `ggGreen` or `ggDarkGreen` where appropriate. For `UIColor.ggGreen` used in `styleTabBarItem`, you'll need to force unwrap the named color like so:

```
UIColor(named: ggGreen)!
```

Finally, open **ProductTableViewController.swift** and find for `UIColor.ggGreen` and `UIColor.ggDarkGreen`. As with the others change these to use `UIColor(named:)` and the appropriate color.

Build and run, and confirm that the colors are working as before.

These colors are also easy to use in storyboards. From the color picker, your color sets will show up under **Named Colors**. Pretty handy!

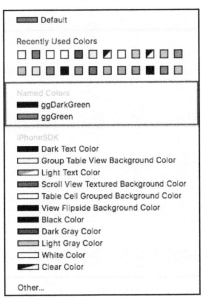

Where to go from here?

In this chapter, you scratched the surface of drag and drop and explored several more modest changes. You also received a rundown of other UIKit updates found elsewhere in this book. Now you know what's new with UIKit, and where to get more info.

For more on drag and drop, be sure to check out Chapters 6 and 7. Check the bulleted list at the start of this chapter for a reference of other UIKit topics covered in this book.

For more high-level UIKit coverage, check out the following WWDC sessions:

- **What's New in Cococa Touch**: apple.co/2vy2mOo
- **Updating Your App for iOS 11**: apple.co/2syu3Tt
- **What's New in Accessibility**: apple.co/2r9EASD

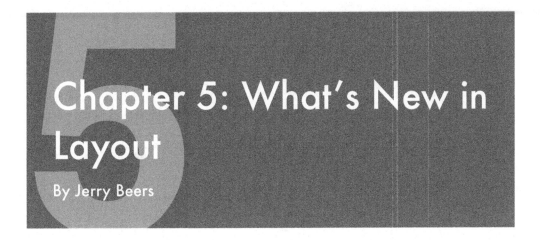

Chapter 5: What's New in Layout

By Jerry Beers

With a new 10.5" iPad, larger navigation bars that change size as you scroll, changes to content insets, and more, it's almost like Apple decided to show developers at WWDC 2017 exactly why they've been telling people to use Auto Layout for the last few years. As if multiple device screen sizes, split screen, and rotation weren't enough, these new features pile on to the list of reasons why Auto Layout is such a powerful tool. In fact, it's pretty much necessary to use Auto Layout for at least part of your interface.

In this chapter, you'll visit the most important of these updates as you migrate an iOS 10 app to use the new Auto Layout features of iOS 11.

Getting st-arrrr-ted

The starter app for this chapter is everyone's favorite pirate app: Pirate Handbook. The app is in the state you left it at the end of the https://videos.raywenderlich.com/courses/75-mastering-auto-layout/lessons/1 video tutorial series on raywenderlich.com. This app shows some different ways to handle adaptive layout, but it was built under iOS 10. In this chapter, you're going to update it for iOS 11 and explore what's new along the way.

Without futher ado, let's launch this voyage!

Large titles

The most obvious change in iOS 11 for apps that have a navigation bar is the new large titles:

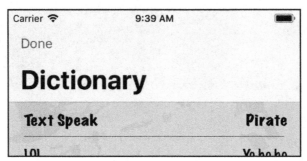

You can control whether view controllers' titles show in this new larger format at the UINavigationController level, using a property on UINavigationBar called prefersLargeTitles. You can also set it in Interface Builder by selecting the navigation bar in a navigation controller scene and then checking the **Prefers Large Titles** checkbox in the Attributes Inspector.

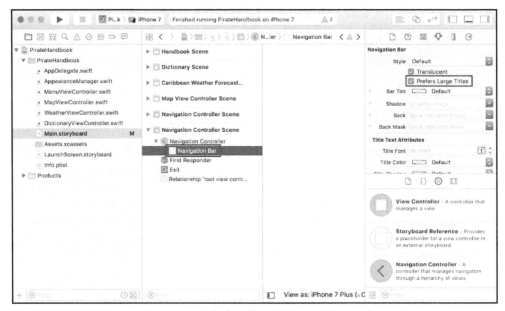

This property serves as a master switch for all view controllers in the navigation controller's hierarchy, and you'll check the box on both of the navigation controllers in your project.

Open the sample project, go to **Main.storyboard**, and click on one of the navigation controller scenes. Select the navigation bar, open the Attributes Inspector (**Command-Option-4** is the keyboard shortcut), and check the checkbox. Repeat for the other navigation controller scene.

Although this property is the master switch, each view controller has its own setting to control if it should show the large or normal title. The largeTitleDisplayMode on UINavigationItem can be set to a value of automatic, always, or never, with a default of automatic. The automatic setting will cause a view controller to inherit the setting of the previous view controller in the navigation stack. The other settings override this behavior, turning on or off the large titles for this view controller.

Typically, you want top-level view controllers to have large titles, but as you drill down, you want view controllers to have smaller titles. You can adjust these settings for your view controllers.

First, select the navigation item in the **Menu View Controller** scene. This controller doesn't yet have a title. In the Attributes Inspector, type **Handbook** for the title. You want this particular title to be large, but not the titles for the map or weather views. Therefore, you set both of those to never. Open the **Caribbean Weather Forecast** scene and select the navigation item. Set the **Large Title** to **Never**.

Repeat these steps for the **Secret Map** scene.

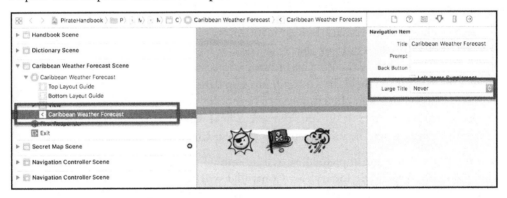

Note: You can control the attributes of the large titles using the largeTitleTextAttributes property on UINavigationBar or its appearance proxy.

Build and run, and you'll see the large title on the home screen. Open the dictionary (in the upper right corner), and if you tap on the map or weather forecast buttons, you'll see a nice transition animation from the large title to the smaller ones.

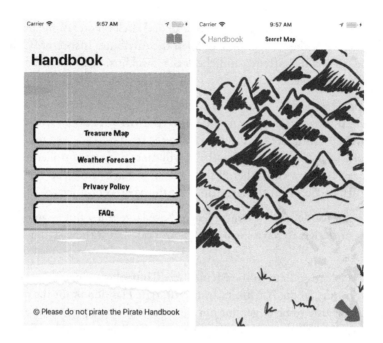

Search controllers

The second change to the navigation bar is the integration of search controllers. UISearchController is not new, but now you can set the searchController property of UINavigationItem to an instance of a search controller and the navigation bar will show the search field drawn inside the bar. UINavigationItem also has a new property, called hidesSearchBarWhenScrolling. If you set this to true, the navigation bar will automatically hide the search field when you scroll. If you want the field to show even when the user is scrolling through content, set this value to false.

Let's try it out. You won't implement search functionality, but you can still see what it would look like. Open **DictionaryViewController.swift** and add this line at the top of the class:

```
private var searchController =
  UISearchController(searchResultsController: nil)
```

Then, in awakeFromNib, after the call to super, add these lines:

```
navigationItem.searchController = searchController
navigationItem.hidesSearchBarWhenScrolling = true
```

Build and run and tap the book icon in the upper right corner to show the dictionary. Nothing looks different at first, but if you pull down on the table, you'll see the search field come into view. This is handy when you're trying to text your friends who don't speak pirate!

Now that navigation bars can be different sizes, and even change while scrolling, you might think it would be a pain to layout your view around the navigation bar. Well, that's where the new safe area concept comes in.

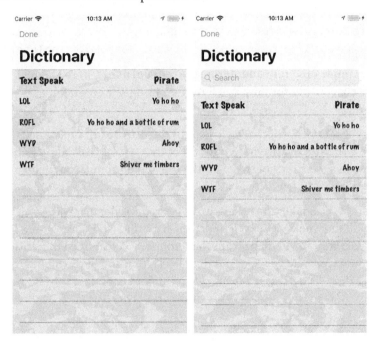

Safe area

When iOS 7 introduced translucency in the navigation and tab bars, it became more confusing as to where the "top" and "bottom" of a view were. If you wanted your view to show through the translucent bars, you'd usually make your top-level view expand to fill the screen and show under the navigation bar.

Then, for content inside that view, you might not want its position to start at the top of the view, but at the bottom of the navigation bar instead. That's why `topLayoutGuide` and `bottomLayoutGuide` on `UIViewController` were introduced, to let you set constraints between your views and the edges of those bars. Those are now deprecated in favor of a new guide, `safeAreaLayoutGuide`, which is a property on `UIView` instead of the controller.

For a view controller's root view, this guide represents the part of the view's visible area that is unobstructed by system views, such as the status bar, or ancestor views, such as the navigation bar. This "safe view area" is also modified and propagated down to child views, representing the portion of their view that is unobstructed.

The `safeAreaLayoutGuide` is perfect for creating constraints between your views and the safe area. But if you only want the measurements of the safe area, `safeAreaInsets` will return those values. And if you want to know when the values change, there are two methods to help: `UIView.safeAreaInsetsDidChange()` and `UIViewController.viewSafeAreaInsetsDidChange()`. If you want to add to the safe area exclusions, you can assign values to the `additionalSafeAreaInsets` property.

You'll see an example of setting `additionalSafeAreaInsets` in the Scroll Views section of this chapter, but for now, you'll turn on using safe area guides for the storyboard.

With the storyboard open, select any element in the storyboard. Open the File Inspector and check the **Use Safe Area Layout Guides** checkbox. Xcode will automatically convert any constraints that were previously set on the top and bottom layout guides to be set on the safe area guide.

One view that the automatic conversion won't get right is the map view. You want the scroll view to fill the whole view, even under the bars, and later you're going to learn how to add to the safe area, so you don't want the scroll view constrained to it. Select the **Scroll View** in the **Secret Map** scene and double-click on any of the **Sibling & Ancestor Constraints** that say Safe Area and change them to **Superview**.

Note: If you were setting constraints to `topLayoutGuide` and `bottomLayoutGuide` before, you'll notice a switch in mindset. The `topLayoutGuide` indicated the area covered by the status bar and navigation bar, but the `safeAreaLayoutGuide` indicates the area *uncovered* by the status and navigation bars. So before, if you wanted to constrain your view to the top, you would have added a constraint between your view's `topAnchor` and the `topLayoutGuide.bottomAnchor`. But in iOS 11, you can create a constraint between your view's `topAnchor` and the `safeAreaLayoutGuide.topAnchor`.

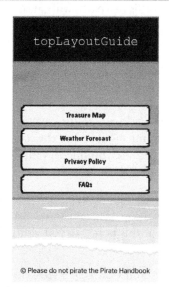 

iPhone X

In portrait orientation, the safe area guide on the iPhone X makes space for the notch at the top (I, for one, welcome our new notch overlords), and for the home indicator at the bottom. In landscape orientation, the safe area makes room on the leading *and* trailing edges of the display for the notch, no matter which way the device is rotated. This provides for a balanced look if you want your content to avoid the notch. But it will be up to you if you want your views to extend to the edges and be cutoff by the notch or respect the safe area to avoid it.

Margins

There are also some changes to margin behavior. The property `directionalLayoutMargins` replaces the now deprecated `layoutMargins`, although the guide remains `layoutMarginsGuide`. The new property allows for changes in reading direction, substituting `leading` and `trailing` for `left` and `right` values.

The values in `directionalLayoutMargins` are added to the ones in `systemMinimumLayoutMargins` to determine the actual margins for a view. If you do not want to respect the system minimum margins, you can set `viewRespectsSystemMinimumLayoutMargins` to `false`.

Finally, there is a new property that ties margins together with safe area: `insetsLayoutMarginsFromSafeArea`. With the default value of `true`, this will cause a view's margins to be relative to the safe area. Setting this to `false` will cause the margins to be relative to the view bounds instead.

Scroll views

When creating constraints to a scroll view prior to iOS 11, the Auto Layout system would employ some logic to determine if the constraint should be to the scroll view's frame or its content area. This could be confusing, because you might want to create a constraint to the frame, but the constraint would attach to the content area.

There are now two different guides for `UIScrollView`: `frameLayoutGuide` and `contentLayoutGuide`. These let you be precise when creating constraints to scroll views. Unfortunately, they're only available in code at this point, so you won't be able to connect to them in Interface Builder.

Another change concerns the content inset when a scroll view is in a view controller that is the child of a navigation controller. The `automaticallyAdjustsScrollViewInsets` property of `UIViewController`, which defaulted to `true`, would cause the content inset of your scroll view to be adjusted so the content wouldn't position under the navigation bar. If you were manually setting the content inset of your scroll view, you would have to be careful to take the system-set value into account.

Starting with iOS 11, the system will no longer set the content inset of your scroll view. Now, `adjustedContentInset` is calculated from the safe area and the values you set in `contentInset`, controlled by `contentInsetAdjustmentBehavior`.

To see how `additionalSafeAreaInsets` works in action, you'll add a legend to the treasure map, and use the new guides for setting constraints.

With the storyboard open, add a new `UIView` to the map scene. This will be the container for the other views. Set the background color to **#B1AA9F** at **90% opacity**.

Set the **top**, **leading**, and **width** constraints, but make them *placeholder* constraints by checking the **Remove at build time** checkbox on the Size Inspector of the constraint. Because these are placeholder constraints, it doesn't matter what values you use for these constraints; simply make the view visible somewhere on the screen somewhere.

I used 8 for leading, 518 for top and 398 for width, but you may need different values for things to look right on your storyboard.

Next, add two image views inside the container: one with the **x** image and one with the **arrow** image. Then, add two labels to the container: one that says **The Spot** and one that says **This Way**. Change the font on both labels to **Marker Felt Thin**.

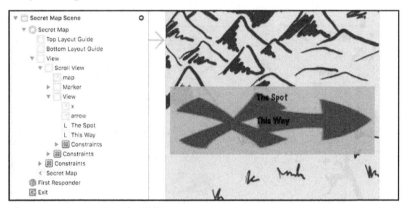

Now, set these constraints on the "x" image view:

- **Leading space**: 0 to superview margin

- **Width**: 33

- **Aspect ratio**: 1:1

- **Top space**: 8 to superview

- **Trailing space**: Standard to "The Spot" label (i.e. 20)

- **Align center y**: To "The Spot" label

- **Bottom space**: 0 to the arrow image view

And add these constraints to the arrow image view:

- **Leading space**: 0 to superview margin

- **Width**: 33

- **Aspect ratio**: 1:1

- **Bottom space**: 8 to superview

- **Trailing space**: Standard to "The Way" label (i.e. 20)

- **Align center y**: To "The Way" label

Update the frames of any views that are misplaced at this time. Everything looks good, but there are two more constraints you need to add.

On both labels, add a constraint from the trailing edge of the label to the trailing margin of the superview that is >= 0. Even though it is unlikely you'll ever need this constraint, if you ever localized your app, long text would run off the right edge. You'd prefer it to resize or clip before running off.

With all the constraints set, your storyboard will look like this:

Now that you have the legend, you need to add code to position it and adjust the safe area insets to account for it. Still in the storyboard, select **Secret Map** and click on the assistant editor to open **MapViewController.swift**.

Create two outlets: Control-drag from the view you just added and name it `legendContainer`, and then Control-drag from the scroll view and name it `scrollView`:

```
@IBOutlet weak var legendContainer: UIView!
@IBOutlet weak var scrollView: UIScrollView!
```

Next, add a couple of constants to `MapViewController`:

```
private let scrollIndicatorMargin: CGFloat = 8
private let legendCornerRadius: CGFloat = 8
```

Add a helper method, `setupLegend()`, to set up the legend view:

```
private func setupLegend() {
  // 1
  legendContainer.layer.cornerRadius = legendCornerRadius
  // 2
  legendContainer.leadingAnchor.constraint(
    equalTo: scrollView.frameLayoutGuide.leadingAnchor,
    constant: scrollIndicatorMargin)
    .isActive = true
  // 3
  legendContainer.trailingAnchor.constraint(
    equalTo: scrollView.frameLayoutGuide.trailingAnchor,
    constant: -scrollIndicatorMargin)
    .isActive = true
  // 4
  legendContainer.bottomAnchor.constraint(
    equalTo: view.safeAreaLayoutGuide.bottomAnchor,
    constant: legendContainer.frame.height)
    .isActive = true
  // 5
  additionalSafeAreaInsets = UIEdgeInsets(
    top: 0,
    left: 0,
    bottom: legendContainer.frame.height +
            scrollIndicatorMargin,
    right: scrollIndicatorMargin)
  // 6
  scrollView.contentInsetAdjustmentBehavior = .never
}
```

Taking this step-by-step:

1. You add rounded corners to make the legend container look nicer.

2. Use the new `frameLayoutGuide` to constrain the legend to the frame of the scroll view. Because you don't want the legend to scroll with the content, you constrain this to the frame and not the `contentLayoutGuide`. Note that you're making a decision here to position the legend container over the iPhone X notch when viewed in landscape. Because the content of the legend is constrained to the view margin, and the margin respects the safe area, the content will avoid the notch.

3. The value for constant is negative here because you're specifying the legend container first and the scroll view `frameLayoutGuide` second. You could switch the order and make this value positive; it simply depends on how your mind views the relationship.

4. On iPhone X, the safe area includes the home indicator on the bottom. You want the legend to be above that, but the next line of code adds additional space to the safe area, so you add a constraint to the bottom of the safe area, but use the constant to add back the height of the legend to position it correctly.

5. The `additionalSafeAreaInsets` property lets you add your own values to the safe area. Because the x/arrow indicator uses the safe area to know where to position, setting this value will make sure the indicator doesn't overlap the legend.

6. You want the contents of the map to start out underneath the navigation bar, so you tell the `scrollView` not to adjust its content using the safe area by setting the `contentInsetAdjustmentBehavior`.

Finally, update `viewDidLoad()` by adding `setupLegend()` right after where it calls `super.viewDidLoad()`:

```
override func viewDidLoad() {
  super.viewDidLoad()
  setupLegend()
  // ... the rest of the code.
}
```

Build and run and you'll see the legend at the bottom of the map and the indicator staying above it.

Self-sizing cells

Self-sizing cells have been around for a while, but in iOS 11 they're on by default. This means that cells will use the constraints between the subviews of the cell and the cell itself to determine the height of the cell. In the past, you could trigger this by setting `rowHeight` to `UITableViewAutomaticDimension` and supplying a value for `estimatedRowHeight`.

Now, the default value for both of these properties is `UITableViewAutomaticDimension` — not just for normal rows, but for headers and footers too. You can turn off automatic cell sizing by setting the `estimatedRowHeight` to `0`. When you add a new table view or table view controller to a storyboard in Interface Builder, these properties will also default to "Automatic".

If you already have a table from a project created in a previous version of Xcode, like the sample project, PirateHandbook, you can set these values in the Size Inspector. Open **Main.storyboard**, select the **Table View** in the **Dictionary** scene, and set the **Row Height** to **Automatic** in the Size Inspector.

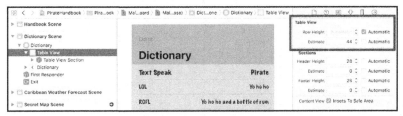

You can set the Estimate value to Automatic, but loading performance of the table view will be improved if you supply a reasonable value. Therefore, set **Estimate** to **44**. Since all the cells you're using have a built-in style, all the constraints are already set.

Build and run and open the Dictionary view to verify that everything still works as expected.

Refresh control

When you add a refresh control to a table view controller hosted in a navigation controller, it will automatically host the refresh control in the navigation bar. Open **DictionaryViewController.swift** and add these lines to the top of `awakeFromNib()` after the call to `super`:

```
refreshControl = UIRefreshControl()
refreshControl?.addTarget(
```

```
        self,
        action: #selector(simulateRefresh),
        for: .valueChanged)
```

Then add the following to the end of `DictionaryViewController`:

```
@objc func simulateRefresh() {
    DispatchQueue.main.asyncAfter(deadline: .now() + 2.5) {
        self.refreshControl?.endRefreshing()
    }
}
```

The method will wait for 2.5 seconds and then stop refreshing. This simulates a refresh that takes a couple of seconds. Now build and run, open the Dictionary view, and pull to refresh. You should see the refresh indicator in the navigation bar:

Insets

You now have more control over how table view cells inset their content and separators. You can set the left and right inset using `separatorInset`, and those values will automatically be flipped in right-to-left languages. You can also control where those insets are measured from using `separatorInsetReference`. If this value is set to `fromCellEdges`, the insets will be measured from the edge of the cell, but if it's set to `fromAutomaticInsets`, it will be inset from the default. You can use that to let iOS perform its usual calculations for the separators, but then add your own adjustments as well. You can also set these values in Interface Builder.

To see this in action, open **Main.storyboard**, and select the **Table View** in the **Dictionary** scene. Open the Attributes Inspector and set the **Separator Inset** to **Custom**, then enter a value of **20** for the **Left** and **Right** inset. You should now see an inset on the left and right side for the separators.

You can also control the content by setting `insetsContentViewsToSafeArea` on a table view. The default for this is `true`, but if you set it to `false`, the cells will ignore the safe area when sizing the content views. In interface builder, you can find this setting on the size inspector for a table view.

Stack views

Stack views are great tools for creating flexible layouts without having to manage a lot of constraints — and iOS 11 makes them more powerful! A stack view's strength is in laying out many views with the same spacing or alignment. But sometimes you have one view that you want to be a little different. Maybe you want to highlight one of the views by adding some spacing around it. Well, now you can.

To illustrate this, you'll add a feature to the weather forecast that toggles a highlight of today's icon.

Still in **Main.storyboard**, select the **Caribbean Weather Forecast** scene, and expand it in the document outline. Add a **UIButton** as a sibling right under the stack view. Add **two constraints** to the button: one to **align the center x** with the stack view, and one for standard, **20pt vertical spacing** between the top of the button and the stack view. Change the text of the button to **Today**. Now, select the **Stack View**. In the Attributes Inspector, notice that the Spacing parameter now has a drop-down arrow. Click that and choose **Use Standard Value**. Before, you had to supply a value, but now you can let the system determine the standard value.

Next, use the assistant editor to create an outlet from the sun icon and name it `todaysWeatherIcon`. Finally, create an `IBAction` for the button you just added by Control-dragging from the storyboard to `WeatherViewController` and naming it `todayTapped()`.

Now, open **WeatherViewController.swift** and add this code below the `IBOutlets`:

```
// 1
private let customSpacing: CGFloat = 40
// 2
private var highlightingToday = false {
  didSet {
    let spacing: CGFloat
    // 3
    if highlightingToday == false {
      spacing = UIStackView.spacingUseDefault
    } else {
      spacing = customSpacing
    }
    // 4
    UIViewPropertyAnimator.runningPropertyAnimator(
      withDuration: 0.5, delay: 0, animations: {
        // 5
        self.stackView.setCustomSpacing(spacing,
          after: self.todaysWeatherIcon)
    })
  }
}
```

Taking this line-by-line:

1. It's always a good idea to create a constant for the hard-coded numeric values you use. That gives a name and some context to the value you're using and makes it more readable.

2. You need a Boolean toggle that indicates if you're highlighting today's icon, so you create that variable with a `didSet` property observer.

3. If you're highlighting today, you'll use the `customSpacing` value, but if you're not, you want to set it back to the value the rest of the views in the stack view are using. The way to do that is using the `UIStackView.spacingUseDefault` value. You can also use the `spacingUseSystem` value to indicate system spacing. In this case, they're the same thing, but be aware that they might not always be the same.

4. The `UIViewPropertyAnimator` class was introduced in iOS 10 and is good for user-interactive animations. Here, you could have also used the basic `UIView` animations - either one is fine.

5. This is how you set the custom spacing in the stack view. Call `setCustomSpacing` with the spacing to use and the view to use the spacing after. If the stack view has a vertical axis, the view refers to the one below the spacing, and if it has a horizontal axis, it refers to the trailing view. You can also read the value that has been set by calling `customSpacing(after:)`.

The only thing left to do is to toggle the Boolean value when the button is pressed. Update the implementation of `todayTapped(_:)` by adding this line:

```
highlightingToday = !highlightingToday
```

Build and run. Now, when you tap the button, the stack view will toggle between custom spacing after the sun icon and standard spacing after it.

Images

While previous versions of Xcode and iOS would let you assign a vector image to an asset, at build time it would generate versions of that image for the different sizes needed. In Xcode 9, you can add vector artwork and tell the system to ship with the vector version using the Preserve Vector Data checkbox. This is quite useful because there are more cases than ever where your image needs multiple sizes. For example, if the user has a large text size selected in the accessibility settings, tab bars will show the tab icon and text scaled up when the user long-presses the tab. And when you rotate a tab bar to landscape, it will show a smaller version of the image side-by-side with the text.

You can use the `landscapeImagePhone` and `largeContentSizeImage` properties on `UIBarItem` to set these to different sized images, but if you use an image with vector data, the system can scale it up or down to show these different sizes for you.

> **Note:** For more information, please refer to Chapter 15, "Dynamic Types".

To see this in action, open **Assets.xcassets** in Xcode and select the **weather-cloudy** image. Open the Attributes Inspector and change the **Scales** value to **Single Scale**. For simplicity, you're going to remove the Compact variant too, so change the **Width Class** value to **Any**. Now, click on one of the images and Command-click on each other image, then press the Delete key. You should be left with one box. In the folder for this chapter, find the **user-images** folder and drag **cloudy.pdf** onto the box. In the Attributes Inspector, check the **Preserve Vector Data** checkbox. Repeat for the other weather icons.

Another accessibility setting you can take advantage of when you have vector images is `adjustsImageSizeForAccessibilityContentSizeCategory`. This property, on `UIButton` and `UIImageView`, will tell the system to automatically scale the size of the image when users have an accessibility content size set.

Build and run; open the Weather Forecast view to verify that everything still works.

Navigation bar custom views

One last thing you'll look at is using constraints to lay out custom views inside a `UINavigationBar` or `UIToolbar`. You'll adjust the title of the map scene to have an image and text, and you'll use constraints to define the size of the custom view and position of the subviews inside it. Like self-sizing cells, you want constraints to fully define the size of the containing view.

Open **Main.storyboard**, and find the **Secret Map** scene. Drag a `UIView` out onto the title area of the navigation bar. Then, drag a `UIImageView` into that view. You'll probably need to drag it over to the document outline to drop it on the right view. Set the image to the **x** image. Then, add a label to the view, change its text to say **Secret Map** and change the font to **Marker Felt Thin 22.0**.

Now you're ready to add the following constraints:

- **Leading space**: 0 from image view to superview

- **Top space**: 0 from image view to superview

- **Bottom space**: 0 from image view to superview

- **Trailing space**: Standard from image view to label

- **Image view width**: 44

- **Image view aspect ratio**: 1:1

- **Align**: Vertical center of image view and label

- **Trailing space**: 0 from label to superview

> **Note:** Unfortunately, there is a bug in Xcode 9's Interface Builder that will prevent you from seeing your layout, but if you build and run, you'll see the view laid out as you'd expect.

The way it is now, you'll see a white background for the container view, but you can change that to clear and it will look correct.

Where to go from here?

There are quite a few changes in iOS 11 that impact Auto Layout. These changes add valuable mechanisms for creating adaptive layouts to handle every device and layout environment. There is lots of information scattered throughout the WWDC videos for all these changes. If I had to pick one, WWDC17 Session 204 - Updating Your App for iOS 11 http://apple.co/2syu3Tt has a good overview of most of what you've covered in this chapter.

For more on iPhone X, see Apple's video: Building Apps for iPhone X http://apple.co/2f5OroX.

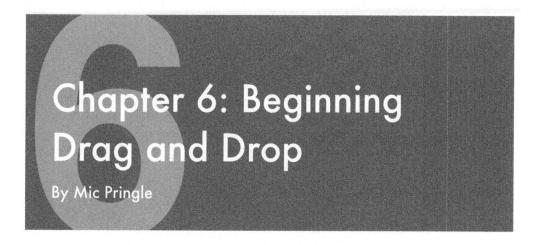

Chapter 6: Beginning Drag and Drop

By Mic Pringle

One of the most anticipated announcements at WWDC '17 was the introduction of Drag and Drop — a true game-changer for mobile devices. In typical Apple fashion, their engineers went above and beyond to deliver an interaction that feels as natural as it does intuitive.

If you haven't yet experienced Drag and Drop in iOS 11 then I highly recommend putting down this book and having a play. If the concept of Drag and Drop interests you now — and it must, you are reading this chapter after all! — your enthusiasm will increase ten-fold once you've actually experienced it.

For developers, the UIKit team provided two sets of APIs to integrate drag and drop in your apps. There are a standard set of APIs that provide for every aspect of the interaction, and then there are a set of higher-level abstractions built specifically for UICollectionView and UITableView.

In this chapter you'll dive straight in and get your hands dirty with the latter set of APIs, by integrating drag and drop into an iPad bug-tracking app known as **Bugray**.

Getting started

The Razeware folks take their engineering efforts pretty seriously, and record each and every bug and feature request in Bugray, which breaks those items into three contexts: **To Do**, **In Progress**, and **Done**. Every item begins its life belonging to the **To Do** context, and moves through the other two contexts as it's worked on.

However, productivity at Razeware has fallen off a cliff since introducing Bugray as there's one massive flaw in the app — it's not quite finished! You see, items can't be moved between the different contexts by the user. It requires a developer to learn and understand the high-level Drag and Drop APIs in iOS 11, and then dive in and finish it.

That developer is *you*.

Locate and open **Bugray.xcodeproj** with Xcode 9. When Xcode has finished launching, select the **iPad Pro (10.5-inch)** simulator and hit Build and Run.

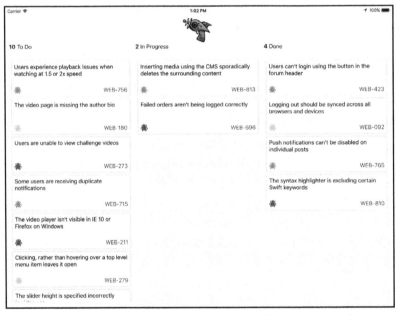

Before jumping in and changing any code, take this brief tour through the existing files and structure of the app.

Open **Main.storyboard** and you'll see everything's been set up for you.

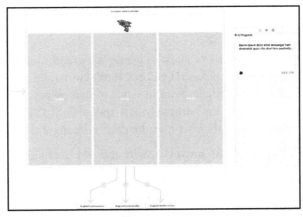

Bugray comprises just two view controllers:

• The main container view controller embeds three instances of the smaller view controller to provide the look and feel of a kanban board.

• The smaller view controller displays a list of all the items in a given context using a collection view. It also displays the number of items in that context in the upper-left corner.

These view controllers are implemented respectively by the following two `UIViewController` subclasses:

1. `ContainerViewController`: Provides each instance of `BugListViewController` with the context it's responsible for displaying.

2. `BugListViewController`: Manages the collection view that displays the items in the current context.

`Bug` is the model object used throughout the app, whereas `BugStore` is a singleton that's responsible for managing all the items in app. It uses `Codable` to load the items from a JSON file that's part of the bundle, and provides methods to insert or remove items from the store.

Now that you're familiar with Bugray and how it works, it's time to knuckle down and add support for Drag and Drop!

> **Note:** This chapter deals exclusively with the drag and drop APIs for `UICollectionView`, but Apple and the `UIKit` team have done a tremendous job providing consistency and parity between `UICollectionView` and `UITableView`. What you learn in this chapter should be directly transferable when working with table views.

Starting a drag

Configuring a `UICollectionView` to allow dragging is incredibly easy: You simply declare an object as conforming to the `UICollectionViewDragDelegate` protocol, implement a single method, and then set an instance of that object as the `dragDelegate` of the collection view. To keep things simple, you'll update `BugListViewController` so it conforms to the protocol, and then set it as the drag delegate of the collection view.

To begin with, open **BugListViewController.swift** and add the following to the bottom of the file:

```
extension BugListViewController: UICollectionViewDragDelegate {

}
```

Here you've created an extension of `BugListViewController` that declares conformance to `UICollectionViewDragDelegate`. Using extensions in this way keeps your code uncluttered and well-organized.

Inside the extension, add the following method:

```
func collectionView(_ collectionView: UICollectionView,
  itemsForBeginning session: UIDragSession,
  at indexPath: IndexPath) -> [UIDragItem] {

  // 1
  let item = UIDragItem(itemProvider: NSItemProvider())
  // 2
  return [item]
}
```

This is the only method that `UICollectionViewDragDelegate` requires you to implement. All others are optional. Inside the method you do the following two things:

1. Initialize an instance of `UIDragItem` with an empty `NSItemProvider`. Internal drag and drop — that is, between views within the same app — doesn't require the use of `NSItemProvider`, hence why you're passing an empty instance here.

You can find out more about inter-app drag and drop, and the role `NSItemProvider` plays in that, in Jeff Rames' **Advanced Drag and Drop** chapter later in this book.

2. Return an array of type `UIDragItem`, which in this case contains just the drag item you initialized in the previous step.

The final step to adopting dragging is to set the controller as the `dragDelegate` of the collection view.

Still in **BugListViewController.swift**, find `viewDidLoad()` and add the following statement to the very bottom:

```
collectionView.dragDelegate = self
```

That's all there is to it! Build and run using the **iPad Pro (10.5-inch)** simulator, and then tap-and-hold on any cell in any of the three collection views.

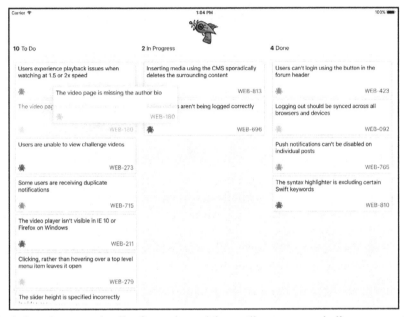

You'll find that the tapped cell, after a short delay, will raise up and allow you to drag it around at will. However, lifting your finger — or mouse button — to drop the cell doesn't actually result in a drop at that location, but instead the collection view simply animates the cell back to its origin.

Accepting the drop

Dragging is useless without the dropping, right? Apple's invested significantly in providing consistency across their Drag and Drop APIs, and configuring the collection view to respond to a user dropping a dragged cell is almost identical to the process you used earlier:

1. Declare an object as conforming to the `UICollectionViewDropDelegate` protocol.

2. Implement the single required method.

3. Set an instance of that object as the `dropDelegate` of the collection view.

With those steps in-mind, open **BugListViewController.swift** and add the following at the foot of the file:

```
extension BugListViewController: UICollectionViewDropDelegate {

}
```

Just as before, you create an extension of `BugListViewController`, but this time declare that it conforms to `UICollectionViewDropDelegate`.

Within the extension, add the following method:

```
func collectionView(_ collectionView: UICollectionView,
  canHandle session: UIDropSession) -> Bool {

  return session.localDragSession != nil ? true : false
}
```

This method allows you to inform the drag process as to whether or not you're willing to handle the drop. It's an optional method, and you're using it here to restrict drag and drop to just those sessions initiated from within the same app. The restriction is enforced by checking if `localDragSession` on the provided `UIDropSession` instance is `nil`. If it is, then it means the drag was initiated from outside of the app, so you return `false` to let the drag process know you're not interested in handling the drop.

Now to implement the only required method of `UICollectionViewDropDelegate` that allows you to handle the drop in all cases where the above method returns `true`.

Still working within the extension, add the following code below the method added in the previous step:

```
func collectionView(_ collectionView: UICollectionView,
  performDropWith coordinator: UICollectionViewDropCoordinator){

  // Intentionally left blank
}
```

For now, just having an empty method stub is enough to change the behavior of drag and drop, as you'll see shortly. You'll flesh out this method later in the chapter. To wrap up *basic* drop handling, you need to set the controller as the `dropDelegate` of the collection view.

In **BugListViewController.swift**, locate `viewDidLoad()` and add the following snippet to the bottom of the method:

```
collectionView.dropDelegate = self
```

Build and run using the **iPad Pro (10.5-inch)** simulator, and then tap-and-hold on any cell to initiate a drag session. Drag the cell into either of the other collection views and you'll notice a small green icon appear in the upper-right corner of the dragged cell:

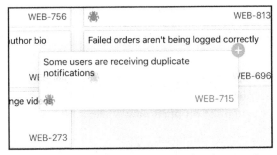

This indicates the collection view is willing to accept the drop. Lift your finger and you'll see a different animation this time: Instead of returning to its origin, the cell now appears *drop* into place. Well... at least until the animation has finished, at which point the cell returns to its original collection view because you've not yet updated the model data and persisted the change.

You'll get to that shortly. But before you do, you need to provide some visual feedback to the user regarding the intent of the drop.

Declaring your intent with drop proposals

As the user drags an object over your collection view, the collection view will ask its drop delegate how it proposes to handle the drop, should the user release their finger at its current location. It will then react visually in a number of different ways depending on how you respond.

The proposal you provide is split into two parts: what operation you'll perform when receiving the drop, and your intention of how to process that operation. Operations are instances of `UIDropOperation`, an enumeration providing the following options:

- `.cancel`: Indicates an operation that doesn't cause data transfer. If you return a drop proposal with this operation then `collectionView(_:performDropWith:)` won't be called on your drop delegate.

- `.forbidden`: Indicates that this interaction would usually perform a different operation, but is explicitly forbidden at this time. You might want to use this when your underlying data model is being updated by a network request on a background thread, and therefore can't be changed at this time. If you use system-provided drag images, then a special symbol will be displayed on that image to provide visual feedback to the user.

- **.copy**: Indicates an operation that will *copy* the dropped item from its source to the destination.

- **.move**: Indicates an operation that's the opposite of **.copy**, and used for operations that *move* the dropped item from its source to the destination.

Intentions are instances of **UICollectionViewDropIntent**, and can be one of the following:

- **.insertAtDestinationIndexPath**: Signals that the dropped item(s) will be inserted at the destination location. A gap will open up at that drop location to simulate the final layout, should the item be dropped now.

- **.insertIntoDestinationIndexPath**: Signals that the item at the drop location is a container, and the dropped item will be placed within it. This intention doesn't open a gap but instead highlights the item at the drop location.

- **.unspecified**: Signals that you will accept the drop but are unsure how the items will be processed. This intention doesn't provide any visual feedback.

Now that you know what operations and intentions are available to you, it's time to put them to good use. As Bugray provides a kanban-like board, it makes sense to be able to drag bugs between the different contexts, and have them stay there permanently. Therefore **.move** and **.insertAtDestinationIndexPath** look like prime candidates to propose that behavior.

Add the following method to the **UICollectionViewDropDelegate** extension in **BugListViewController.swift**:

```
func collectionView(_ collectionView: UICollectionView,
    dropSessionDidUpdate session: UIDropSession,
    withDestinationIndexPath destinationIndexPath: IndexPath?)
    -> UICollectionViewDropProposal {

    return UICollectionViewDropProposal(operation: .move,
        intent: .insertAtDestinationIndexPath)
}
```

Here you return an instance of **UICollectionViewDropProposal** initialized with the operation and intention decided earlier.

Build and run. As before, tap-and-hold on any cell to initiate a drag session. Drag the cell into either of the other collection views to see the new behavior.

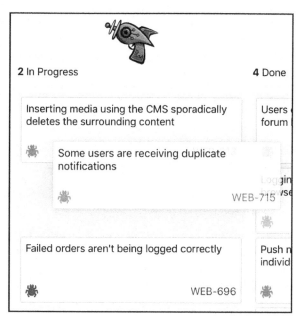

Cells now move apart to open a gap, signaling where the dragged item would be dropped, and the green icon is no longer visible. This is because .copy is the default operation, but you're now declaring that you intend to move items instead.

As a nice side-effect of using the .move operation, you can also now drag the cell around within its current context, effectively providing bug reordering for free! Go ahead and try it.

Model coordination

The APIs the UIKit team have added to UICollectionView — and UITableView — do a very good job at abstracting away the communication with the drag process and coordinating the necessary visual changes. But there's one thing they don't cater for and that's updating your model layer. That's very much left up to the developer!

There are two approaches you can take depending on the complexity of the drag and drop interaction:

1. If you are dragging a single item between two views of different classes, such as a custom UIView and a UICollectionView, then you can attach the model object to UIDragItem via its localObject property. When you receive the drop, you ask the drop coordinator for the drag item, and then retrieve the model object back from localObject.

2. If you are dragging one or more items between two or more collection-based views, such as `UITableView`, and you need to be able to track which index paths were affected, as well as which items were dragged, then that use case is beyond what the first approach can offer. Instead, it makes more sense to create a custom coordinator object that can track things, such as the source view, the destination view, the source index paths that were flocked (multiple items in a single drag) etc., and then pass that object between the drag and drop session using the `localContext` property on `UIDragSession`.

The rest of this section will focus on how to implement the latter in Bugray.

Adding model coordination

With the theory of model coordination out of the way, it's worth taking a moment and breaking down your implementation into practical terms. What exactly would a coordinator need to know to successfully coordinate between a drag session and a Bugray model update?

A coordinator would need to know the following things:

• The source context of the drag, so the bugs being dragged can be easily located, and later removed.

• The index paths of the item(s) being dragged. Index paths are useful because they not only represent the visual position of the cells in the collection view in its native tongue, but you can use their indexes to locate the associated bugs in the underlying data model.

• The destination context of the drop, so you know into which context to insert the dragged bugs.

• The index path(s) of where the dragged item(s) will be inserted.

• If the drag is a move or a reorder operation. You'll leverage different `UICollectionView` APIs depending on whether a drag is a move or a reorder, so you'll need to be able to ask the coordinator what type of drag it is.

• If the drag operation finished, so you can update the source collection view if necessary.

Now you have a checklist to work through, it's time to get cracking!

Right-click on the **Coordinators** group in the Project Navigator and select **New File...**. In the template chooser select **Swift File** and click **Next**. Name the file **BugDragCoordinator** and click **Create**.

Open **BugDragCoordinator.swift** and replace its contents with the following:

```
import UIKit

class BugDragCoordinator {
  let source: Bug.Context

  init(source: Bug.Context) {
    self.source = source
  }
}
```

This is the bare-bones implementation of the class that will be responsible for the coordination between the drag session and your data model. The initializer receives the source context of the drag and assigns it to the source property.

Next, add the following property declarations to the top of BugDragCoordinator:

```
var sourceIndexPaths: [IndexPath] = []
var sourceIndexes: [Int] {
  get {
    return sourceIndexPaths.map { $0.item }
  }
}
```

Here you declare an array to store the index paths of the items being dragged, within the context of the source collection view. You also add a computed property that uses map to return an array of just the indexes from those index paths. You do this so that you can query either the collection view or the underlying data model and receive exactly the same model objects.

With the source of the drag taken care of, it's now time to handle the destination. Add the following properties just below those added in the previous step:

```
var destination: Bug.Context?
var destinationIndexPaths: [IndexPath]?
var dragCompleted = false
```

Both destination and destinationIndexPaths are optionals because you don't know the destination of a drop until it happens. You store the destination context and destination index paths so you can update the data model and destination collection view respectively. You also add a Bool to store whether or not the drag operation has completed.

That's five of the six items on the list covered. All that's remaining is a way to determine if the drag operation is a reorder.

Add the following computed property directly below those you added in the previous step:

```
var isReordering: Bool {
  get {
    guard let destination = destination else { return false }
    return source == destination
  }
}
```

In the `getter` for this property you first attempt to unwrap `destination`, and return `false` if it fails. It's impossible to determine what kind of operation is taking place if you don't know the destination. You then check to see if `source` and `destination` are the same, and return the result: `true` if they are, in which case it's a reorder, and `false` otherwise.

With every item on the list now checked off, add the following convenience method to the bottom of `BugDragCoordinator`:

```
func dragItemForBugAt(indexPath: IndexPath) -> UIDragItem {

  sourceIndexPaths.append(indexPath)
  return UIDragItem(itemProvider: NSItemProvider())
}
```

You'll remember that earlier you added code to create the drag item in `collectionView(_:itemsForBeginning:at:)`, but you move it here so that you can record the index path of the drag item by appending it to `sourceIndexPaths`.

And that's it for the coordinator implementation, at least for now. The next step is to update the drag and drop delegates to use the coordinator.

Open **BugListViewController.swift** and locate `collectionView(_:itemsForBeginning:at:)` in the `UICollectionViewDragDelegate` extension. Replace the current implementation with the following:

```
// 1
let dragCoordinator = BugDragCoordinator(source: context)
// 2
session.localContext = dragCoordinator
// 3
return [dragCoordinator.dragItemForBugAt(indexPath: indexPath)]
```

Here's the breakdown of what's happening:

1. You initialize an instance of `BugDragCoordinator` using the context of the current controller. This represents the source of the drag.

2. You assign the coordinator to the `localContext` property on the drag session that's passed to this method. This is so you can access the coordinator from the other methods in both the drag and the drop delegates.

3. You ask the coordinator to create a drag item for the bug at the provided index path, and then return it wrapped in an array.

Next, find `collectionView(_:performDropWith:)` in the `UICollectionViewDropDelegate` extension and replace the comment with the following lines of code:

```
// 1
guard let dragCoordinator =
  coordinator.session.localDragSession?.localContext
  as? BugDragCoordinator
  else { return }
// 2
let indexPath = coordinator.destinationIndexPath ??
  IndexPath(item: collectionView.numberOfItems(inSection: 0),
    section: 0)
// 3
dragCoordinator.destinationIndexPaths = [indexPath]
// 4
dragCoordinator.destination = context
// 5
print(dragCoordinator.source, dragCoordinator.destination!,
  dragCoordinator.sourceIndexPaths.first!,
  dragCoordinator.destinationIndexPaths!.first!)
```

Here's the play-by-play of what's happening above:

1. This method is passed an instance of `UICollectionViewDropCoordinator`, which provides access to the drop session via its `session` property. The property returns an instance of `UIDropSession`, which itself provides access to the drag session, if available, via `localDragSession`. It's on this property that you can access the local context to which, in the previous step, you assigned your instance of `BugDragCoordinator`. Since `localDragSession` could be `nil`, and you need to cast the value of `localContext` to the type `BugDragCoordinator`, you wrap everything up in a `guard` statement.

2. `UICollectionViewDropCoordinator` will provide you with the destination index path of the drop, if the drop location is somewhere within the range of the first and last cells of the collection view, otherwise it'll return `nil`. To account for this, you use nil coalescing (`??`) to set the value of `indexPath` to either the destination index path, or to one you instantiate that represents the next available cell. This means that if a drop happens *within* the bounds of the collection view, but *not* over an existing cell, the dropped cell will always be inserted at the end of the collection view.

3. You set `destinationIndexPaths` on the drag coordinator to an array containing the index path from step #2. An array is used so the coordinator can cope with **Flocking** — multiple items per drag session — which you'll implement shortly.

4. You set the destination context of the drag coordinator to be the context of the current controller.

5. You print the information contained within the drag coordinator as a sanity check to make sure everything is working as expected. This is just temporary as you'll replace this line in the next section.

Build and run. Tap-and-hold the first cell in the **To Do** context to initiate a drag, then drop it at the bottom of **In Progress**. You should see the following output in the console:

```
toDo inProgress [0, 0] [0, 2]
```

This shows that you dragged the first item in the `toDo` context, and dropped it as the third item in the `inProgress` context.

Performing the drop

Now you're confident that the coordinator is accurately recording the information required to successfully coordinate the drop with the underlying data model, it's time to actually perform that drop and have those changes persist.

Open **BugListViewController.swift** and add the following private method declaration to the `UICollectionViewDropDelegate` extension:

```
private func moveBugs(using dragCoordinator: BugDragCoordinator,
    performingDropWith
    dropCoordinator: UICollectionViewDropCoordinator) {

}
```

It's within this method you'll update the bugs data store, remove any cells from the source collection view, and insert any cells into the destination collection view. For this to happen you need access to both the drag coordinator *and* the drop coordinator, hence why they're both passed as parameters.

Next, add the following `guard` statement to the top of the method:

```
guard let destination = dragCoordinator.destination,
    let destinationIndexPaths =
      dragCoordinator.destinationIndexPaths
    else { return }
```

To be able to perform the drop you need both the destination context *and* the destination index paths. If one or both of these are missing then you exit early.

Now, add the following just below the `guard` statement:

```
let bugs = BugStore.sharedStore.deleteBugs(
  at: dragCoordinator.sourceIndexes, in: dragCoordinator.source)
```

Here you use `deleteBugs(at:in:)` on `BugStore` to remove the bugs at the given indexes from the source context in the underlying data store. The method returns an array of the bugs it removed, so you hold onto them as you'll need them in just a moment.

Next, add the following to the bottom of `moveBugs(using:performingDropWith:)`:

```
// 1
for (index, item) in dropCoordinator.items.enumerated() {
  // 2
  let sourceIndexPath = dragCoordinator.sourceIndexPaths[index]
  let destinationIndexPath = destinationIndexPaths[index]
  // 3
  collectionView.performBatchUpdates({
    // 4
    BugStore.sharedStore.insert(bugs: [bugs[index]],
      into: destination, at: destinationIndexPath.item)
    // 5
    if dragCoordinator.isReordering {
      self.collectionView.moveItem(at: sourceIndexPath,
        to: destinationIndexPath)
    } else {
      self.collectionView.insertItems(
        at: [destinationIndexPath])
    }
  }, completion: { _ in
    // 6
    self.setBugCount()
  })
  // 7
  dropCoordinator.drop(item.dragItem,
    toItemAt: destinationIndexPath)
}
```

Here's the breakdown:

1. Iterate over the items provided by the drop coordinator, each one being an instance of `UICollectionViewDropItem`. You use `enumerated()` because you need access to both the index of the iteration and the item itself.

2. Retrieve the source and destination index paths for the given item.

3. Use `performBatchUpdates(_:completion:)` to wrap any changes to the collection view in a single batch operation, so they are performed efficiently and in parallel.

4. Take the bug at the current index from the temporary `bugs` array, and insert it into the destination context using the `item` property of `destinationIndexPath` as its new index.

5. If the current operation is a reorder then ask the collection view to move the cell at `sourceIndexPath` to `destinationIndexPath`, otherwise simply insert a new cell at `destinationIndexPath`. `insertItems(at:)` expects an array, so you provide one containing just the single index path.

6. Once the batch update has completed update the bug count displayed at the top of each context.

7. Finally, tell the drop coordinator to animate the current item's drag item to the destination index path, completing the drop of that particular item.

Once the enumeration has finished and all items have been dropped you need to tell the drag coordinator that the drag is now considered complete.

Add the following statement to the very bottom of `moveBugs(using:performingDropWith:)`:

```
dragCoordinator.dragCompleted = true
```

The final step to hooking everything up is to actually call this new method. Locate the `print` statement in `collectionView(_:performDropWith:)` and replace it with the following:

```
moveBugs(using: dragCoordinator,
   performingDropWith: coordinator)
```

Build and run using the **iPad Pro (10.5-inch)** simulator. Initiate a drag with any cell in the **To Do** context, and then drop it to a different location within that same context. You'll see that the drop now persists and the collection view updates visually:

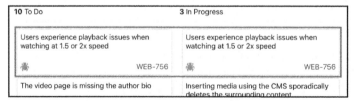

However, if you try to drag a cell from one context and drop it onto another, and then drag that cell back to its original context, you'll notice two things: the visual state of the source collection view doesn't update giving the impression there are now multiple instances of the same bug, and the app crashes with a familiar `UICollectionView` exception:

```
*** Terminating app due to uncaught exception
'NSInternalInconsistencyException', reason: 'Invalid update:
invalid number of items in section...
```

Both of these issues are caused by the fact that the visual state of the source collection view isn't updated after a successful drag and drop, and therefore its internal state becomes out-of-sync with its data source. You'll fix this in the following section.

Updating the source

When a drag session ends, the drag delegate of the source collection view is informed via a delegate method. You'll use this method to delete the cells that were dragged out of the collection view, keeping it in sync with the underlying data model.

Open **BugListViewController.swift** and add the following delegate method to the bottom of the `UICollectionViewDragDelegate` extension:

```swift
func collectionView(_ collectionView: UICollectionView,
  dragSessionDidEnd session: UIDragSession) {
}
```

This method is called whenever the drag session ends, regardless of whether the drop was successful or not. This is the reason you added the ability to record whether the drop was completed to `BugDragCoordinator`.

Next, add the following `guard` statement to the top of this new method:

```swift
guard let dragCoordinator = session.localContext
  as? BugDragCoordinator,
  dragCoordinator.source == context,
  dragCoordinator.dragCompleted == true,
  dragCoordinator.isReordering == false else { return }
```

There are four conditions being checked in this `guard` statement:

1. First, you make sure you can access the coordinator via `localContext` and cast it to the type `BugDragCoordinator`.

2. Next, you check whether the source context is the same as the context of the current controller. You do this because you only want to delete cells from the collection view where the drag originated.

3. Next, you make sure the current drag has completed.

4. Finally, you make sure the current operation *isn't* a reorder, because you don't want to delete any cells if it is.

Assuming all those conditions are met, you then need to ask the collection view to delete the items located at `sourceIndexPaths`.

Now add the following snippet just below the `guard` statement:

```
collectionView.performBatchUpdates({
  collectionView.deleteItems(
    at: dragCoordinator.sourceIndexPaths)
}, completion: { _ in
  self.setBugCount()
})
```

Here you once again use `performBatchUpdates(_:completion:)` to delete the items at the given index paths from the collection view, and then in the completion closure update the bug count that's displayed at the top of each context in the kanban board.

Build and run. You can now drag items between the different contexts and see both the source and destination collection views update accordingly, and you don't have any more crashes! Nice work.

You *could* consider the drag and drop implementation complete at this point, but wouldn't it be even better if you could drag multiple bugs between contexts at the same time? It sure would! Luckily, Apple agrees and provides some APIs to allow you to do just that.

Flocking

To enable flocking of drag items, that is, to add one or more cells to an already in-flight drag session, you simply need to implement a single method declared on the `UICollectionViewDragDelegate` protocol. Don't you just love how easy Apple has made all of this?

Open **BugListViewController.swift** and add the following method declaration to your `UICollectionViewDragDelegate` extension:

```
func collectionView(_ collectionView: UICollectionView,
  itemsForAddingTo session: UIDragSession,
  at indexPath: IndexPath, point: CGPoint) -> [UIDragItem] {

}
```

This method is called each time a cell is tapped and there's already an active drag session. Within it, you need to return an array of the drag items that you wish to add to the flock. Add the following snippet to the method to achieve that:

```
guard let dragCoordinator =
    session.localContext as? BugDragCoordinator,
    dragCoordinator.source == context
  else { return [] }

return [dragCoordinator.dragItemForBugAt(indexPath: indexPath)]
```

Here you use a `guard` statement to make sure you can access the drag coordinator via `localContext`, and that it can be cast to the type `BugDragCoordinator`. You also make sure that the source context of the drag is the same as the context of the current controller. You do this to restrict flocking to just bugs from the same context; mixing contexts within a flock is substantially more complex and out-of-scope for this chapter. If one or both of these conditions fail you return an empty array. Otherwise, you ask the drag coordinator for a drag item corresponding to the bug at the given index path and return that, wrapped in an array.

That takes care of adding items to the flock, but what about dropping them? The drop coordinator passed to `collectionView(_:performDropWith:)` only provides the index path of the location of the drop, which is fine for a single item, but when dealing with multiple items you need one index path per item.

Given you know the index path of the drop, and can determine the number of items in the flock via the drop coordinator, you can add a method to the drag coordinator to take that information and calculate the necessary index paths.

Open **BugDragCoordinator.swift** and add the following method to the bottom of the class:

```
func calculateDestinationIndexPaths(from indexPath: IndexPath,
  count: Int) {

  // 1
  let indexes = Array(indexPath.item..<(indexPath.item + count))
  // 2
  destinationIndexPaths =
    indexes.map { IndexPath(item: $0, section: 0)}
}
```

Here's what's happening in the method above:

1. Instantiate an `Array` of `Int` using a range, starting at the index of `indexPath` and having `count` number of elements. This array represents the indexes of where the new items will be inserted.

2. Use `map` to convert the values of `indexes` into an array of index paths, and then set `destinationIndexPaths` to that array.

Now you just need to update your drop delegate to use this new method.

Open **BugListViewController.swift** and, in your `UICollectionViewDropDelegate` extension, find `collectionView(_:performDropWith:)`. Within that method, locate the following statement:

```
dragCoordinator.destinationIndexPaths = [indexPath]
```

Replace it with this one:

```
dragCoordinator.calculateDestinationIndexPaths(
  from: indexPath, count: coordinator.items.count)
```

Bugray is now all set up to handle flocking!

Build and run, using the **iPad Pro (10.5-inch)** simulator. Initiate a drag with the first cell in the **To Do** context, then press **Control** and release your mouse button. This will keep the drag session active while you select other cells to add to the flock. Tap each of the next two cells in the **To Do** context to add them to the flock:

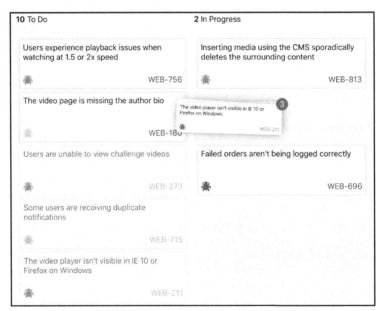

With the left mouse button pressed, you can now release **Control** and drag the flock around. Drop the flock on either of the other contexts and see all three cells inserted.

Where to go from here?

If this is your first experience with the Drag and Drop APIs in iOS 11, I congratulate you. Not only have you acquired the knowledge you need to add the power and convenience of drag and drop to your `UICollectionView`-powered iOS apps, you've made the Razeware team far more productive since they can finally move bugs into the **In Progress** and **Done** contexts of their kanban board!

Before you move on, play around with drag and drop in Bugray. Familiarize yourself with the gestures and key-combinations, see how many items you can add to a flock, and see if you can clear one of the contexts completely.

The power of drag and drop doesn't end here! Head over to Chapter 7, "Advanced Drag and Drop", to learn all about `UIDragInteractionDelegate` and `UIDropInteractionDelegate`, `NSItemProvider` and `UIDragItem`, adding drag and drop support to custom views, and spring loading. See you there!

Chapter 7: Advanced Drag and Drop

By Jeff Rames

Drag and drop has finally arrived with iOS 11, and once you've experienced it, you'll realize how important this feature really is. While Apple's implementation is quite straightforward, there's a lot to know to use it effectively.

In Chapter 6, "Beginning Drag and Drop", you learned the basics while focusing on collection views. In this chapter you'll learn how to drag and drop between apps. You'll also dive deeper, and learn some flexible APIs for working with custom views.

The stars of this show are `UIDragInteractionDelegate` and `UIDropInteractionDelegate`. These protocols define behavior for dragging and dropping, respectively. Their core functionality is similar to `UICollectionViewDragDelegate` and `UICollectionViewDropDelegate`, but they offer far more options for customization, particularly around animation and security.

A drag starts in the source app, and generates a *drag session*: an OS-managed object that oversees the drag. The drop occurs in the destination app, and generates a drop session. `UIDragSession` and `UIDropSession` provide the drag and drop delegates with information about the items being dragged, including their locations, and the actual data.

For a view to accept drags, it needs a `UIDragInteraction` configured with a `UIDragInteractionDelegate`. When a drag is initiated on that view, the delegate must return one, or more, `UIDragItem` objects. Each `UIDragItem` uses an `NSItemProvider` to share the object being dragged.

When the user releases the drag over a view containing a `UIDropInteraction`, the corresponding `UIDropInteractionDelegate` is asked if it can handle the drop. The delegate can then obtain the `UIDragItem` objects from the drop session, and load their data using `NSItemProvider` objects.

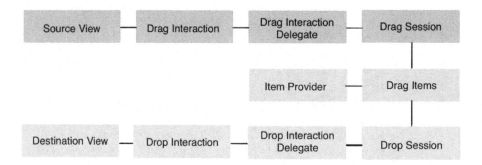

Getting started

You'll be working with two sample apps in this chapter. **National Parks** allows you to view basic info about various U.S. National Parks. It will act as the source app. **Hike Journal** presents a map of a park you'll be hiking, and allows you to record notes, and pictures. It will act as the destination app.

Open **ParkHiker.xcworkspace** in the starter project folder. Select the **NationalParks** scheme, and chose any iPad simulator, or device.

Build and run **NationalParks**, and you'll see a paging view that displays park names, descriptions, and coordinates.

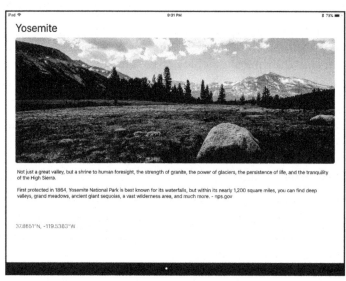

To make setting up split screen a little easier, drag **NationalParks** from the Springboard to your dock.

Now build and run the **HikeJournal** scheme on the same device. You'll see various blank views you'll use for displaying info about your hike.

Swipe up from the bottom to reveal the dock. Drag National Parks to the left of Hike Journal, taking half the screen. You'll work in this configuration through most of this chapter.

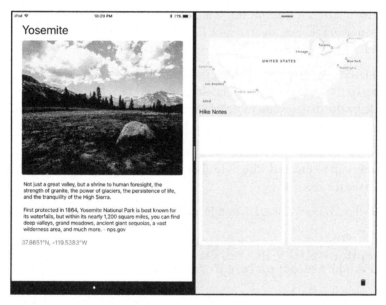

Adding drag support

Tap and hold the park image in National Parks, and nothing will happen. Making the image draggable is a great place to start.

For a view to respond to drags, it needs a `UIDragInteraction` to accept the gesture, and a `UIDragInteractionDelegate` to respond to `UIDragSession` requests. The system creates a `UIDragSession` when a view with a `UIDragInteraction` is touched. The session then asks the interaction's delegate if it should proceed with a *lift*.

Open **ParkViewController.swift**, and add the following extension at the end of the file:

```
extension ParkViewController: UIDragInteractionDelegate {
  func dragInteraction(_ interaction: UIDragInteraction,
                       itemsForBeginning session: UIDragSession)
    -> [UIDragItem] {
      guard let parkImage = imageView.image else { return [] }
      let provider = NSItemProvider(object: parkImage)
      let dragItem = UIDragItem(itemProvider: provider)
      return [dragItem]
  }
}
```

You've implemented `dragInteraction(_:itemsForBeginning:)`, the only required method in `UIDragInteractionDelegate`. It contains information about the `UIDragSession`, and returns an array of `UIDragItem` objects representing the content being dragged.

This creates an `NSItemProvider`, passing it the unwrapped `imageView.image` corresponding to the park photo you'll be dragging. `NSItemProvider` is considered as a promise made by the drag session to deliver the given item. `UIDragItem`, the object representing the data to the session, is created with the provider and returned.

When `dragInteraction(_:itemsForBeginning:)` returns a `UIDragItem`, the session gives the thumbs up to proceed with a lift. Before it can happen, something has to create a session to make the request!

Add the following code in `viewDidLoad` just after the call to `super`:

```
imageView.isUserInteractionEnabled = true
let dragInteraction = UIDragInteraction(delegate: self)
stackView.addInteraction(dragInteraction)
```

`isUserInteractionEnabled` is first set to `true` to allow the user to interact with the `imageView`. A `UIDragInteraction` is then created with `self` as the delegate, allowing it to call the `UIDragInteractionDelegate` method you just defined. `addInteraction` ties the interaction to the `stackView` containing all of the park info.

Build and run the **NationalParks** scheme, and long press anywhere on the park listing. The entire stack view lifts up, but has nowhere to go!

Hike Journal isn't yet set up for image drops, but **Photos.app** is! Position the Photos app in Hike Journal's pane, and drag a park image to it. When you drag over Photos, a **+** badge will appears over it indicating the view can accept that drop. Release, and the park image will be copied to your photo library.

A number of cool things just happened for free. A drag preview icon was created that matches the source view (the park's `stackView`). You also saw animations at the start of the drag, and during the drop. You'll see later in this chapter how easy these are to customize.

Multiple representations with item providers

The image you just dragged worked because `UIImage` conforms to the `NSItemProviderWriting` protocol. This means a `UIImage` is able to tell its `NSItemProvider` what types of data it can provide, and then actually load it.

The `Park` model used in this example has more than the image data you just transferred to Photos. It also contains the park name, description, and coordinates. Wouldn't it be handy if portions of the data, or even the entire object, were made available, depending on what the receiving app could handle?

Open **Park.swift**, and add the following lines just below the existing imports:

```
import MobileCoreServices

public let parkTypeId = "com.razeware.park"
```

MobileCoreServices contains UTI definitions which are used by drag and drop to identify types of data. To learn more about UTI, read up here: apple.co/2t5cN7E. parkTypeId is a custom ID string that will be used to identify a Park object.

Next, add an extension to the bottom of the file:

```
extension Park: NSItemProviderWriting {
  // 1
  public static var writableTypeIdentifiersForItemProvider:
    [String] {
    return [parkTypeId,
            kUTTypePNG as String,
            kUTTypePlainText as String]
  }

  // 2
  public func loadData(
    withTypeIdentifier typeIdentifier: String,
    forItemProviderCompletionHandler completionHandler:
    @escaping (Data?, Error?) -> Void) -> Progress? {
    // 3
    if typeIdentifier == kUTTypePNG as String {
      if let imageData = UIImagePNGRepresentation(image) {
        completionHandler(imageData, nil)
      } else {
        completionHandler(nil, nil)
      }
    } else if typeIdentifier == kUTTypePlainText as String {
      completionHandler(name.data(using: .utf8), nil)
    } else if typeIdentifier == parkTypeId {
      let data =
        NSKeyedArchiver.archivedData(withRootObject: self)
      completionHandler(data, nil)
    }
    return nil
  }
}
```

Park now fully conforms to NSItemProviderWriting. Here's a closer look at what's happening:

1. writableTypeIdentifiersForItemProvider needs to return an array of UTI Strings to identify types of data this object can provide. These must be provided in fidelity order, with the highest fidelity item first. Here, the entire Park object is preferred, followed by PNG, with plain text being the least preferred.

2. When a drop session requests data from an item provider, it calls loadData to get it. typeIdentifier indicates the data format preferred by the requesting drop session. The closure is responsible for loading data based on the requested type.

3. For the custom `parkTypeId`, `NSKeyedArchiver` is used to archive the `Park` object. For `kUTTTypePNG`, `UIImagePNGRepresentation` is used to load data from the Park's `image`. For `kUTTypePlainText`, the Park `name` is encoded with `utf8`.

Open **ParkViewController.swift**, and locate `dragInteraction(_:itemsForBeginning)`. Replace the contents with the following:

```
guard let park = park else { return [] }
let provider = NSItemProvider(object: park)
let dragItem = UIDragItem(itemProvider: provider)
return [dragItem]
```

This now passes the entire `park` object to `NSItemProvider`, rather than the image.

Build and run the **NationalParks** scheme, drag a park to Photos, then to Reminders. You'll see the park image drop for Photos, and the name for Reminders.

> **Note:** If you get a compiler error complaining that `park` does not conform to `NSItemProviderWriting`, you may need to restart Xcode. The build actually succeeds but the error may still be flagged in the Xcode source editor window.

Nothing exists that can accept the entire `Park` object — *yet*. Time to make that happen!

Adding drop support

When you drag a park from the National Parks app you want it to populate the title label, map, and first image in the Hike Journal when dropped. First, you need to implement the other `NSItemProvider` protocol: `NSItemProviderReading`.

Open **Park.swift**, and the following to the bottom of the file:

```
extension Park: NSItemProviderReading {
  public static var readableTypeIdentifiersForItemProvider:
    [String] {
    return [parkTypeId]
  }
}
```

`readableTypeIdentifiersForItemProvider` looks like its `NSItemProviderWriting` counterpart, but provides UTI types the item provider can read. You pass `parkTypeId` because Hike Journal will only accept `Park` object drops.

`NSItemProviderReading` also requires another method. Add the following at the bottom of the extension you just created:

```
public static func object(withItemProviderData data: Data,
                    typeIdentifier: String) throws -> Self {
  switch typeIdentifier {
  case parkTypeId:
    guard let park = NSKeyedUnarchiver
      .unarchiveObject(with: data) as? Park
      else { throw EncodingError.invalidData }
    return self.init(park)
  default:
    throw EncodingError.invalidData
  }
}
```

`data` contains the `Data` you formatted via `loadData` in the `Park` class. `typeIdentifier` is the UTI String identifying the data type. Between these, the method has the archived `Data`, and knows it contains a `Park` object. It accordingly initializes a `Park`.

`Park` is now capable of being dropped as a `UIDragItem`. The next step is to prepare Hike Journal to receive it by implementing `UIDropInteractionDelegate`.

Open **HikeViewController.swift**, and add the following at the bottom:

```
extension HikeViewController: UIDropInteractionDelegate {
  // 1
  func dropInteraction(
```

```
    _ interaction: UIDropInteraction,
    canHandle session: UIDropSession) -> Bool {
      return session.canLoadObjects(ofClass: Park.self)
  }

  // 2
  func dropInteraction(_ interaction: UIDropInteraction,
                       sessionDidUpdate session: UIDropSession)
    -> UIDropProposal {
      return UIDropProposal(operation: .copy)
  }

  // 3
  func dropInteraction(_ interaction: UIDropInteraction,
                       performDrop session: UIDropSession) {
    guard let dropItem = session.items.last else { return }
    // 4
    dropItem.itemProvider.loadObject(ofClass: Park.self) {
      [weak self] object, _ in
      guard let `self` = self else { return }
      self.park = object as? Park
      // 5
      DispatchQueue.main.async {
        self.displayPark()
      }
    }
  }
}
```

`UIDropInteractionDelegate` has no required methods, but a few that need to be implemented for a drop to work. Here's a look at those you've added:

1. `dropInteraction(_:canHandle:)` is the first method called by a drop session. Its response indicates if the interaction is interested in the drop. `canLoadObjects` is called to determine if the session has any `Park` drop items. If it does, you want to accept the drop.

2. `dropInteraction(_:sessionDidUpdate:)` is called when a drag enters the interaction's view, and repeatedly as the drag continues. Its primary responsibility is to return a `UIDropProposal` to tell the session what it wants to do with the item. In this case it returns a proposal for a copy operation, indicating it wants a copy of the object being dropped.

3. `dropInteraction(_:performDrop:)` is called when the user releases the item over the view, and is your only opportunity for requesting data from the drop items. You access the drop items via the session (`session.items`), pulling only the `last` because this view expects a single item.

4. `loadObject` asynchronously loads the dropped data, and fires a closure when done.

In the closure, the view controller's `park` property is set to the newly loaded `object`.

5. Because loading occurs on a background thread, you need to dispatch on the main queue before updating the UI. `displayPark` is included in the starter, and populates the Hike Journal UI with data from the newly stored `park`.

> **Note:** There are several drop operation types in addition to `copy`:
>
> **cancel** indicates no data should be transferred. A default badge is added to these previews showing a drop there would cancel.
>
> **forbidden** indicates a location where a move or copy would normally be available, but isn't currently. This also uses a unique badge.
>
> **move** indicates the drop will result in data being removed from the source, and copied to the destination.

In `viewDidLoad`, add the following after the call to `super`:

```
let dropInteraction = UIDropInteraction(delegate: self)
view.addInteraction(dropInteraction)
```

This defines the drop interaction, and adds it to the `view`. Hike Journal is now ready to accept Park drops!

Build and run **HikeJournal**. In split view, drag a park from National Parks over to Hike Journal. You'll now see the park name, map location, and first image load from the dropped Park!

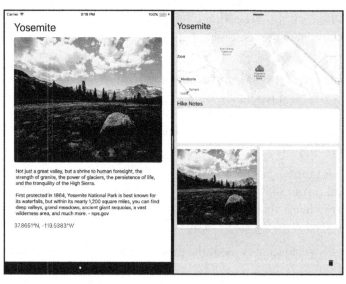

> **Note:** Again, you may get a compiler error complaining that `park` does not conform to `NSItemProviderReading`. As before, you may need to restart Xcode. The build actually succeeds but the error may still be flagged in the Xcode source editor window.

Animating drag & drop

You're now successfully dragging and dropping a park between two apps, though the visuals leave something to be desired.

When you drop, there's no indication anything has happened until the data suddenly appears after a delay. If you cancel a drag outside of a drop area by lifting your finger, the preview expands out from the touch point, and disappears. These behaviors kill the illusion that you've actually dragged the park from one area to another.

Fortunately, `UIDragInteractionDelegate` and `UIDropInteractionDelegate` have you covered! Here's a high-level look at the delegate calls involved in animation, and the order in which they act.

First, the `UIDragInteractionDelegate` side triggers:

1. `dragInteraction(_:previewForLifting:session:)` lets you provide a preview for the dragged item.

2. `dragInteraction(_:willAnimateLiftWith:)` lets you add your own animations to the source view, alongside system animations.

3. `dragInteraction(_:didEndWith:)` is called when the drag ends, either by canceling, or successfully dropping. This is your opportunity to revert any changes you made to the view during the drag.

4. `dragInteraction(_:previewForCancelling:withDefault:)` allows you to provide a preview image for each canceled drag item along with info on where they should animate to in the source view.

5. `dragInteraction(_:item:willAnimateCancelWith:)` is called when the cancel animation is about to start, and allows you to animate changes alongside the system animation.

`UIDropInteractionDelegate` provides similar callbacks on the destination end:

1. `dropInteraction(_:sessionDidUpdate:)` is called when the drag enters the drop interaction's view, and periodically as it moves. It can be used to alter the destination view based on location of the drag.

2. `dropInteraction(_:previewForDropping:withDefault:)` is called when the drop occurs, and is responsible for creating a preview, and animation, to move dropped items to their final position.

3. `dropInteraction(_:item:willAnimateDropWith:)` is called when the drop is about to occur, and allows you to animate changes to the destination view along with the system animations.

4. `dropInteraction(_:concludeDrop)` is called when the drop completes, and is responsible for configuring the destination view to its final state.

There is a *lot* to digest here (and this isn't even all of the available calls), but these provide you control throughout the progression of a drag and drop. You're also given the opportunity to customize the drag previews, and sync custom animations alongside the system's. Fear not, you'll walk through most of these in the pages ahead!

Adding animation

You'll start where it all begins: the lift. The entire park stack view lifts off the view, but it would be nicer to have a concise drag representation, so you'll create a custom preview.

Open **ParkViewController.swift**, and add the following to the `UIDragInteractionDelegate` extension:

```swift
func dragInteraction(_ interaction: UIDragInteraction,
                     previewForLifting item: UIDragItem,
                     session: UIDragSession)
  -> UITargetedDragPreview? {
    // 1
    guard let park = park, let dragView = interaction.view
      else {
        return UITargetedDragPreview(view: interaction.view!)
    }
    // 2
    let parkView = ParkDragView(park.image, name: park.name)
    let parameters = UIDragPreviewParameters()
    parameters.visiblePath =
      UIBezierPath(roundedRect: parkView.bounds,
                   cornerRadius: 20)
    // 3
    let dragPoint = session.location(in: dragView)
    let target = UIDragPreviewTarget(container: dragView,
                                     center: dragPoint)
    return UITargetedDragPreview(view: parkView,
                                 parameters: parameters,
                                 target: target)
}
```

This method creates a `UITargetedDragPreview` which consists of a view, and target location from which it animates. Here's a closer look:

1. You grab a reference to `interaction.view`, which is the stack view where the drag interaction was configured. If this, or the `park`, are unavailable, you create a preview from the source view. This would be the default behavior, had you not implemented this method.

2. `ParkDragView` displays the park name above its image, surrounded by a white border. You configure it with the `park`. `UIDragPreviewParameters` are used to apply a `UIBezierPath` to round the corners of the visible preview.

3. `location(in:)` helps you identify the point in the source view's frame where the drag occurred. The point is used to create a `UIDragPreviewTarget` to specify where the preview should originate. You then return a `UITargetedDragPreview` that will result in your rounded preview image presenting from the drag point.

Build and run **NationalParks**, and long tap on a park until it lifts. This time you'll see the new preview image appear from your touch point!

It looks a bit strange that the preview represents the park during the drag while the park is still fully visible. Dimming it is a great way to emphasize what the drag preview represents, so you'll do that next.

Add the following to the `UIDragInteractionDelegate` extension:

```
// 1
func dragInteraction(
  _ interaction: UIDragInteraction,
  willAnimateLiftWith animator: UIDragAnimating,
  session: UIDragSession) {
  animator.addAnimations {
    self.imageView.alpha = 0.25
  }
}
```

```
// 2
func dragInteraction(_ interaction: UIDragInteraction,
                     session: UIDragSession,
                     didEndWith operation: UIDropOperation) {
  if operation == .copy {
    imageView.alpha = 1.0
  }
}

// 3
func dragInteraction(
  _ interaction: UIDragInteraction,
  item: UIDragItem,
  willAnimateCancelWith animator: UIDragAnimating) {
  animator.addAnimations {
    self.imageView.alpha = 1.0
  }
}
```

Here's some detail on the three methods you implemented:

1. UIDragAnimating allows you to add animations to run along with system animations. addAnimations takes an animation closure which you use to dim the park imageView via its alpha.

2. When the drop completes, you need to revert the dimmed state for copy operations because the item should still be there. If you were doing a move, this is where you'd want to clear the data from the source view.

3. For drag cancellations, you're again provided an animator to gracefully revert your source view changes. In this case, you fade the imageView back in.

Build and run, and you'll see the background dim as the preview image animates in. Drag, and cancel it. Next, try dragging all the way to a successful drop in Hike Journal. In both cases, the park image will return to its prior state.

Try dragging the preview within National Parks, and dropping before getting to Hike Journal. You'll see the preview explode out from its current position and fade away. It would make more sense in this case if it popped back towards the park image to clarify the drag was ineffective.

Add the following to the `UIDragInteractionDelegate`:

```
func dragInteraction(
  _ interaction: UIDragInteraction,
  previewForCancelling item: UIDragItem,
  withDefault defaultPreview: UITargetedDragPreview)
  -> UITargetedDragPreview? {
    guard let superview = imageView.superview
      else { return defaultPreview }

    let target = UIDragPreviewTarget(container: superview,
                                     center: imageView.center)
    return UITargetedDragPreview(
      view: imageView,
      parameters: UIDragPreviewParameters(),
      target: target)
}
```

This returns a `UITargetedDragPreview` that provides a view, and target location for the cancel. `defaultPreview` is the behavior you observed when testing cancel, and you return it if the `guard` fails.

A `UIDragPreviewTarget` is created from the center of the `imageView` in the source view. The same `imageView` is used as the `UITargetedDragPreview` view. Together, this means the drag preview will animate into the `imageView` frame while transforming from the drag preview to the `imageView`.

Build and run, and test dragging to the far end of the National Parks view then releasing. You'll see the image snap back in place.

Indicating progress

It can take a while to load large data items in `dropInteraction(_:performDrop:)`. You've probably noticed some lag when dropping in Hike Journal. You're going to address this by adding a drop preview with a loading indicator.

In **HikeViewController.swift**, add the following properties near the top of the class:

```
var progress: Progress?
var loadingView: LoadingView?
```

`Progress` is a Foundation object allowing you to track progress and cancel processes. It's used by item providers for both of these purposes. You'll be relying on default behavior of `loadData` in `NSItemProviderWriting` to update this, but you can also do so manually by returning a `Progress` value in that method.

`LoadingView` is a custom view included in the starter project that displays a blurred background with a label in the center for displaying progress complete.

Now you'll place a progress indicator view over the entire Hike Journal while the drop loads. Add the following to your `UIDropInteractionDelegate` extension:

```
func dropInteraction(
  _ interaction: UIDropInteraction,
  item: UIDragItem,
  willAnimateDropWith animator: UIDragAnimating) {
  // 1
  guard let progress = progress,
    let interactionView = interaction.view else { return }
  // 2
  loadingView = LoadingView(interactionView.bounds,
                            progress: progress)
  // 3
  interactionView.addSubview(loadingView!)
}
```

`dropInteraction(_:item:willAnimateDropWith:)` is called when the drop animation is ready to start. In this case, you're not actually animating the drop, but hiding it behind a blurred loading screen. Here's how you did it:

1. Unwrap the `progress` property as well as the drop interaction's view (`interaction.view`). You'll populate `progress` shortly.

2. `LoadingView` will produce a blurred background covering the `interactionView.bounds`, and update a label with `progress` values using KVO. Open **LoadingView.swift**, part of the starter, and check out `observeValue` to see how `progress.fractionCompleted` is used to display percent completed.

3. Add `loadingView` to the `interactionView`, temporarily covering it.

When the drag is completed, and the data loaded, you want to remove this loading view to unveil the copied park.

Add the following to the top of `dropInteraction(:performDrop:)`, just below the `guard`:

```
session.progressIndicatorStyle = .none
```

`progressIndicatorStyle` is an enum with two values: `none`, and `default`. The default will pop up an alert based progress indicator for long running loads (you may have seen it in earlier testing). As you've now implemented your own indicator, you've turned the default one off.

In this same method, replace the existing `loadObject` call, and its closure, with:

```
// 1
progress = dropItem.itemProvider.loadObject(ofClass: Park.self)
{ [weak self] object, _ in
  guard let `self` = self else { return }
  self.park = object as? Park

  DispatchQueue.main.async {
    self.displayPark()
    // 2
    self.loadingView?.removeFromSuperview()
    self.loadingView = nil
  }
}
```

You've made two changes here:

1. The return value of `loadObject` is now stored in `progress`. This controller will now have access to progress updates, which the loading view observes.

2. Once the UI is updated with the loaded park, you remove the `loadingView` to unveil the updated destination view.

Build and run **HikeJournal**, and drag a park from National Parks. This time, you'll see a progress view cover the journal, displaying percent complete, and dismissing when complete.

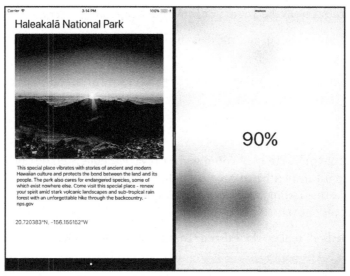

In this case, there isn't much data to transfer, so you're not likely to see this view for long. Consider a case where your drop has to pull data from iCloud, or another network source. Then, you shouldn't count on the destination app running, much less being in the foreground, by completion.

In such a case, you'd want to use a `FileProvider` extension for background loading. You can read more about it here: apple.co/2eG2qF3

> **Note:** You've obfuscated the actual drop animation with the loading view. This makes sense because the `Park` isn't dropping to any specific subview, but rather updating the entire Hiking Journal.
>
> Another common use case would be dropping one, or more, items into specific views, such as the image views in Hike Journal. In this case, you'd use `dropInteraction(_:previewForDropping:withDefault:)` to create a drop preview, and target it to land in the destination frame.

Data privacy

When you're enabling the ability to drag any kind of data to other apps, security and privacy should be at the forefront of your mind. The good news is drag and drop allows granular control over where your data can be dropped.

In this chapter, you initialized `NSItemProvider` directly with objects conforming to `NSItemProviderWriting`. However, the item provider offers several other methods for registering data.

One example is `registerDataRepresentationforTypeIdentifier:visibility:loadHandler:)`, which takes a type identifier and a closure that loads the required data. The `visibility` parameter is where it differs from what you've done thus far.

`NSItemProviderRepresentationVisibility` dictates which apps can accept a drag from this item provider. It allows data access based on the following options:

- **all**: Allows any app.

- **group**: Allows apps sharing the same app group.

- **ownProcess**: Allows only the source app.

- **team**: Allows any process created by the same development team.

An even simpler method is available for restricting drags to the source application. Open **ParkViewController.swift**, and add the following to the `UIDragInteractionDelegate`:

```
func dragInteraction(
  _ interaction: UIDragInteraction,
  sessionIsRestrictedToDraggingApplication
    session: UIDragSession) -> Bool {
  return true
}
```

This returns a `Bool` indicating whether the drag session should be limited to the current app.

Build and run **NationalParks**, and attempt to drag to Hike Journal. You'll no longer see a + badge when the drag preview enters Hike Journal, and releasing will cancel the drag. Your public domain park data is now safe from misguided thieves!

Since this isn't really necessary or helpful for this example, replace the `return` in `dragInteraction(_:sessionIsRestrictedToDraggingApplication:)` with:

```
{ return false }
```

Changing the return type to `false` again allows drops to Hike Journal. Make sure you build **NationalParks** again to load this update.

Spring loading

Spring loading allows controls to fire their actions when receiving a drop. It also allows you to launch apps by dropping onto their icons in the SpringBoard, or Dock.

You may have noticed the trash can in the bottom right of Hike Journal. Tapping it will clear your current hike data. You're going to take it a step further by spring loading that operation when dragging your hike data.

First, you need to enable dragging. Open **HikeViewController.swift**, and add the following extension:

```
extension HikeViewController: UIDragInteractionDelegate {
  func dragInteraction(_ interaction: UIDragInteraction,
                       itemsForBeginning session: UIDragSession)
    -> [UIDragItem] {
    guard let park = park else { return [] }
    let provider =
      NSItemProvider(object: NSString(string: park.name))
    let dragItem = UIDragItem(itemProvider: provider)

    return [dragItem]
  }
}
```

You've implemented `dragInteraction(_:itemsForBeginning:)`, and provided the current park's name to the item provider.

In `viewDidLoad()`, add the following after the code that adds a `dropInteraction` to the view:

```
clearButton.isSpringLoaded = true
let dragInteraction = UIDragInteraction(delegate: self)
stackView.addInteraction(dragInteraction)
```

`clearButton` is the trash can, and setting `isSpringLoaded` is all you need to do to force it to fire when hovered over by a drag. You also add a drag interaction to the `stackView` containing your journal info so it can be dragged to the trash.

Build and run **HikeJournal**, and drag a park from National Parks. Next, drag the Hike Journal, and hover over the trash icon for about a second. You'll see the button action fire, and the journal clear.

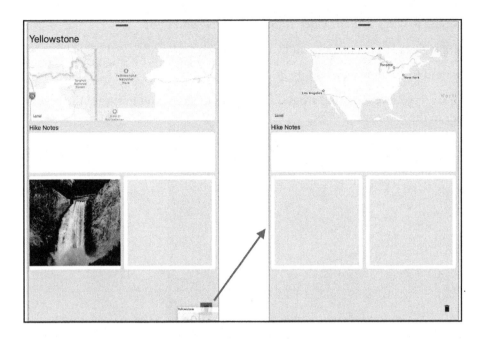

Where to go from here?

With little work, you set up a basic drag and drop between custom views in two different apps, complete with some canned animation. With a little more work, you were able to smooth out the edges and make it look natural. You also implemented a basic progress indicator, and learned how to protect your data with visibility controls.

There is still a lot more to learn:

- **Multiple Item Drag** is simple to implement, and allows you to add items to a drag with a tap.

- **More Animations and Visual Indicators** are possible with a more methods in `UIDragInteractionDelegate`, and `UIDropInteractionDelegate` as well as capabilities of `NSItemProvider`.

- **Sharing File URLs** is possible with `NSItemProvider`, and allows you to edit files in place; sharing updates made in the destination app with the source app!

There are several great WWDC sessions from 2017 that cover these topics, and more:

- Introducing Drag and Drop: <u>apple.co/2vO46Q4</u>

- Mastering Drag and Drop: <u>apple.co/2vOhvYA</u>

- Data Delivery with Drag and Drop: <u>apple.co/2tszCCm</u>

Also be sure to check out our video tutorials on Drag and Drop:

- Multiple Data Representations and Custom Views: bit.ly/2eGhceO

- Table and Collection Views: bit.ly/2unOBAH

Sory to say, if you were waiting around for info on dragons, you misheard the keynote. It happens to the best of us!

Chapter 8: Document Based Apps

By Michael Ciurus

iOS is pretty good at protecting your privacy. That's because every app has its own sandbox other apps can't access without permission. Thanks to that, one app's files are kept nice and safe from the reach of others.

However, this approach comes with a small drawback: managing files is a little more complicated. You can't freely browse files, and you need specialized tools and processes to allow sharing files between apps on iOS.

With iOS 11, Apple introduced a new tool for managing files: `UIDocumentBrowserViewController`. This brand-new view controller lets you create document browser apps, just like the new **Files** app on iOS 11, which lets you freely manage documents across all of your available locations.

In this chapter you'll create your own document browser app named **ColorBrowser** which manages custom files named with a **.color** extension.

> **Note:** The sample app in this chapter does not work well on the simulator. You will need a device running iOS 11 to build and test the app.

Documents on iOS

Before you dive into creating the document browser, you need to understand how iOS documents work. `UIDocument` is a powerful class that runs almost every document-based app. `UIDocument` is a wrapper over a physical file. It can be on your device or even in iCloud. It can asynchronously read/write to a file, auto-save, do file versioning and much more.

You're not forced to use `UIDocument`, but doing so is highly recommended as it solves a lot of problems for you. For example, you can work on the same iCloud file on your iPhone and your MacBook, and `UIDocument` will take care of everything for you.

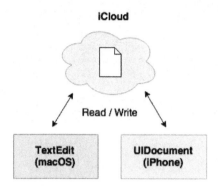

Document Provider

The Document Provider extension lets other apps work on your files that would otherwise be sandboxed. `UIDocumentPickerViewController` is a part of that extension; it's the visual interface that other apps will display to select documents from your app. The document provider allows other apps to import files from your app, which means that the file will be duplicated and your original file remains unchanged.

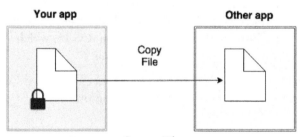

Import File

You can also allow other apps to directly open the files in your app, work on them and overwrite the original files.

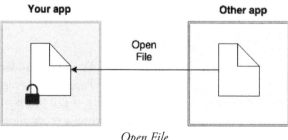

Open File

Document Browser

`UIDocumentBrowserViewController`, the hero of this chapter, is something else entirely. The document browser is not an extension for your app; it is a *type* of an app. Your customized `UIDocumentBrowserViewController` subclass must be the root view of your app. Simply put, it's a custom implementation of the iOS 11 **Files** app.

Play around with the **Files** app to get comfortable with the idea of a document browser app. You can use the document browser to open popular file extensions like `.txt`, `.pdf` or `.mp3`, but `UIDocumentBrowserViewController` shines when it comes to supporting custom file extensions.

Imagine that you have an iOS UI design app that uses proprietary **.color** extension files to describe RGB colors. Thanks to `UIDocumentBrowserViewController`, you can create a document browser that will manage **.color** files on your device, iCloud or any other available location.

Getting started

Go to the starter project folder for this chapter and open **ColorBrowser.xcodeproj**. Run the project.

This is the default `UIDocumentBrowserViewController`. All you can do is browse files. You can't open them or create new ones, since your custom `UIDocumentBrowserViewController` doesn't know how to do that yet.

In order for `UIDocumentBrowserViewController` to work, it needs to be the root view controller of the app. It also needs to have the `UISupportsDocumentBrowser` key set to YES in **Info.plist**. This is set up for you when you create a new project from the *Document Based App* Xcode template. It's also already been configured for you in the starter project. :]

Custom extensions

Files that use the custom **.color** extension are simple text files consisting of RGB color values separated by commas. So, for example, a white color file would contain the text 255,255,255. In order to support a custom **.color** extension in your document browser app, you need to register a new Uniform Type Identifier (UTI). Then you need to associate that new file type with your app.

Select the **ColorBrowser** project file in Xcode, then the **ColorBrowser** target, then open the **Info** tab.

You declare custom file types within the *Imported UTIs* and *Exported UTIs* dropdowns. Imported UTIs are for extensions that already exist, but don't belong to you, such as the Photoshop **.psd** format. Exported UTIs are for proprietary formats, just like your custom **.color** extension!

Expand **Exported UTIs**, click the + to add a new UTI and fill out these values:

- **Description**: A general description of the file extension. Enter **RGB Color file**.

- **Identifier**: The identifier of your proprietary data format. Enter **com.razeware.colorExtension**.

- **Conforms To**: UTI can conform to other types, just like subclassing. For example `public.html` conforms to `public.text`, because HTML is a specialization of simple text. Enter **public.text**, because .color is also a specialization of simple text.

You also need to specify the name of the extension. Expand the **Additional Exported UTI properties** section and create a dictionary called **UTTypeTagSpecification**. Inside this new dictionary, create an array called **public.filename-extension**. Add an item to the array with a value of **color**. This is the name of the file extension.

After you've defined this new UTI, you must associate it with your app in the **Document Types** section. Enter the name **Color Extension**, and in the **Types** field, enter the UTI identifier you just just defined: **com.razeware.colorExtension**.

Finally, you need to describe the role in which your app uses this document. In the **Additional document type properties** section, add a **CFBundleTypeRole** key with a string value of **Editor** and a **LSHandlerRank** key with a string value of **Owner**. The former indicates that your app can edit documents of this type; you could have set it to

Viewer if you only wanted the app to be able to view the documents instead. The latter identifies your app as the owner of the document type.

You can find out more about UTIs here: http://apple.co/2v0FiHO

That takes care of things. You've now defined a custom **.color** extension and associated it with your app!

Creating files

At the moment, nothing happens when you try to create a new file in your current browser, it just doesn't know how to do it yet. So you need to implement some of the the `UIDocumentBrowserViewControllerDelegate` methods.

Open **DocumentBrowserViewController.swift** and add the following to the bottom of the file:

```
extension DocumentBrowserViewController:
  UIDocumentBrowserViewControllerDelegate {
  func documentBrowser(_ controller:
    UIDocumentBrowserViewController,
    didRequestDocumentCreationWithHandler importHandler:
    @escaping (URL?, UIDocumentBrowserViewController.ImportMode)
    -> Void) {
    // 1
    let url = Bundle.main.url(forResource: "Untitled",
                              withExtension: "color")
    // 2
    importHandler(url, .copy)
  }
}
```

In order to create a new document, you need to provide a URL to a file template that the document browser will use. In other words, creating a file is importing a template file. You can create a blank file in the app temporary folder or simply load a template shipped with the app bundle. Here's how:

1. This obtains the URL to the **Untitled.color** file shipped with the starter project. Open the file in Xcode and take a look. It's a simple text file containing 150,150,150, which describes a gray color.

2. You always need to call the importHandler closure. In this case, you specify the URL to import along with the copy mode, which says that you want to copy the template file without removing it. If you specified move here instead, that would copy the file and remove the original.

Before going any further, you need to implement viewDidLoad():

```
override func viewDidLoad() {
  super.viewDidLoad()
  delegate = self
  allowsDocumentCreation = true
}
```

Here you make this class the delegate and enable the UI to allow the user to create new documents.

Creating a new document is an asynchronous operation, and the result can be success or failure. Therefore, you need to handle both cases. You must also handle what to do when a document is chosen by the user.

Add the following to the extension at the bottom of the file:

```
// 1
func documentBrowser(_ controller:
UIDocumentBrowserViewController,
                  didImportDocumentAt sourceURL: URL,
                  toDestinationURL destinationURL: URL) {
  // 2
  presentDocument(ColorDocument(fileURL: destinationURL))
}

// 3
func documentBrowser(_ controller:
UIDocumentBrowserViewController,
                  failedToImportDocumentAt documentURL: URL,
                  error: Error?) {
  showAlert(title: "Failed", text: "Failed to import")
}

// 4
func documentBrowser(_ controller:
UIDocumentBrowserViewController,
                  didPickDocumentURLs documentURLs: [URL]) {
  presentDocument(ColorDocument(fileURL: documentURLs[0]))
}
```

Here's what these delegate methods do:

1. `documentBrowser(_:didImportDocumentAt:toDestinationURL:)` is called when a new document is imported successfully.

2. This presents the new document in a `DocumentViewController`. `presentDocument(_:)` is a helper method delivered with the starter. It accepts a `ColorDocument` object. `ColorDocument` is a subclass of `UIDocument` contained in the starter and is responsible for saving and loading color files. You'll use the `ColorDocument` later in `DocumentViewController` to preview and edit color files.

3. `documentBrowser(_:failedToImportDocumentAt:error:)` is called when a new document fails to import, such as when you don't have access to the file passed in the `importHandler` closure.

4. `documentBrowser(_:didPickDocumentURLs)` is called when user picks files to open in the document browser. `UIDocumentBrowserViewController` supports opening multiple files. You don't need that in your app, so you should use the first URL: `documentURLs[0]`.

Run the app. You should be able to create new files and open them. All of your files will be imported with the same filename as the template file: *Untitled*.

You can change the name of the file in the browser by holding your finger down on the file and choosing the **Rename** action.

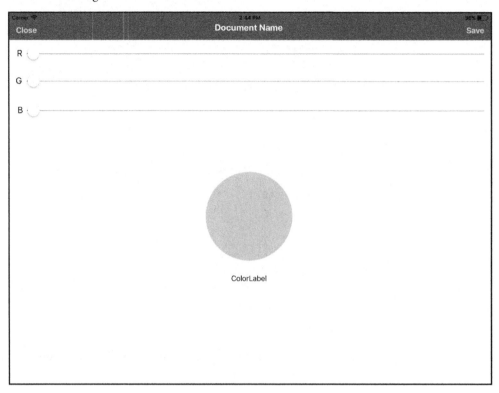

Displaying files

At the moment, `DocumentViewController` is presented, but you can't preview the color documents or save them.

Open **DocumentViewController.swift** and add the following to the bottom of the class:

```
override func viewWillAppear(_ animated: Bool) {
  super.viewWillAppear(animated)
  guard let document = document else {
    return
  }
  // 1
  if document.documentState == .normal {
    updateUI()
  } else {
    // 2
    document.open { success in
```

```
      if success {
        self.updateUI()
      } else {
        self.showAlert(title: "Error",
                          text: "Can't open document")
      }
    }
  }
}
```

This opens the document when the view appears. Specifically:

1. Here you check if the document is already loaded. If `documentState` is `.normal`, the file is already open so call `updateUI()`, which is a pre-supplied method that refreshes the UI with the current color.

2. Load the `UIDocument`. This reads the file URL that was passed to it at initialization and deserializes it. As mentioned above, `ColorDocument` contains the deserialization code.

In order to support saving you need to implement `didTapSave(_:)`. Replace the method stub with the following:

```
@IBAction func didTapSave(_ sender: Any) {
  guard let document = document  else {
    return
  }
  // 1
  document.color = RGBColor(R: Int(RSlider.value),
                            G: Int(GSlider.value),
                            B: Int(BSlider.value))
  // 2
  document.save(to: document.fileURL, for: .forOverwriting)
  { success in
    // 3
    if success {
      self.showAlert(title: "Success", text: "Saved file")
    } else {
      self.showAlert(title: "Error",
                        text: "Failed to save file")
    }
  }
}
```

Taking this step-by-step:

1. Update the document values with the values read from the sliders.

2. Save the updated values to the file.

3. Indicate to the user the result of the save operation.

Build and run the app. You can now preview and save colors.

Opening from other apps

You can create and open files in your app. One thing that still doesn't work is opening files passed to the app by the system. Go to the **Files** app and try opening a color file. It doesn't work! The app gets opened, because you associated your app with **.color** extension, but the `DocumentViewController` isn't presented.

This is because the file was opened outside of your app. The iOS interface for communicating actions happening outside of your app's process is the `AppDelegate`. When iOS wants your app to open a file, it calls `application(_:open:options:)`. Open **AppDelegate.swift** and add this code to your `AppDelegate` class:

```
func application(_ app: UIApplication, open inputURL: URL,
    options: [UIApplicationOpenURLOptionsKey: Any] = [:])
    -> Bool {
  guard inputURL.isFileURL else { return false }

  // 1
  guard let documentBrowserViewController =
    window?.rootViewController as? DocumentBrowserViewController
  else { return false }

  // 2
  documentBrowserViewController.revealDocument(at: inputURL,
    importIfNeeded: true) { (revealedDocumentURL, error) in
      guard let revealedDocumentURL = revealedDocumentURL,
        error == nil else {
          return
      }
    // 3
    documentBrowserViewController.presentDocument(
      ColorDocument(fileURL: revealedDocumentURL))
  }
  return true
}
```

This opens documents when prompted by the system:

1. First, access the current `UIDocumentBrowserViewController` root controller.

2. `revealDocument(at:importIfNeeded:completion:)` asynchronously prepares the document for you. This can either import (copy) the original file or work directly on the original file. This sets `importIfNeeded` to `true` to indicate that the document browser should try importing the file if opening directly isn't an option. Opening a file directly is disabled by default; you need to allow it in **Info.plist**.

3. Present the `ColorDocument`.

As mentioned above, you need to enable the open-in-place feature, opening documents from other apps in your app and working on them directly. Open the **Info.plist** file and find the key called **Supports opening documents in place** and set its value to **YES**.

Build and run the app and try opening a **.color** file from **Files** app again, this time it should open directly in your app.

Customizing the document browser

`UIDocumentBrowserViewController` has a couple of options to allow you to customize it. You can change the document browser style, tint color, add a custom action or add a new bar button item.

Open **DocumentBrowserViewController.swift** and add the following code to the class:

```swift
func customizeBrowser() {
  // 1
  view.tintColor = UIColor(named: "MarineBlue")
  // 2
  browserUserInterfaceStyle = .light
  // 3
  let action = UIDocumentBrowserAction(
    identifier: "com.razeware.action",
    localizedTitle: "Lighter Color",
    availability: .menu) { urls in
      let colorDocument = ColorDocument(fileURL: urls[0])

      colorDocument.open { success in
        if success {
          // 4
          colorDocument.color =
            colorDocument.color!.lighterColor(by: 60)
          self.presentDocument(colorDocument)
        }
      }
  }

  // 5
  action.supportedContentTypes =
    ["com.razeware.colorExtension"]
  // 6
  customActions = [action]

  // 7
  let aboutButton = UIBarButtonItem(
    title: "About",
```

```
      style: .plain,
      target: self,
      action: #selector(openAbout))
    // 8
    additionalTrailingNavigationBarButtonItems = [aboutButton]
  }

  @objc func openAbout() {
    showAlert(title: "About",
              text: "ColorBrowser 1.0.0\n By Ray Wenderlich")
  }
```

Here's a breakdown:

1. Change the tint color to `MarineBlue`. This color was shipped along with the starter in `Assets.xcassets`.

2. Change the style of the document browser. There are three styles: `dark`, `light` and `white`. You can't change colors of the document browser beyond the tint color and the style.

3. When you hold your finger on a file in the browser, you'll see various actions. Here, you create a custom action by using `UIDocumentBrowserAction`.

4. Your custom action opens an existing document with a color that's lighter by 60 points for each of the red, green and blue components.

5. `supportedContentTypes` is an array of UTI identifiers that the custom action supports. You pass `com.razeware.colorExtension` as it was the UTI identifier you defined earlier.

6. Assign the custom action to the `customActions` array of `UIDocumentBrowserViewController` to make the action available in the browser.

7. Create a new bar button item.

8. Assign the custom bar item to the `additionalTrailingNavigationBarButtonItems` property of the document browser.

To call your new method, add the following to the bottom of `viewDidLoad()`:

```
customizeBrowser()
```

Build and run to see your new effects!

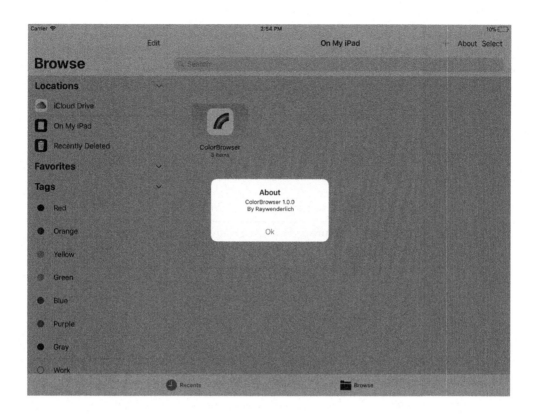

Animation controller

UIDocumentBrowserViewController lets you enable an alternate presentation
animation. Open **DocumentBrowserViewController.swift** and add the following
property to the top of the class:

```
var transitionController: UIDocumentBrowserTransitionController?
```

Now add the following extension at the bottom of the file:

```
extension DocumentBrowserViewController:
  UIViewControllerTransitioningDelegate {

  func animationController(forPresented presented:
    UIViewController, presenting: UIViewController,
    source: UIViewController)
    -> UIViewControllerAnimatedTransitioning? {
    return transitionController
  }
}
```

This will return the `transitionController` property that you will instantiate in the next snippet. In `presentDocument(_:)`, add the following code, just before you present `documentViewController`:

```
// 1
documentViewController.transitioningDelegate = self
// 2
transitionController = transitionController(
  forDocumentURL: document.fileURL)
```

Here's what this does:

1. Set this class to be the delegate to handle the transition.

2. The `transitionController` property is used to define what is returned in the `animationController(forPresented:presenting:source:)` delegate method. `transitionController(forDocumentURL:)` is a `DocumentBrowserViewController` method that creates a `UIDocumentBrowserTransitionController`. This conforms to `UIViewControllerAnimatedTransitioning` and defines the transition that should be used when a file is opened.

By returning a custom transition controller in the delegate method you enable the predefined alternate animation for opening documents.

Run the app and open a **.color** document to see your cool new animation.

Custom activities

When you hold on a document in your browser and tap **Share**, it opens the list of possible activities. You can create a custom activity for this as well.

In order to do that, you need to create a `UIActivity` subclass. You'll build an activity that copies a string representation of a **.color** file to your pasteboard. Open **CopyStringActivity.swift** and add the following:

```
class CopyStringActivity: UIActivity {

  let colorDocument: ColorDocument

  // 1
  init(colorDocument: ColorDocument) {
    self.colorDocument = colorDocument
  }

  override class var activityCategory: UIActivityCategory {
```

```
    // 2
    return .action
  }

  override var activityType: UIActivityType? {
    // 3
    return UIActivityType(rawValue: "ColorBrowserCopy")
  }

  // 4
  override var activityTitle: String? {
    return "Copy"
  }

  // 5
  override var activityImage: UIImage? {
    return UIImage(named: "copy_activity_icon")
  }

  // 6
  override func canPerform(
    withActivityItems activityItems: [Any]) -> Bool {
    return true
  }

  // 7
  override func perform() {
    colorDocument.open { success in
      if success {
        UIPasteboard.general.string =
          try! self.colorDocument.stringRepresentation()
        self.activityDidFinish(true)
      }
    }
  }
}
```

Going through this step-by-step:

1. In the constructor, assign the supplied `colorDocument` for which the activity will be used for.

2. Specify the activity type as `action`. You can also define a `share` activity.

3. Return a unique identifier for the activity type. You can use any identifier you want.

4. Return the title that will be presented below the activity in the UI.

5. Return the image that will serve as an icon for the activity.

6. This activity can be performed on all items in this app, so you return `true`.

7. This defines what happens when the user taps on the activity. You open the
   `colorDocument` and copy the value of `stringRepresentation()` to the
   pasteboard. `stringRepresentation()` is a method of `ColorDocument` shipped
   with the starter project. After the activity finishes you call `activityDidFinish(_)`.

In order to enable `CopyStringActivity` in your browser, you need to return its
instance. Go back to **DocumentBrowserViewController.swift** and add the following
code to the `UIDocumentBrowserViewControllerDelegate` extension:

```
func documentBrowser(_ controller:
  UIDocumentBrowserViewController,
  applicationActivitiesForDocumentURLs
  documentURLs: [URL]) -> [UIActivity] {
  let colorDocument = ColorDocument(fileURL: documentURLs[0])
  return [CopyStringActivity(colorDocument: colorDocument)]
}
```

This returns the available custom activities; in this case, an array of one object:
`CopyStringActivity`.

Build and run the project. Tap the **Select** button in the top right and choose a file, then
hit the **Share** button that appears along the bottom. From the activity menu, select the
Copy activity and *voilà* — now you can paste the value of the color into any other iOS
app!

Where to go from here?

`UIDocumentBrowserViewController` is a useful addition to iOS that helps to manage, share and edit your files across all kinds of cloud providers. As you've just experienced, one of its biggest advantages is the deep integration of custom document types.

If you want to know more about the document browser, check out this WWDC Video, "Building Great Document-based Apps in iOS 11": http://apple.co/2wdUjDg

Chapter 9: Core ML & Vision Framework

Michael Katz

We are visual creatures. According to *Time* magazine, 7 of the 10 most popular non-game apps in 2016 were either solely or significantly about image and or/video sharing. Some of these apps, like Facebook, Snapchat, and Instagram, provide users more than basic image display. They provide image correction, add filters, identify faces, and more.

In iOS 11, the new **Vision** framework, built on top of Core Image and Core ML, provides several out-of-box features for analyzing images and video. Its supported features include face tracking, face detection, face landmarks, text detection, rectangle detection, barcode detection, object tracking, and image registration.

In this chapter, you'll learn to detect faces, work with facial landmarks, and classify scenes using Vision and Core ML.

Getting started

Open the starter project: **GetReady**. GetReady looks at your pictures and decorates your friends and families for the occasion. These occasions include hiking and going to the beach. Hikers can be accessorized with ranger hats, and sunbathers will get sunglasses.

The image detail controller **ImageViewController.swift** is where most of the tutorial's code will go.

Build and run the app; you'll be presented with a blank screen. Tap the "+" button in the upper right-hand corner to open the picture chooser.

> **Note:** You can safely ignore any warnings or log messages that appear in the console due to opening the image picker.

If you're using the iOS Simulator, it comes preloaded with some pretty flowers and waterfalls. But since this tutorial is all about images with faces, these won't be helpful. Fortunately, the iOS 11 Simulator now makes it easy to add images!

You can use one of your own images, or you can grab the sample **hiker.jpg** from the **GetReady\images** folder and simply drag it into the Photos app. This will import it into the Simulator and make it available to its apps.

Back to our app, tap the plus button at top right, then select the new image. The image will appear as a thumbnail in a collection view.

Tap the thumbnail and it will open larger in its own screen. This is the view controller where all the image decorating will happen.

This guy looks like he's having fun hiking, but something's missing. Ah — he's *sans-chapeau*! Let's get the dude a hat to protect that magnificent scalp.

Detecting faces

To figure out where to put a hat involves finding the dimensions of each head in the picture. Fortunately, one of the things **Vision** does quite well is identify the bounding rectangles of a face.

> **Note:** The Core Image `CIDetector` class is also able to identify faces in images. The new Vision face detection is more powerful, able to identify smaller faces, faces in profile, and faces blocked by objects, hats, and glasses. The downside is that Vision is slower and requires more compute power (read "battery").

For this first part, the goal will be to draw a ranger hat on top of every recognized head in a photo. Later on, you'll use additional data to orient the hat and to place sunglasses on beachgoers' faces.

Face rectangle detection

Open **ImageViewController.swift** and replace `viewWillAppear(_:)` with:

```swift
override func viewWillAppear(_ animated: Bool) {
  super.viewWillAppear(animated)

  // 1
  guard let cgImage = image.cgImage else {
    print("can't create CIImage from UIImage")
    return
  }

  // 2
  let orientation = CGImagePropertyOrientation(
    image.imageOrientation)

  // 3
  let faceRequest = VNDetectFaceRectanglesRequest(
    completionHandler: handleFaces)

  // 4
  let handler = VNImageRequestHandler(cgImage: cgImage,
                                      orientation: orientation)
  // 5
  DispatchQueue.global(qos: .userInteractive).async {
    do {
      // 6
      try handler.perform([faceRequest])
    } catch {
```

```
            print("Error handling vision request \(error)")
        }
    }
}
```

This code sets up the call to the Vision API:

1. Vision does not work on `UIImage`s, but instead on raw image data, a pixel buffer, or either a `CIImage` or `CGImage`.

2. Specifying the orientation makes sure the detected bounds line up in the same direction as the image.

3. This creates the face detection request. The completion handler is a class instance method that you will supply shortly.

4. You need an image request handler to process one or more requests for a single image.

5. Vision requests can be time-intensive, so it's best to perform them on a background queue.

6. `perform(_:)` takes a list of requests and performs the detection work. The request callbacks are invoked on the background queue at the end of the detection process.

The completion handler

As its name suggests, `VNDetectFaceRectanglesRequest` finds the rectangles that bound faces in an image. A Vision request calls its completion handler with an array of detected objects, called *observations*.

Build out the completion handler by replacing `handleFaces(request:error:)` with:

```swift
func handleFaces(request: VNRequest, error: Error?) {
  // 1
  guard let observations = request.results
    as? [VNFaceObservation] else {
      print("unexpected result type from face request")
      return
  }

  DispatchQueue.main.async {
    // 2
    self.handleFaces(observations: observations)
  }
}
```

This implementation does the following:

1. Confirms that the request has a valid `results` array of `VNFaceObservation` elements.

2. Bounces the actual hard work to another function on the `main` queue.

This function is not defined yet, and Xcode is likely telling you so. To solve that, insert the following observation-handling method after `handleFaces()`:

```swift
func handleFaces(observations: [VNFaceObservation]) {
  var faces: [FaceDimensions] = []

  // 1
  let viewSize = imageView.bounds.size
  let imageSize = image.size

  let widthRatio = viewSize.width / imageSize.width
  let heightRatio = viewSize.height / imageSize.height
  let scaledRatio = min(widthRatio, heightRatio)

  let scaleTransform = CGAffineTransform(scaleX: scaledRatio,
                                         y: scaledRatio)
  let scaledImageSize = imageSize.applying(scaleTransform)

  let imageX = (viewSize.width - scaledImageSize.width) / 2
  let imageY = (viewSize.height - scaledImageSize.height) / 2
  let imageLocationTransform = CGAffineTransform(
    translationX: imageX, y: imageY)

  let uiTransform = CGAffineTransform(scaleX: 1, y: -1)
    .translatedBy(x: 0, y: -imageSize.height)

  for face in observations {
    // 2
    let observedFaceBox = face.boundingBox

    let faceBox = observedFaceBox
      .scaled(to: imageSize)
      .applying(uiTransform)
      .applying(scaleTransform)
      .applying(imageLocationTransform)

    // 3
    let face = FaceDimensions(faceRect: faceBox)
    faces.append(face)
  }
  // 4
  annotationView.faces = faces
  annotationView.setNeedsDisplay()
}
```

This method iterates over all observations, with the purpose of translating coordinates and define regions within the image where faces have been detected:

1. Here you locate the actual bounds of the image within the containing image view. Because the image view's content mode is specified as **Aspect Fit**, it is shrunk down so it fills at least one dimension of the image view. This means that the other dimension won't line up with the coordinates of the image view. Choosing a different mode, such as **Scale to Fill**, would simplify the math, but won't look very nice.

2. For each observation, you translate its coordinates to `imageView` coordinates.

3. You encapsulate the face bounds in a custom `FaceDimensions` struct and push it into an array. The struct is used to pass the face data around the app.

4. Finally, you add all face dimensions to `annotationView`, which will draw custom images over the original photo.

Step 2 is required because an observation's `boundingBox` is normalized in Core Graphics coordinates, with an origin at the bottom left. Before being drawn on a view, you need to do the following to the bounding box:

* Denormalize it to the input image size.

* Flip it into UIKit coordinates.

* Scale it to the drawn aspect ratio.

* Translate it to where the image is within the image view.

Before moving on, you probably want to see this code in action. Open **annotationView.swift** and change the `drawDebug` variable at the top to `true`:

```
class AnnotationLayer: UIView {
  var drawDebug = true
  ...
```

This will draw green boxes around the identified faces. Build and run, and select a photo. After a short time, you will see a green rectangle around all the identified faces.

Put a hat on it

Now that you can find a face, the next step is to style the head with a hat:

In **AnnotationView.swift**, replace `drawHat(faceRect:)` with:

```
private func drawHat(faceRect: CGRect) {
  let hatSize = hat.size
  let headSize = faceRect.size
  // 1
  let hatWidthForHead = (3.0 / 2.0) * headSize.width
  let hatRatio = hatWidthForHead / hatSize.width

  let scaleTransform = CGAffineTransform(scaleX: hatRatio,
                                         y: hatRatio)
  let adjustedHatSize = hatSize.applying(scaleTransform)

  // 2
  let hatRect = CGRect(
          x: faceRect.midX - (adjustedHatSize.width / 2.0),
          y: faceRect.minY - adjustedHatSize.height,
          width: adjustedHatSize.width,
          height: adjustedHatSize.height)

  // 3
  hat.draw(in: hatRect)
}
```

The general idea is to fit the hat on the head, with a little bit of brim extending beyond the head. By going with a 2/3 horizontal ratio of head to hat, you can draw hats by:

1. Computing the 3/2 scale factor and applying it to the hat's size.

2. Creating a rectangle centered horizontally on the face, and resting just above the top of the face. This will have the brim cover up the brow, which gives it a worn look rather than floating above the head.

3. Asking the hat to draw itself on the annotation view.

Build and run again. Now a hat will appear above each head.

Working with landmarks

Finding a face rectangle is nothing new in iOS, although the added accuracy in Vision is nice. Vision's capabilities get interesting when identifying additional face landmarks, such as the location of eyes, noses, mouths, and chins.

What can you do with these landmarks? Well, this app should be able to deliver cool shades to people out in the hot sun on a beach. To do that, the app will need to draw a sunglasses image over the eyes.

Detecting facial landmarks

The first thing is to use a `VNDetectFaceLandmarksRequest` to get all the landmarks. Back in **ImageViewController.swift**'s `viewWillAppear(_:)` change:

```
let faceRequest = VNDetectFaceRectanglesRequest(
    completionHandler: handleFaces)
```

...to

```
let faceRequest = VNDetectFaceLandmarksRequest(
  completionHandler: handleFaces)
```

Then, in `handleFaces(observations:)` replace:

```
let face = FaceDimensions(faceRect: faceBox)
```

...with:

```
var leftEye: [CGPoint]?
var rightEye: [CGPoint]?
if let landmarks = face.landmarks {
  leftEye = compute(feature: landmarks.leftEye,
                    faceBox: faceBox)
  rightEye = compute(feature: landmarks.rightEye,
                     faceBox: faceBox)
}

let face = FaceDimensions(faceRect: faceBox,
                          leftEye: leftEye,
                          rightEye: rightEye)
```

This queries the `landmarks` property of the `VNFaceObservation`, which is a class that contains an optional property of all the possible landmarks that can be detected. Here, you're using the `leftEye` and `rightEye` properties.

Now complete the code by adding the following `compute` method:

```
private func compute(
  feature: VNFaceLandmarkRegion2D?,
  faceBox: CGRect) -> [CGPoint]? {

  guard let feature = feature else {
    return nil
  }

  var drawPoints: [CGPoint] = []
  for point in feature.normalizedPoints {
    // 1
```

```
        let cgPoint = CGPoint(x: CGFloat(point.x),
                              y: CGFloat(1 - point.y))
        // 2
        let scale = CGAffineTransform(scaleX: faceBox.width,
                                      y: faceBox.height)
        // 3
        let translation = CGAffineTransform(
                          translationX: faceBox.origin.x,
                          y: faceBox.origin.y)
        let adjustedPoint =
            cgPoint.applying(scale).applying(translation)
        drawPoints.append(adjustedPoint)
    }
    return drawPoints
}
```

Face landmarks are a path of points normalized to the overall face rectangle and are in a "flipped" CIImage coordinate system. For each point, this method does the following:

1. Flips the point to core graphics orientation, with the origin in the upper left.

2. Scales the normalized point to the face's size.

3. Translates the point to the face's origin.

The result is a `CGPoint` array in the image view's coordinates that form the contour of the given feature.

If `drawDebug` is still set to `true`, you can build and run to see lines drawn around the eyes.

Adding the sunglasses

Now that the eyes are identified, you can go ahead and draw some sunglasses.

In **AnnotationView.swift** replace `drawGlasses(left:right:)` with:

```
private func drawGlasses(left: [CGPoint], right: [CGPoint]) {
  let total = left + right
  let minX = total.reduce(CGFloat.infinity) { min($0, $1.x) }
  let minY = total.reduce(CGFloat.infinity) { min($0, $1.y) }
  let maxX = total.reduce(0) { max($0, $1.x) }
  let maxY = total.reduce(0) { max($0, $1.y) }

  let width = max(maxX - minX, 16.0)
  let x = (maxX - minX) / 2.0 + minX - width / 2.0

  let height = max(maxY - minY, 8.0)
  let y = (maxY - minY) / 2.0 + minY - height / 2.0

  let eyesRect = CGRect(x: x, y: y,
                        width: width, height: height)

  glasses.draw(in: eyesRect)
}
```

In order to have sunglasses that sit across the face, they have to cover both eyes. Since the eyes are represented by a series of points, this method finds a box that encloses all the points from both eyes. Then it makes sure the bounds are at least 16 points wide and 8 points tall so that the image is discernible when drawn. Finally, it takes the sunglass image and draws it in the calculated rectangle.

Wanna see sunglasses in action? Build and run.

It's also a good time to check out an image with people on a beach. If you don't have one handy, drag in **kids_at_beach.jpg** and open it up!

Oops! The kids have both ranger hats and sunglasses. You'll need to determine whether this is a hiking or beach scene somehow.

Core ML: Scene Classification

The app's goal is to draw a situation-appropriate accessory on the heads in an image. In this case, it's a ranger hat in a forest and sunglasses on a beach. Right now the app is doing both, so you're going to fix that.

In an iOS 10 world, you might present a chooser to the user to select what type of scene is depicted. In iOS 11, you can access machine learning through Core ML. That means you can have a neural network automatically identify the image. Apple provides several ready-to-use models for image classification at https://developer.apple.com/machine-learning/. This means no need to learn Python and code train a model yourself!

The Core ML Model

This app uses the **Places205-GoogLeNet** model. This model tries to categorize the background of an image's scene as one of 205 places, such as a lighthouse, igloo, shoe shop, train platform, and so on. It has already been included in the project, as **GoogLeNetPlaces.mlmodel**. Open the model in the Project Navigator.

▼ Machine Learning Model			
Name	GoogLeNetPlaces		
Type	Neural Network Classifier		
Size	24.8 MB		
Author	B. Zhou, A. Lapedriza, J. Xiao, A. Torralba, and A. Oliva		
Description	Detects the scene of an image from 205 categories such as airport, bedroom, forest, coast etc.		
License	Creative Common License. More information available at http://places.csail.mit.edu		

▼ Model Class			
	GoogLeNetPlaces		
	Generated interface available after next build		

▼ Model Evaluation Parameters			
Name		Type	Description
▼ inputs			
	sceneImage	Image<RGB,224,224>	Input image of scene to be classified
▼ outputs			
	sceneLabelProbs	Dictionary<String,Double>	Probability of each scene
	sceneLabel	String	Most likely scene label

The top section is the model's metadata. The most important value is the model Type, which is a Neural Network Classifier. A classifier looks at the input and assigns a label. In this case, the neural network evaluates an image and returns a location description. And if neural networks are not good enough for you, Core ML also supports tree ensembles, support vector machines, and pipeline models.

> **Note:** You can find more information about these models and how Core ML supports them in Apple's developer documentation at http://apple.co/2sjpAXw.

The bottom section, Model Evaluation Parameters, describes the inputs and outputs of the model.

There is one input: `sceneImage`. This is a 224x224 RGB image. Vision automatically massages the input image so it fits a model's required size.

There are two outputs: `sceneLabel`, and `sceneLabelProbs`. `sceneLabel` is the classification label. This is the most likely scene type and is a `String`. `sceneLabelProbs` is a dictionary that lists the probabilities that the image is of every known scene. Machine learning is imprecise, and some images can be hard to classify. Therefore, images might have multiple labels that are close in probability, or all labels might have really low probability. This means the most likely `sceneLabel` might just be noise.

For example, a picture of a rooftop garden at a hotel bar with a mountain in the background might score almost as well for a bar, garden, hotel, and mountain since it contains features for all of those classifications. Depending on the inputs that were used to train the model, several classifications might be equally probably, or one type of classification might be a clear winner. Either way, only one value with the highest absolute probability will be the sceneLabel in this case.

In the middle of the model file's editor is the Model Class. Core ML exposes a model to the app's code through an automatically generated class.

Click the arrow next to GoogLeNetPlaces to open the Swift file. It has a class GoogLeNetPlacesInput for the inputs, GoogLeNetPlacesOutput for the outputs, and GoogLeNetPlaces for the model itself. The input class wraps a CVPixelBuffer for the image. As you'll see in the next section, Vision handles building the input for you.

Using the Model

Vision provides a special request type, VNCoreMLRequest for running a Core ML classification on an image. Back to **ImageViewController.swift**, in viewWillAppear(_:) replace everything after:

```
let handler = VNImageRequestHandler(cgImage: cgImage,
                                    orientation: orientation)
```

...with:

```
var requests: [VNRequest] = [faceRequest]

// 1
let leNetPlaces = GoogLeNetPlaces()
// 2
if let model = try? VNCoreMLModel(for: leNetPlaces.model) {
  // 3
  let mlRequest = VNCoreMLRequest(model: model,
                  completionHandler: handleClassification)
  requests.append(mlRequest)
}

DispatchQueue.global(qos: .userInteractive).async {
  do {
    // 4
    try handler.perform(requests)
  } catch {
    print("Error handling vision request \(error)")
  }
}
```

Taking each numbered comment in turn:

1. This first creates an instance of the model GoogLeNetPlaces.

2. The model is wrapped in a `VNCoreMLModel` container.

3. The model is fed to a `VNCoreMLRequest`.

4. The request handler then performs this request, along with the original face landmarks request.

Fix the compilation error by adding the following method:

```
func handleClassification(request: VNRequest, error: Error?) {
  guard let observations = request.results
    as? [VNClassificationObservation] else {
      print("unexpected result type from VNCoreMLRequest")
      return
  }
  guard let bestResult = observations.first else {
    print("Did not a valid classification")
    return
  }

  DispatchQueue.main.async {
    let scene = SceneType(classification: bestResult.identifier)
    self.annotationView.classification = scene
    print("Scene: '\(bestResult.identifier)' "
        + "\(bestResult.confidence)%")
  }
}
```

The classification will be returned as a `VNClassificationObservation` in the results field of the request. This result is then wrapped as a custom `SceneType` enum and passed to the annotation view, which will choose which annotations to draw.

GoogLeNetPlaces provides a whopping 205 possible places for an image scene. However, this is hardly exhaustive. In fact, neither forest or beach is in its list of known places! Check out **IndoorOutdoor_places205.csv** in the project directory for a complete listing. The `SceneType` enum helps map some of the known places to a possible forest or beach. As more types of places are added to the things the app cares about, this logic could get quite interesting.

Build and run. This time when an image is opened, the best classification is printed in the console. For our hiker, it guesses `Scene: 'rope_bridge' 0.202607%`. This seems like a reasonable guess given his stance. For a bigger shocker, try the kids on the beach. This says: `Scene: 'playground' 0.0852083%`. Only 9% is not very confidence-inspiring, since the image is not of a playground!

Using only one at a time

With the classification done and with the help of a magic enum, the app is now ready to use the classification to draw only one type of accessory.

Open **AnnotationView.swift**. At the top of `drawHat(faceRect:)`, add:

```
guard classification == .forest else { return }
```

At the top of `drawGlasses(left:right:)`, add:

```
guard classification == .beach else { return }
```

Build and run, and now only one type of accessory will be drawn on an image. You can also set `drawDebug` back to `false` for a cleaner result.

Tipping the hat

These overlay accessories sure look great, but they aren't always believable. Heads are not always going to be lined up vertically like it's a mug shot. The way to determine a face's orientation is with its median line, which is literally a line down the middle of a face. It will be oriented in the same direction as the face, so if the face is tilted then the line will be at a corresponding angle, rather than straight up and down.

Go back to **ImageViewController.swift**, locate `handleFaces(observations:)` and replace the last half of the `for face in observations` loop with:

```
var leftEye: [CGPoint]?
var rightEye: [CGPoint]?
var median: [CGPoint]?
if let landmarks = face.landmarks {
  leftEye = compute(feature: landmarks.leftEye,
                    faceBox: faceBox)
  rightEye = compute(feature: landmarks.rightEye,
                     faceBox: faceBox)
  median = compute(feature: landmarks.medianLine,
                   faceBox: faceBox)
}

let face = FaceDimensions(faceRect: faceBox,
                          leftEye: leftEye,
                          rightEye: rightEye,
                          median: median)
faces.append(face)
```

This retrieves the `medianLine` property from the landmarks and adds it to data passed to the annotation view.

Next, in **AnnotationView.swift** add the following method:

```
private func drawAngled(to median: [CGPoint]?,
                        in accessoryRect: CGRect,
                        image: UIImage) {
  if let median = median, median.count >= 2 {

    let top = median.first!
    let bottom = median.last!
    let estimatedSlope = (top.y - bottom.y)
      / (top.x - bottom.x )
    let degrees = atan2(1, estimatedSlope)
      + (estimatedSlope < 0 ? CGFloat.pi : 0)

    let context = UIGraphicsGetCurrentContext()
    context?.saveGState()

    context?.translateBy(x: accessoryRect.midX,
                         y: accessoryRect.midY)
    let angle: CGFloat = -degrees
    context?.rotate(by: angle)

    context?.translateBy(x: -accessoryRect.width / 2
      - (accessoryRect.midX - top.x),
                         y: -accessoryRect.height / 2)
    let drawRect = CGRect(origin: .zero,
                          size: accessoryRect.size)
    image.draw(in: drawRect)
```

```
        context?.restoreGState()
    } else {
        image.draw(in: accessoryRect)
    }
}
```

This computes a face angle by finding the slope between the top and bottom points of the median line. Then it rotates the draw context around the face midpoint and draws the accessory image.

Make sure this new method gets called by both drawing methods.

In `drawFaceAnnotations()` replace the call to `drawHat(faceRect:)` with:

```
drawHat(faceRect: faceRect, median: face.median)
```

Then update the signature of `drawHat(faceRect:)` to:

```
private func drawHat(faceRect: CGRect, median: [CGPoint]?) {
```

Then replace `hat.draw(in: hatRect)` with:

```
drawAngled(to: median, in: hatRect, image: hat)
```

Next do the same for the sunglasses. In `drawEyeAnnotations()` replace the call to `drawGlasses` with:

```
drawGlasses(left: left, right: right, median: face.median)
```

Change the signature of `drawGlasses(left:right:)` to:

```
private func drawGlasses(left: [CGPoint], right: [CGPoint],
                         median: [CGPoint]? ) {
```

And finally replace `glasses.draw(in: eyesRect)` with:

```
drawAngled(to: median, in: eyesRect, image: glasses)
```

Build and run. Boom! The hats and glasses are now aligned with each face's rotation.

Where to go from here?

One obvious next step is adding more fun accessories, based on other scenes and face landmarks. For example, adding clown noses to people at a circus. Additional scenes can be mapped from the classification labels to the SceneType enum.

In addition, the Vision Framework provides lots of other new functionality. Image registration can be used to straighten pictures or stitch together multiple photos into a single image. Rectangle detection can be used to pick out signs, flat surfaces, or boxes. Barcode detection can identify all sorts of common bar codes. Text detection can pick out words and letters from an image, and you could combine that with OCR or Core ML to do a live translation.

In addition to images, all Vision requests also work with video content. That means these annotations can be combined with the camera to provide live filters. For video content, the Vision framework provides object tracking: An identified object, such as a face or rectangle, can be tracked across multiple frames, even if it moves, scales, and rotates!

You could solve the beach scene confidence issue by replacing GoogLeNetPlaces with a broader or more accurate classifier. Or you could create a model that automatically determines the most appropriate fun accessory. Or even replace one background in a scene with another. We can't wait to see what you come up with!

Chapter 10: Natural Language Processing

By Michael Katz

In science fiction, omniscient computers understand a user's every spoken request. Imagine if you could just speak what you desire, as you would to a servant, and it would fulfill that request. With each iteration of operating systems and hardware, our mobile devices inch ever closer to making that a reality.

Current-day computers understand free-form text through a group of technologies called *Natural Language Processing*. This is a broad topic in computer science that covers many types of text features, and many, many techniques for processing the text.

Apple's operating systems provide functions to understand text using the following techniques:

- Language identification

- Lemmatization (identification of the root form of a word)

- Named entity recognition (proper names of people, places, and organizations)

- Parts of speech identification

- Tokenization

In iOS, you access these through the NSLinguisticTagger Foundation class. This API has actually been around since iOS 5, but in iOS 11 it received a significant upgrade by being rewritten on top of **Core ML**.

As a user of iOS, you'll notice the impact machine learning can have through the improvements it makes in areas such as determining when it's best to update your apps, what news you read more, or what apps you use more at certain times of the day. For your own apps, using NSLinguisticTagger is significantly more accurate, faster, and supports more languages than ever before.

The natural language processing APIs in Foundation use machine learning to deeply understand text using features such as language identification, tokenization, lemmatization, part of speech, and named entity recognition.

In this tutorial, you'll build an app that analyzes movie reviews for salient information. It will identify the review's language, any actors mentioned, calculate sentiment (whether the reviewer liked, or hated, the movie), and provide text-based search.

Getting started

Here's a quick peek at what the final project will look like:

Open the starter project in Xcode 9, run it, and check out its three tabs:

- **All**: Shows all movie reviews, as loaded from the *server*. You will add language identification to this screen.

- **By Movie**: Groups the reviews by their respective movie. You will add a *tomato* rating on this screen based on the average review sentiment.

- **By Actor**: Groups the reviews by mentioned actor. Actors will be automatically identified from the review text.

The review data comes from the included **reviews.json** file so you don't actually have to connect to a server in order to get the data for this tutorial.

Right now the app doesn't show the language of a review, the sentiment of a review, or include any search functionality. Let's work on the first issue: identifying the language.

Language identification

New to iOS 11 is the ability of `NSLinguisticTagger` to tell you the dominant, or primary, language of a string.

In **NLPHelper.swift**, replace `getLanguage(text:)` with the following:

```
func getLanguage(text: String) -> String? {
  return NSLinguisticTagger.dominantLanguage(for: text)
}
```

This will try to identify the most significant language from the supplied text. For most strings, it's likely there will only be one language present, so the dominant language will be the same as the language. A string such as *"That boy with a ballon has a real joie de vivre."* will be identified as English even though *"joie de vivre"* is a French expression.

Build and run. Country flags representing the language of a review will now show up beneath each review string:

> **Note:** I've greatly oversimplified the languages with flag emoji here, as there is no simple one-to-one mapping between languages or countries (or even different languages within countries). NSLinguisticTagger isn't smart enough to tell the difference between things like American English and British English, so country iconographies such as flag emoji are, of course, better suited for representing *where* the review was written rather than its language. However, they serve as a quick way to showcase this functionality in this chapter — no offense intended to any of you beautiful Earthlings out there!

Adding a search feature

Next, you'll add smart search to the app so users are able to find interesting reviews just by filtering for words that appear in the review.

A naïve approach

One approach is to create a mapping between a review and all the words in that review. But how do you even *get* the words in a string? Splitting a string on spaces seems like a good idea, but that can get messy when you have to work around punctuation. If you start capturing all the rules that define what a word *is*, and before you know it, you've built a complex parser to capture all the edge cases of a language.

Better yet, you can again leverage NSLinguisticTagger to figure out the words for you.

In **NLPHelper.swift** replace getSearchTerms(text:block:) with:

```
func getSearchTerms(text: String, block: (String) -> Void) {
  // 1
  let tagger = NSLinguisticTagger(tagSchemes: [.tokenType],
                                  options: 0)
  tagger.string = text
  // 2
  let options: NSLinguisticTagger.Options = [.omitWhitespace,
                                             .omitPunctuation,
                                             .omitOther,
                                             .joinNames]
  // 3
  let range = NSRange(text.startIndex..., in: text)
  // 4
  tagger.enumerateTags(in: range, unit: .word,
                    scheme: .tokenType, options: options)
  { tag, tokenRange, _ in
```

```
    guard tag != nil else { return }
    // 5
    let token = Range(tokenRange, in: text)!
    block(text[token].lowercased())
  }
}
```

This method iterates over the words of the input `text`, and sends them back to `block`. It does the following:

1. Sets up an `NSLinguisticTagger` to look for tokens.

2. Specifies the options for enumeration. When calling the enumeration block, these options will skip whitespace, punctuation, and unidentified characters. In addition, `.joinNames` will combine names into a single token so "John Smith" will be a single token instead of "John" and "Smith" being separate tokens.

3. Creates the range to enumerate over. `NSLinguisticTagger` is a `Foundation` class that still relies on `NSString` behavior, including `NSRanges`. Swift 4 introduces support for easily converting between `NSRange` and `Range<String.Index>`.

4. Performs the enumeration over the string's words, finding the tags with the specified options.

5. Since all the tags will be legitimate words, as all other types were omitted in `options`, it's safe to get the text from the original string. The enumeration provides `tokenRange`, an `NSRange`, to describe the word. Again, use the Swift 4 support to obtain the appropriate `Range<String.Index>` and use that to extract the word.

Build and run the app. Once launched, pull down on the table to reveal the search bar. Type **music** to only show reviews that contain the word "music":

This even works with multiple languages. Try searching for **mucho** to filter to a Spanish review. *¡Muy bueno!*

Now try searching for that one review talking about dancing by typing **dance**. No reviews. Hrm.

There has got to be a better way to do this!

A less naïve approach

Users have grown accustomed to rather forgiving search functionality. When typing "dance", "dances", or "dancing", a user will expect a match for "dance". A proper search engine indexes the text and does this for you, but those operations typically run server-side.

Direct word matching only goes so far. Fortunately NSLinguisticTagger is once again here to help! It provides *lemmatization* of tags. A lemma is the root, or *base*, form of a word excluding any modification for tense, gender, pluralization, etc.

The lemma of "dancing" is "dance", and the lemma of "dances" is also "dance". Instead of adding words as found in the text, add their lemmas instead.

Replace getSearchTerms(text:block:) with this updated version:

```
func getSearchTerms(text: String, block: (String) -> Void) {
  // 1
  let tagger = NSLinguisticTagger(tagSchemes: [.lemma],
                                  options: 0)
  tagger.string = text
  let options: NSLinguisticTagger.Options = [.omitWhitespace,
                                             .omitPunctuation,
                                             .joinNames,
                                             .omitOther]
  let range = NSRange(text.startIndex..., in: text)
  // 2
  tagger.enumerateTags(in: range, unit: .word,
                       scheme: .lemma, options: options)
  { tag, _, _ in
    guard let tag = tag else { return }
    block(tag.rawValue.lowercased())
  }
}
```

Like the previous version, this enumerates over all the words in the supplied text. There are three subtle changes that result in quite different functionality:

1. NSLinguisticTagScheme.lemma now tells the tagger to process for lemmas instead of token types.

2. The enumeration is for lemmas as well.

3. The `tag` is now the lemma, so its `rawValue` will contain the actual lemma, whereas `tokenRange` will still contain the original, non-lemmatized word.

Build and run again. Searching for **dance** now yields a result that contains a review with the word "dancing". Search for **good**, and you'll see reviews that contain "best".

Now, try searching specifically for **best**. Again, no results!

When building a search list with lemmas, it's good to also lemmatize the search input. This way, the input query will match the search dictionary keys.

There is one little gotcha: Lemmatization is language-dependent. Because of the machine learning algorithms that power `NSLinguisticTagger`, it's more accurate in determining the language, and the actual word, the more text that is provided.

However, a single search query is often not enough context, so it can use a little help.

For the third and final time, replace `getSearchTerms(text:block:)`:

```
// 1
func getSearchTerms(text: String, language: String? = nil,
                    block: (String) -> Void) {
  let tagger = NSLinguisticTagger(tagSchemes: [.lemma],
                                  options: 0)
  tagger.string = text
  let options: NSLinguisticTagger.Options = [.omitWhitespace,
                                              .omitPunctuation,
                                              .joinNames,
                                              .omitOther]
  let range = NSRange(text.startIndex..., in: text)

  // 2
  if let language = language {
    tagger.setOrthography(NSOrthography
      .defaultOrthography(forLanguage: language), range: range)
  }

  tagger.enumerateTags(in: range, unit: .word,
                       scheme: .lemma, options: options)
  { tag, _, _ in
    guard let tag = tag else { return }
    block(tag.rawValue.lowercased())
  }
}
```

In this version:

1. The caller can provide an optional language to help the tagger determine the lemma.

2. To set the tagger's language you have to actually set its **orthography**. The orthography describes not only the language, but the *script* as well.

An easy shorthand to understand script is to think about the alphabet, or character set, such as Latin for English, or Cyrillic for Russian.

Next, open **ReviewsTableViewController.swift**, and replace findMatches(_:) with:

```
func findMatches(_ searchText: String) {
  var matches: Set<Review> = []
  getSearchTerms(text: searchText,
                 language: Locale.current.languageCode)
  { word in
    if let founds = ReviewsManager.instance.searchTerms[word] {
        matches.formUnion(founds)
    }
  }
  reviews = matches.filter {baseReviews.contains($0) }
}
```

Instead of using the searchText directly, this reuses the previous lemmatization code to process the user's input text. The user's current Locale is assumed for the search language. A complete case would cover at least the same set of languages as the total review set since you can no longer properly search for reviews in different languages.

Build and run again. Searching for **best** will now return viable results!

Using named entities

Another great feature is *named entity recognition*: the ability to identify mentioned people, places, and organizations in the text. You will use this feature to identify the actors mentioned in the reviews.

In **NLPHelper.swift** replace getPeopleNames(text:block:) with:

```
func getPeopleNames(text: String, block: (String) -> Void) {
  // 1
  let tagger = NSLinguisticTagger(tagSchemes: [.nameType],
                                  options: 0)
  tagger.string = text
  let options: NSLinguisticTagger.Options = [.omitWhitespace,
                                              .omitOther,
                                              .omitPunctuation,
                                              .joinNames]
  let range = NSRange(text.startIndex..., in: text)

  tagger.enumerateTags(in: range, unit: .word,
                       scheme: .nameType, options: options)
  { tag, tokenRange, _ in
    // 2
    guard let tag = tag, tag == .personalName else { return }
```

```
        let token = Range(tokenRange, in: text)!
        block(String(text[token]))
    }
  }
}
```

This pattern should look very familiar at this point. You set up the
NSLinguisticTagger, and iterate over the tokens. The differences this time are:

1. The tag scheme used is nameType, which means the tagger is on the lookout for named entities.

2. Since there are a few types of named entities, this makes sure that the tag found is a person's name.

Build and run again. Tap the **By Actor** tab.

Now the list of actors is populated. Tapping on a name will show the list of reviews associated with them. As you can see, this list is pretty good, but not perfect, with a few false positives, such as "O". That's a tradeoff, though, when you're being forgiving in your search results.

Sentiment analysis

No movie review app is complete without determining if a movie is good or not, based on its reviews. In natural language processing parlance, figuring out the emotional content of a text is called sentiment analysis. **SMDB** has a simple measure of a review's sentiment: either the writer liked, or disliked the movie.

NSLinguisticTagger is mighty powerful, but sentiment is one feature that it does not yet tag. You'll have to build this feature yourself. There's no straightforward algorithm for sentiment analysis, but there are general patterns for identifying positive and negative reviews. This scenario is a great candidate for machine learning.

New in iOS 11, the Core ML framework lets you run machine learning algorithms in apps. Apple provides a few powerful models for image analysis, but as of this writing, none yet for text. This means you will have to model this yourself.

The Core ML model

First, you'll build out the sentiment analysis feature, and then see how it works.

Locate **Sentiment.mlmodel** in the **Project Navigator**, and open it. This is the editor for the pre-trained model for this app's sentiment analysis.

The top section is the model's metadata. The most important value is the model **Type** which is a Generalized Linear Classifier. A Classifier looks at the input and assigns a label. An image classifier might look at an image of a dog, and label its breed. In your case, the label for the text sentiment will be either *positive*, or *negative*.

The *Generalized Linear* part describes the type of math used in the model; this process will be described in the next section. Other popular types of supported models include neural networks, tree ensembles, support vector machines, and pipeline models. A description, and use, of those model types are outside the scope of this chapter.

> **Note:** You can find more information about these models and how Core ML supports them in Apple's developer documentation at http://apple.co/2sjpAXw

The bottom section, **Model Evaluation Parameters**, describes the inputs, and outputs, of the model.

There is one **input**: `wordCount`. This is a frequency count of all the known words as they occur in a review. This is a `MultiArray` (`Double 189`). This means that the input is a 1x189 array. This is because the model uses the frequency of only 189 words.

It may seem like the model doesn't scale well for all the words in English, and that is true. A more fully-fledged app, however, would likely input the whole input string, or a dictionary of word counts, and perform the vectorization on the model side, which is a lot more complicated.

Due to the limited set of known words, this model only supports analyzing reviews in English.

There are two **outputs**: `sentiment`, and `classProbability`. Sentiment is the classification label. This is the most likely sentiment, and is an `Int64`. The value will be `0` for a negative review, and `1` for a positive one.

Machine learning algorithms are not perfect, and some input can be hard to classify. Consider the following review:

"The special effects were amazing, but the plot was predictable."

Is that a positive, or negative review? In a case like this, the model might assign a Class Probability of 51% to negative and 49% to positive. The predicted `sentiment` value would be `0` because that is the more likely scenario, but it doesn't tell the whole story. This output probability dictionary allows you to build a UI that exposes that ambiguity to the user.

In the middle of the **Sentiment.mlmodel** file's editor is the **Model Class**. Core ML exposes a model to the app's code through an automatically generated class.

Click the arrow next to `Sentiment` to open the Swift file. It has a class `SentimentInput` for the inputs, `SentimentOutput` for the outputs, and `Sentiment` for the model itself. There is an initializer, and only one function to worry about: `prediction(wordCount:)`.

Using the model

It's time to put the model to use. Open **NLPHelper.swift**, and replace
`predictSentiment(text:)` with:

```
func predictSentiment(text: String) -> Int? {
  // 1
  let counts = tokenizeAndCountWords(text: text)
  // 2
  let model = Sentiment()
  // 3
  let input = try! MLMultiArray(shape:
    [1, NSNumber(value: words.count)], dataType: .int32)
  // 4
  for (index, counts) in counts.enumerated() {
    input[index] = NSNumber(value: counts)
  }

  // 5
  let prediction = try! model.prediction(wordCount: input)
  // 6
  let sentiment = prediction.sentiment
  // 7
  return Int(sentiment)
}
```

This method organizes a review's text into the required form for the model, and performs the classification. Here's how each step works:

1. Find the word frequencies in the review with this soon-to-be-added helper method.

2. Instantiate an object of type `Sentiment`, which was generated by the Core ML model.

3. Create an `MLMultiArray` object to match the required input shape. Core ML uses Foundation types, thus the explicit `NSNumber` conversion.

4. Fill the model input with values.

5. Run the model, and find the prediction.

6. Grab the most likely classification label. The output of a prediction is also an object, as described by the model file.

7. Cast the result, an `Int64`, to a Swift `Int` before returning.

To get the word counts, replace `tokenizeAndCountWords(text:)` with the following:

```
func tokenizeAndCountWords(text: String) -> [Int] {
  // 1
  let tagger = NSLinguisticTagger(tagSchemes:
    [.lemma, .lexicalClass], options: 0)
  tagger.string = text
  let options: NSLinguisticTagger.Options =
    [.omitWhitespace, .omitPunctuation, .joinNames, .omitOther]
  let range = NSRange(text.startIndex..., in: text)
  // 2
  var wordCount = Array(repeating: 0, count: words.count)
  tagger.enumerateTags(in: range, unit: .word,
                   scheme: .lemma, options: options)
  { tag, _, _ in
    guard let tag = tag else { return }

    let word = tag.rawValue
    // 3
    if let index = words.index(of: word) {
      wordCount[index] += 1
    }
  }
  return wordCount
}
```

This iterates over the lemmas, looks up the lemma in a list, and increments a counter at the corresponding index each time. Here's a breakdown of the method:

1. Use an `NSLinguisticTagger` to find the lemmas.

2. Set up an array with a count of 0 for each known word. The complete list of words in the model is included below as the `words` array.

3. Get the index, and increment the corresponding count if the lemma is in the word list.

The resulting array is what is then passed to the model. The model used here doesn't actually know anything about words. It treats each "word" as an anonymous feature represented by an Integer. When using models like this one, it's important to make sure the same "feature list" that was used for training is the same for the prediction inputs.

Build and run the app. Now, if a sentiment is determined, it will be marked with either a happy or sad emoji accordingly.

With the app running, tap the **By Movie** tab. For each movie, an average sentiment is calculated, and assigned a value in terms the Internet understands for movie quality: tomatoes!

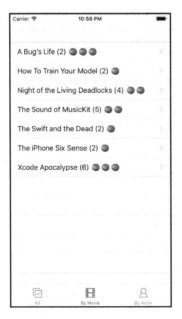

For each actor mentioned, the tab now shows an average sentiment.

How Linear SVC works

That's interesting, but how does this all work behind the scenes?

The *Linear Support Vector Classifier (SVC)* model is basically a fancy linear regression; that is, it fits a line to a bunch of points. The basic idea is to map the domain onto a space, and figure out how to divide up that space so each classification fits neatly into its own area.

Take an example with four simple reviews. The first two are positive reviews, and the last two are negative:

```
* The movie was great. Loved it!
* I really loved the movie.
* That was the worst movie, ever.
* I hated all the things!
```

One common way of treating text for machine learning is called *Bag of Words*. This theory is that the meaningful part of a text is the words in it, and the relative frequency of those words. With lemmatization your input becomes:

```
* great is it love movie the
* i love movie really the
* ever is movie that the worst
* all hate i movie the
```

The next step is finding the relative count of each word where the total word list is [all, ever, great, hate, I, is, it, love, movie, really, that, the, worst]. Each input now looks like the following:

```
* [0, 0, 1, 0, 0, 1, 1, 1, 1, 0, 0, 1, 0]
* [0, 0, 0, 0, 1, 0, 0, 1, 1, 1, 0, 1, 0]
* [0, 1, 0, 0, 0, 1, 0, 0, 1, 0, 1, 1, 1]
* [1, 0, 0, 1, 1, 0, 0, 0, 1, 0, 0, 1, 0]
```

You can think of each word as a *feature*, or *dimension*. This means each review can be plotted as a point in N-dimensional space. In this example, there are 13 dimensions. In the app, there are 189 features for each review. In a full-fledged sentiment classifier text analyzer, there might be 20,000 to 40,000 words considered.

In order to illustrate this example on paper, consider a two-dimensional space with the words "I", and "love". These can be plotted on an axis:

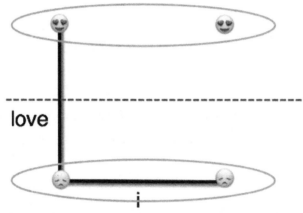

Four reviews plotted against frequency of the words "love", and "i". The blue line is the fit that divides the space into positive, and negative reviews. Orange loops are groupings by class.

There are two groupings for the reviews: the positive reviews are at the top, and the negative reviews at the bottom. The blue line evenly bisects these two spaces, which, for this contrived example, would be the linear classifier that fit this data. Take this two-dimensional example, and scale it up to thousands of dimensions, and that is how a Linear Support Vector Classifier works.

In a three-dimensional example, a plane would be fit so it divides the space between reviews.

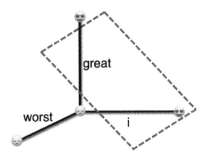

Four reviews plotted against frequency of the words "great", "worst" and "i". Blue plane is the fit that divides the space into positive, and negative.

If the word *movie* were chosen instead of *love*, then there would not be a clear grouping, and the classifier would have a harder time figuring things out. As both the number of examples for training increases, and the total number of features increases, the more accurate, and general, the classifier becomes.

More sophisticated models use N-grams instead of Bag of Words. These not only consider the frequency of words, but also the location of those words relative to each other.

Where to go from here?

There are more things that can be identified by `NSLinguisticTagger`, including parts of speech and script. Identified tokens can be used to build lists for type-ahead search, analytics, input for interactive fiction games, translation, or input validation.

In this app, the search mechanism is a dictionary lookup, which can soak up memory as the number of reviews increases. A better implementation would offload this lookup to a search index, or a database that provides full-text searching.

There are many, many different ways to analyze text, and an equally large number of ways to leverage Core ML in your apps. Some great machine learning applications for NLP that you can investigate on your own include translation, style identification, spam filtering, data mining, type-ahead prediction, or converting data to identify appointments, travel plans, or contact information *à la* Google Inbox.

I'm excited to see where your forays into natural language processing take you!

Chapter 11: Introduction to ARKit

By Michael Ciurus

Mainstream augmented reality was nothing but a distant dream not so long ago. So it's no wonder ARKit, a new iOS framework that lets developers create augmented reality apps, took the world by storm after it was introduced at WWDC '17. All you need to run AR apps is an iOS device — no extra accessories needed.

Need to set the mood? ARKit has you covered!

The result is simply stunning. By the end of the chapter, you'll have created an app that'll make you the hero of any social gathering: **HomeHero**. This is an AR app that helps you measure, plan and visualize the interior design of your home.

Getting started

Go to the starter project folder for this chapter and open **HomeHero.xcodeproj**. Choose your development team in the **General** tab, after you select the **HomeHero** project file and target.

> **Note:** ARKit doesn't work with the simulator. It works best with an iOS device with an A9 processor or better.

Run the project on an iOS 11 device:

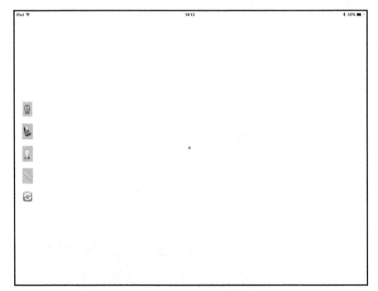

No magical worlds yet, just some plain good ol' UIButtons. You'll need to configure ARKit and render it, but first you need to get comfortable with the building blocks of ARKit.

ARKit uses your device's camera and motion sensors to detect changes in device position over time. Camera images are also used for recognizing depth, planes and lighting conditions. That's why ARKit works best in good lighting conditions in backgrounds with a lot of objects and rich texture. ARKit is so accurate you can measure real world objects with its help.

ARKit session

Imagine that your iOS device is a robot: it has eyes and it can feel its motion. ARSession is the brain of that robot and it communicates what it sees and feels through its API. ARSession operates on two building blocks to communicate with you:

- **ARAnchor**: A class that represents the real world position and orientation of an object. You can manually add anchors to the session to track objects, or ARSession can add them automatically when detecting certain objects. For example, when you turn on automatic plane detection, ARPlaneAnchor objects (an ARAnchor subclass) are added automatically.

- **ARFrame**: ARKit captures video frames, analyzes the motion data of each and returns the digested data in ARFrame, one for each video frame. ARFrame contains the captured video image, light estimation data and all tracked ARAnchor objects. ARFrame provides ARCamera, which is a representation of the physical camera and its position. ARFrame also contains detected **feature points**, which are interesting features in the real world 3D coordinates. More stuff happening on video means you have more feature points.

ARSesssion has an ARSessionDelegate delegate that keeps you up to date with all that's happening.

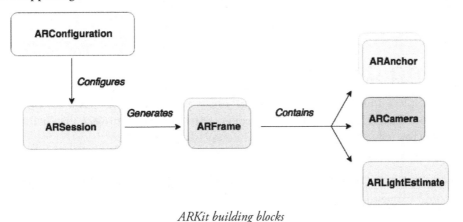

ARKit building blocks

Session configuration

You'll need ARConfiguration to run ARSession. Using ARConfiguration directly is not recommended, because it only detects the rotation of the device, not its position. It supports devices that don't have an A9 processor, so it should be only used if you want to fallback and support older devices. Instead, use ARWorldTrackingConfiguration (a subclass of `ARConfiguration`), which tracks all degrees of movement and gives the best results.

`ARWorldTrackingConfiguration` lets you opt in for:

- **Light Estimation**: Executes additional calculations to estimate the lighting conditions and return them in the `ARFrame` objects. It's used by the renderers to help the virtual objects match the real world light to intensify the illusion.

- **Plane Detection**: Detects planes in the real world and tracks them by automatically adding `ARPlaneAnchor` objects. As of now, only horizontal planes are detected. ARKit detects planes on floors, tables, couches etc. ARKit continually gathers data as you move the camera so the plane's position and extent change, or even merge together to make one plane.

Rendering

ARKit is just a robot's brain, containing the raw data of its observations. It doesn't render anything. You can use any renderer like SceneKit, Metal or even SpriteKit to render your augmented reality objects. Fortunately, Apple has provided you with `ARSCNView` which helps you in rendering ARKit data using SceneKit. `ARSCNView` holds an `ARSesssion` instance and maps the `ARCamera` to an `SCNCamera`, so the rendered SceneKit objects move when you move your device. It does a lot of heavy-lifting for you, as you'll find out soon enough.

Setting up ARKit

In order to place and render your first virtual object you need to set up `ARSession` and `ARSCNView`. Open **HomeHeroViewController.swift**. The starter project already includes an `ARSCNView`, which is connected to the `sceneView` property in `HomeHeroViewController`.

Create a `HomeHeroViewController` extension that conforms to `ARSCNViewDelegate`:

```
extension HomeHeroViewController: ARSCNViewDelegate {
}
```

This is where `ARSCNView` will update you about the `ARSession` and renderer state. You'll implement its methods later.

Add the following method to the `HomeHeroViewController` class:

```
func runSession() {
  // 1
```

```
    sceneView.delegate = self
    // 2
    let configuration = ARWorldTrackingConfiguration()
    // 3
    configuration.planeDetection = .horizontal
    // 4
    configuration.isLightEstimationEnabled = true
    // 5
    sceneView.session.run(configuration)
    // 6
    #if DEBUG
       sceneView.debugOptions = ARSCNDebugOptions.showFeaturePoints
    #endif
}
```

This method configures and runs `ARSession`. This is how it works:

1. Registers `HomeHeroViewController` as `ARSCNView` delegate. You'll use this later to render objects.

2. Uses `ARWorldTrackingConfiguration` to make use of all degrees of movement and give the best results. Remember, it supports A9 processors and up.

3. Turns on the automatic horizontal plane detection. You'll use this to render planes for debugging and to place objects in the world.

4. This turns on the light estimation calculations. `ARSCNView` uses that automatically and lights your objects based on the estimated light conditions in the real world.

5. `run(_:options)` starts the `ARKit` session along with capturing video. This method will cause your device to ask for camera capture permission. If the user denies this request, ARKit won't work.

6. `ASRCNView` has an extra feature of rendering feature points. This turns it on for debug builds.

To call `runSession()` in `viewDidLoad()` of `HomeHeroViewController`, change the already existing `viewDidLoad()` to the following:

```
override func viewDidLoad() {
   super.viewDidLoad()
   runSession()
   trackingInfo.text = ""
   messageLabel.text = ""
   distanceLabel.isHidden = true
   selectVase()
}
```

This will run the `ARKit` session when the view loads.

Run the app; you'll need to grant camera permissions as well. ARSCNView does all the work for you: it shows the captured video images in the background and it renders the feature points. If it weren't for ARSCNView, you'd have to do all that hard work yourself!

Drawing planes

Before placing objects, you need to understand how ARKit sees the world. You're familiar with feature points, but they're hardly an accurate model of the world. Fortunately, ARKit provides a more accurate representation of the world: planes.

ARPlaneAnchors are added automatically to the ARSession anchors array, and ARSCNView automatically converts ARPlaneAnchor objects to SCNNode nodes. This is convenient because all you have to do is implement a ARSCNViewDelegate delegate method and render new planes there. Implement renderer(_:didAdd:for:) in the ARSCNViewDelegate extension of HomeHeroViewController:

```
func renderer(_ renderer: SCNSceneRenderer,
            didAdd node: SCNNode,
            for anchor: ARAnchor) {
  // 1
  DispatchQueue.main.async {
    // 2
    if let planeAnchor = anchor as? ARPlaneAnchor {
      // 3
      #if DEBUG
        // 4
        let planeNode = createPlaneNode(
          center: planeAnchor.center,
          extent: planeAnchor.extent)
        // 5
        node.addChildNode(planeNode)
      #endif
    }
  }
}
```

When ARSession recognizes a new plane, ARSCNView automatically adds a new ARAnchor for that plane and calls the renderer(_:didAdd:for:) delegate methods. This is what happens in your implementation:

1. Renderer delegate methods are called on a separate queue. The easiest solution to prevent multithreading problems is to dispatch to the main queue.

2. This checks if the newly added ARAnchor is indeed an ARPlaneAnchor subclass.

3. Show only for debug builds.

4. createPlaneNode(center:extent:) is a helper function included with the starter project. This is SceneKit-specific code that creates a blue plane SCNNode with given a center and extent taken from ARPlaneAnchor.

5. node argument is an empty SCNNode that is automatically added to the scene by ARSCNView at a coordinate that corresponds to the anchor argument. All you need to do is attach a child to this empty node using addChildNode(_:), and this child (your plane in this example) will be in the correct position automatically.

You also need to support the cases where a plane's size or position changes, or where it's removed altogether. For these, you need to implement the renderer(_:didUpdate:for:) and renderer(_:didRemove:for:) delegate methods:

```
func renderer(_ renderer: SCNSceneRenderer,
              didUpdate node: SCNNode,
              for anchor: ARAnchor) {
  DispatchQueue.main.async {
    if let planeAnchor = anchor as? ARPlaneAnchor {
      // 1
      updatePlaneNode(node.childNodes[0],
                      center: planeAnchor.center,
                      extent: planeAnchor.extent)
    }
  }
}

func renderer(_ renderer: SCNSceneRenderer,
              didRemove node: SCNNode,
              for anchor: ARAnchor) {
  guard anchor is ARPlaneAnchor else { return }
  // 2
  removeChildren(inNode: node)
}
```

This takes care of updating the state of your planes. renderer(_:didUpdate:for:) is called when a corresponding ARAnchor is updated, and renderer(_:didRemove:for:) is called when an ARAnchor is removed. Here are the details:

1. Update the child node, which is the plane node you added earlier in renderer(_:didAdd:for:). updatePlaneNode(_:center:extent:) is a function included with the starter that updates the coordinates and size of the plane to the updated values contained in ARPlaneAnchor.

2. Removes the plane from the node if the corresponding ARAnchorPlane has been removed. removeChildren(inNode:) was provided with the starter project as well.

Run the app and walk around to see planes being visualized in the real world:

Creating AR objects

You're ready! It's time to enter the virtual world and mold it to your will. You'll start by placing objects on detected planes. ARSCNView contains very useful hit detection methods, so you'll use it to detect the point where the tap of the finger touches a detected plane in the virtual world.

Add the following new method in **HomeHeroViewController.swift**:

```
override func touchesBegan(_ touches: Set<UITouch>,
                           with event: UIEvent?) {
  // 1
  if let hit = sceneView.hitTest(
      viewCenter,
      types: [.existingPlaneUsingExtent]).first {
    // 2
    sceneView.session.add(anchor:
        ARAnchor(transform: hit.worldTransform))
    return
  }
}
```

This will add a new anchor in the hit test result point. Here's how it works:

1. hitTest(_:types:) returns all hit test results for given screen coordinate and types. You're passing viewCenter as the coordinate which is the screen's center, where the gray dot is drawn. viewCenter is a helper property provided with the starter project. You're using existingPlaneUsingExtent hit test option to indicate that you're

interested in hit testing with existing planes, while respecting the plane's limited size (the extent).

2. If there's a result, you use `add(anchor:)` on `ARSession` to create an anchor to represent the point in world where your object will be placed.

This adds an anchor but doesn't render anything. `ARSCNView` calls the `renderer(_:didAdd:for:)` delegate method when a new `ARAnchor` is added. This is where you'll handle rendering your new object.

Change the `renderer(_:didAdd:for:)` implementation to the following:

```
func renderer(_ renderer: SCNSceneRenderer,
              didAdd node: SCNNode,
              for anchor: ARAnchor) {
  DispatchQueue.main.async {
    if let planeAnchor = anchor as? ARPlaneAnchor {
      #if DEBUG
        let planeNode = createPlaneNode(
            center: planeAnchor.center,
            extent: planeAnchor.extent)
        node.addChildNode(planeNode)
      #endif
      // 1
    } else {
      // 2
      switch self.currentMode {
      case .none:
        break
      // 3
      case .placeObject(let name):
        // 4
        let modelClone = nodeWithModelName(name)
        // 5
        self.objects.append(modelClone)
        // 6
        node.addChildNode(modelClone)
      // 7
      case .measure:
        break
      }
    }
  }
}
```

This code will place the selected model in the world like so:

1. `else` means that `ARAnchor` is not `ARPlaneAnchor` subclass, but just a regular `ARAnchor` instance you added in `touchesBegan(_:with:)`

2. `currentMode` is a `HomeHeroViewController` property already added in the starter.

It represents the current UI state: `placeObject` value if the object button is selected, or `measure` value if the measuring button is selected. The switch executes different code depending on the UI state.

3. `placeObject` has an associated `string` value which represents the path to the 3D model **.scn** file. You can browse all the 3D models in **Models.scnassets**.

4. `nodeWithModelName(_:)` creates a new 3D model `SCNNode` with the given path name. It's a helper function provided with the starter project.

5. Append the node to the `objects` array provided with the starter.

6. Finally, you add your new object node to the `SCNNode` provided to the delegate method.

7. You'll implement measuring later.

Run the project, point the gray dot at an existing plane and tap the screen:

Placing objects at feature points

You can't expect the user to run around the apartment hunting for ARKit planes, so you need some other means of hit detection. You'll use feature points as a backup if no planes were found. It's actually very easy; you simply need to modify `touchesBegan(_:with:)`. Replace it with the following:

```
override func touchesBegan(_ touches: Set<UITouch>,
                           with event: UIEvent?) {
    if let hit = sceneView.hitTest(
        viewCenter,
        types: [.existingPlaneUsingExtent]).first {
      sceneView.session.add(
```

```
      anchor: ARAnchor(transform: hit.worldTransform))
    return
  } else if let hit = sceneView.hitTest(
    viewCenter,
    types: [.featurePoint]).last {
  sceneView.session.add(
      anchor: ARAnchor(transform: hit.worldTransform))
    return
  }
}
```

This adds a new type of hit test — `featurePoint` — for when you haven't found any results with `existingPlaneUsingExtent` test. The feature point hit results are sorted from nearest to farthest, so you should use the `last` result rather than `first`, because it gives the best user experience most of the time.

Run HomeHero and try it out. You might notice that this hit detection is pretty good but far from perfect: It places the object at *some* feature point you know nothing about. You'll have a chance to improve that later in a challenge.

Oops...

Measuring distances

It's time to work on another interesting feature in your app: measuring distances. ARKit places and tracks objects so accurately that you can use it to measure real world distances. 1 coordinate point in SceneKit is 1 meter in the real world. You'll measure distances in the app by placing two AR spheres and calculating the distance between them. To do that, you need to modify `renderer(_:didAdd:for:)` and implement the `measure` case in the `switch` statement:

```
func renderer(_ renderer: SCNSceneRenderer,
              didAdd node: SCNNode,
              for anchor: ARAnchor) {
  DispatchQueue.main.async {
    if let planeAnchor = anchor as? ARPlaneAnchor {
      #if DEBUG
        let planeNode = createPlaneNode(
            center: planeAnchor.center,
            extent: planeAnchor.extent)
        node.addChildNode(planeNode)
      #endif
    } else {
      switch self.currentMode {
      case .none:
        break
      case .placeObject(let name):
        let modelClone = nodeWithModelName(name)
        self.objects.append(modelClone)
        modelClone.position = SCNVector3Zero
        node.addChildNode(modelClone)
      case .measure:
        // 1
        let sphereNode = createSphereNode(radius: 0.02)
        // 2
        self.objects.append(sphereNode)
        // 3
        node.addChildNode(sphereNode)
        // 4
        self.measuringNodes.append(node)
      }
    }
  }
}
```

This code will create measuring nodes when you have the measuring tool selected in UI. It's fairly straightforward:

1. Create the sphere node using the `createSphereNode(radius:)` helper function included with the starter project.

2. Add the object the objects array.

3. Add the sphere to the node passed to the delegate.

4. Add the sphere to the `measuringNodes` array provided in the starter project to keep track of the measuring nodes.

You need to create logic that calculates the distance between two measuring nodes. Add the following new method in **HomeHeroViewController.swift**:

```swift
func measure(fromNode: SCNNode, toNode: SCNNode) {
  // 1
  let measuringLineNode = createLineNode(
      fromNode: fromNode,
      toNode: toNode)
  // 2
  measuringLineNode.name = "MeasuringLine"
  // 3
  sceneView.scene.rootNode.addChildNode(measuringLineNode)
  objects.append(measuringLineNode)
  // 4
  let dist = fromNode.position.distanceTo(toNode.position)
  let measurementValue = String(format: "%.2f", dist)
  // 5
  distanceLabel.text = "Distance: \(measurementValue) m"
}
```

This method creates a line between two nodes and updates the UI. Here's how it works:

1. `createLineNode(fromNode:toNode:)` is a helper function provided with the starter project. It creates a straight line node between two nodes.

2. Names the line node so it's easier to delete later.

3. Adds the line node to the scene.

4. Measures the distance between the two nodes. The distance between virtual objects corresponds to the distance in meters of the objects in real world position.

5. Updates the UI to show the distance to the user.

You need to add some logic that will update the measurement state depending on the number of spheres. Add the following method to **HomeHeroViewController.swift**:

```swift
func updateMeasuringNodes() {
  guard measuringNodes.count > 1 else {
    return
  }
  let firstNode = measuringNodes[0]
  let secondNode = measuringNodes[1]
  // 1
  let showMeasuring = self.measuringNodes.count == 2
  distanceLabel.isHidden = !showMeasuring
  if showMeasuring {
    measure(fromNode: firstNode, toNode: secondNode)
  } else if measuringNodes.count > 2 {
    // 2
    firstNode.removeFromParentNode()
    secondNode.removeFromParentNode()
```

```
    measuringNodes.removeFirst(2)
    // 3
    for node in sceneView.scene.rootNode.childNodes {
      if node.name == "MeasuringLine" {
        node.removeFromParentNode()
      }
    }
  }
 }
}
```

The logic is as follows:

1. Shows measure results only if there are two spheres.

2. Removes old measurement nodes if there are more than 2 nodes.

3. Removes old measuring lines.

Now you only need to call `updateMeasuringNodes()` at an appropriate time.
`renderer(_:didAdd:for:)` is too early, because at that time the nodes passed in the delegate method don't yet have a valid position. Because
`renderer(_:didUpdate:for:)` is called right after `renderer(_:didAdd:for:)`, the node passed in the `for` argument has the correct scene position, which means you can start the measuring.

With that in mind, change `renderer(_:didUpdate:for:)` to:

```
func renderer(_ renderer: SCNSceneRenderer,
              didUpdate node: SCNNode,
              for anchor: ARAnchor) {
  DispatchQueue.main.async {
    if let planeAnchor = anchor as? ARPlaneAnchor {
      updatePlaneNode(node.childNodes[0],
                      center: planeAnchor.center,
                      extent: planeAnchor.extent)
    } else {
      self.updateMeasuringNodes()
    }
  }
}
```

Calling `updateMeasuringNodes()` will update your measuring logic when a new ARAnchor has been added, mapped to a SCNNode, and updated.

Run the app and experience for yourself the magical accuracy of ARKit. You might want to find a plane to test on for more accurate hit testing.

ARSession state

ARSession, the running brain of ARKit, has different "moods" depending on the conditions in the real world. Sometimes it's running perfectly because the lighting and number of details on the screen is great; sometimes it has problems with the tracking. You'll use the state information provided in ARFrame to let the user know when there are tracking problems.

Add the following method to **HomeHeroViewController.swift**:

```
func updateTrackingInfo() {
  // 1
  guard let frame = sceneView.session.currentFrame else {
    return
  }
  // 2
  switch frame.camera.trackingState {
  case .limited(let reason):
    switch reason {
    case .excessiveMotion:
      trackingInfo.text = "Limited Tracking: Excessive Motion"
    case .insufficientFeatures:
      trackingInfo.text =
          "Limited Tracking: Insufficient Details"
    default:
      trackingInfo.text = "Limited Tracking"
    }
  default:
    trackingInfo.text = ""
```

```
  }
  // 3
  guard
    let lightEstimate = frame.lightEstimate?.ambientIntensity
    else {
    return
  }
  // 4
  if lightEstimate < 100 {
    trackingInfo.text = "Limited Tracking: Too Dark"
  }
}
```

This code takes the current `ARFrame` information and communicates it to the user if conditions are poor. Here's how this works:

1. You can get the current `ARFrame` thanks to the `currentFrame` property on the `ARSession` object.

2. The `trackingState` property can be found in the current frame's `ARCamera` object. The `trackingState` enum value `limited` has an associated `TrackingStateReason` value which tells you the specific tracking problem.

3. You turned on light estimation in the `ARWorldTrackingConfiguration`, so it's measured and provided in each `ARFrame` in the `lightEstimate` property.

4. `ambientIntensity` is given in lumen units. Less than 100 lumens is usually too dark, so you communicate this to the user.

You need to update the tracking information for each rendered frame, so you do that in the `renderer(_:updateAtTime:)` delegate method. Add this method in the `ARSCNViewDelegate` extension of **HomeHeroViewController.swift**:

```
func renderer(_ renderer: SCNSceneRenderer,
              updateAtTime time: TimeInterval) {
  DispatchQueue.main.async {
    // 1
    self.updateTrackingInfo()
    // 2
    if let _ = self.sceneView.hitTest(
        self.viewCenter,
        types: [.existingPlaneUsingExtent]).first {
      self.crosshair.backgroundColor = UIColor.green
    } else {
      self.crosshair.backgroundColor = UIColor(white: 0.34,
                                               alpha: 1)
    }
  }
}
```

This method does the following:

1. Updates tracking info for each rendered frame.

2. If the dot in the middle hit tests with `existingPlaneUsingExtent` type, it turns green to indicate high quality hit testing to the user.

Run the app and test the tracking info by feeding the camera with some bad conditions.

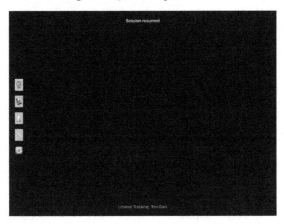

Session interruptions

Sometimes the `ARSession` will be interrupted, such as when sending the app to background. This cuts the video feed, making the `ARSession` completely blind. The session is interrupted, so the next time you enter the app and resume the session, your device probably won't be in the same position and rotation as before so the tracking will be completely broken. When that happens, you need to restart the session.

`ARSession` signals all session interruptions and general errors to its delegate via the `ARSessionObserver` protocol. `ARSCNViewDelegate` implements `ARSessionObserver`, so all you need to do is add these methods to your `ARSCNViewDelegate` implementation in **HomeHeroViewController.swift**:

```
func session(_ session: ARSession,
             didFailWithError error: Error) {
  // 1
  showMessage(error.localizedDescription,
              label: messageLabel,
              seconds: 2)
}

// 2
func sessionWasInterrupted(_ session: ARSession) {
  showMessage("Session interrupted",
              label: messageLabel,
```

```
           seconds: 2)
  }

  func sessionInterruptionEnded(_ session: ARSession) {
    showMessage("Session resumed",
    label: messageLabel,
    seconds: 2)
    // 3
    removeAllObjects()
    runSession()
  }
```

This code takes care of most `ARSession` problems that can occur. Here are the details:

1. `showMessage(_:label:seconds:)` is a helper method included with the starter project. It shows a message in a label for a given number of seconds. `session(_:didFailWithError:)` is called in case of general `ARSession` errors like a device not supporting AR.

2. `sessionWasInterrupted(_:)` is called when a session is interrupted, like when your app is backgrounded.

3. When `sessionInterruptionEnded(_:)` is called, you should remove all your objects and restart the AR session by calling the `runSession()` method you implemented before. `removeAllObjects()` is a helper method provided with the starter project.

Run the app on your device and try to interrupt the session by sending it to background, then resume the app again.

Where to go from here?

In this chapter, you had a chance to grasp most of what ARKit has to offer. Past that point, it's up to SceneKit and math to create jaw-dropping AR apps. ARKit will surely revitalize the App Store with exciting new experiences. The app you created has proven that AR is not only good for entertainment, but also for useful features like measuring, visualizing or education.

Before diving into designing awesome AR experiences, make sure to check out the Apple Human Interface Guidelines for ARKit here: apple.co/2xOwp1Q

For more details check out the WWDC ARKit Video here: apple.co/2t4UPlA

Challenge

The ARKit WWDC Demo App that you can find in the above link has a solution for more accurate placing of objects using feature points. The challenge is to improve the problematic hit testing in HomeHero by reading the ARKit WWDC Demo App code and introducing a similar algorithm. You're going to need trigonometry and algebra knowledge to solve that problem.

You can find the solution in the **challenge** folder. Of course, you can cheat a little and peek at the challenge solution — the point is for you to understand the math and algorithms so you can use it in your future ARKit projects.

Chapter 12: PDFKit

By Andy Pereira

The PDF specification was first made available by Adobe in 1993, and has since gone through many changes and improvements. However, these changes have seen the PDF Reference grow to over 1300 pages, which can be a little daunting for the average developer.

Working easily with PDFs is something macOS developers have been able to do for years with PDFKit. Meanwhile, iOS developers have been forced to use low-level code or third-party libraries to accomplish those same PDF tasks.

Apple has finally made PDFKit available to iOS developers in iOS 11, and they have also introduced many improvements to simplify working with PDFs for everyone!

In this chapter, you will learn how to use PDFKit in your iOS applications. You'll see how to create thumbnail previews of your documents and how to add text, input fields, radio buttons, checkboxes, watermarks, and more to your PDF projects.

Getting started

Open **WenderlichBeverage.xcodeproj** in the starter project folder for this chapter. The application is a tool used by the fictional sales representatives for Ray's new fictional beverage company, Wenderlich Beverages. The sales reps will need to be able to show sales documents and draw up contracts with customers.

Build and run the app to get familiar with it:

The initial screen has two image view placeholders you'll change later. The first thing you're going to add is the ability to show a PDF when you tap on one of these images.

Displaying a PDF

Open **HomeViewController.swift** and replace showDocument(_:) with the following:

```
@IBAction func showDocument(_ sender: UITapGestureRecognizer) {
  guard let view = sender.view as? UIImageView else { return }
  let document: String
  if view === imageView1 {
    document = SalesDocument.wbCola.nameWithExtension()
  } else {
    document = SalesDocument.wbRaysReserve.nameWithExtension()
  }
  let urlPath = URL(fileURLWithPath:
      FileUtilities.documentsDirectory()
        .appending("/\(document)"))
  let pdfDocument = PDFDocument(url: urlPath)
  performSegue(withIdentifier:
    SegueIdentifiers.showDocumentSegue.rawValue,
              sender: pdfDocument)
}
```

Here's what you're doing above:

1. Determine which image was tapped, and get the corresponding PDF document's URL.

2. Create a `PDFDocument` object with the URL.

It's very simple to create a `PDFDocument` object, and displaying one is no different.

Next, replace `prepare(for:sender:)` with the following:

```
override func prepare(for segue: UIStoryboardSegue,
                      sender: Any?) {
  guard let identifier = segue.identifier else { return }
  if identifier == SegueIdentifiers.showDocumentSegue.rawValue {
    if let document = sender as? PDFDocument,
      let upcoming = segue.destination
        as? DocumentViewController {
      upcoming.document = document
      upcoming.title = "Sales Document"
    }
  }
}
```

This code simply passes the `PDFDocument` you created in the previous step to the `DocumentViewController`. At this point, however, the view controller has no way to display the PDF.

Open **Main.storyboard** and find the **DocumentViewController** scene. Add a `UIView` to the scene, and set the constraints to **0** for all four sides, as shown:

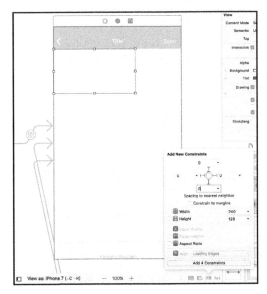

With the `UIView` selected, open the Identity Inspector and change the sublcass to **PDFView**. Finally, connect the `PDFView` to a new outlet in **DocumentViewController.swift** named `pdfView`.

> **Note:** You will not be able to select **PDFView** from the drop-down list. You must type it in explicitly.

In **DocumentViewController.swift**, replace `viewDidLoad()` with the following:

```
override func viewDidLoad() {
  super.viewDidLoad()
  if let document = document {
    pdfView.displayMode = .singlePageContinuous
    pdfView.backgroundColor =
      UIColor.lightGray.withAlphaComponent(0.25)
    pdfView.autoScales = true
    pdfView.document = document

    if addAnnotations {
      // This will come later.
    } else {
      navigationItem.rightBarButtonItem = nil
    }
  }
}
```

Here's what this code does:

- Sets the display mode of the `pdfView`.

- Enables **autoScales** on the view. With this set, a `PDFView` will automatically make the document's pages to scale to fit the view in which they're displayed.

- Sets the `document` object of the `PDFView`. This is all you need to do to show a PDF to a user.

There are a total of four display modes that are available to you, and they all display PDFs differently:

1. **singlePage**: Shows one page at a time, with scrolling only affecting the displayed page.

2. **singlePageContinuous**: The document displays all of the pages to user, defaulting to a vertical flow.

3. **twoUp**: Show two pages, side by side, with scrolling applying to only the two pages.

4. **twoUpContinuous**: Show all the pages of the document, by twos, side by side.

Build and run, and select either of the grey images. You'll be directed to the **DocumentViewController**, with the PDF in full splendor:

Sometimes, the default vertical direction won't work for your PDFs. Fortunately, it's very simple to change the document to scroll horizontally.

Test this out by adding the following to **DocumentViewController.swift**, inside `viewDidLoad()`, just before the point where you set the `displayMode`:

```
pdfView.displayDirection = .horizontal
```

Build and run, go to either document, and you'll see the display direction has now changed. You can remove the added line of code when you've finished exploring.

Under my thumb...nail

You've seen that displaying PDFs in iOS 11 is quite easy to do. However, there are times when you won't want to keep all of your PDF document data around, but still need to display a single page to the user. Keeping with the theme of "easy", `PDFDocument` provides a simple way to get thumbnail images from your PDFs.

Open **HomeViewController.swift**, and add the following methods below
`preloadDocuments()`:

```
private func loadDocumentThumbnails() {
  // 1.
  let document1Path = FileUtilities.documentsDirectory()
    .appending("/\(SalesDocument.wbCola.nameWithExtension())")
  let colaDocument =
    PDFDocument(url: URL(fileURLWithPath: document1Path))
  let document2Path = FileUtilities.documentsDirectory()
    .appending(
      "/\(SalesDocument.wbRaysReserve.nameWithExtension())")
  let rrDocument = PDFDocument(url:
      URL(fileURLWithPath: document2Path))
  // 3.
  imageView1.image = thumbnailImageForPDFDocument(document:
colaDocument)
  imageView2.image = thumbnailImageForPDFDocument(document:
rrDocument)
}

private func thumbnailImageForPDFDocument(
      document: PDFDocument?) -> UIImage? {
  guard let document = document,
    let page = document.page(at: 0) else { return nil }
  // 2.
  return page.thumbnail(
    of: CGSize(
      width: documentsStackView.frame.size.width,
      height: documentsStackView.frame.size.height / 2),
    for: .cropBox)
}
```

Breaking down what you've added:

1. For each PDF thumbnail you want, you first create a `PDFDocument` object.

2. Get the page for your thumbnail and call `thumbnail(of:for:)`. You need to supply
   the size of the image you want along with the type of `PDFDisplayBox` you need.

3. Add the thumbnail images to the `imageViews`.

`PDFDisplayBox` defines how much content should display from your PDF page.
Sometimes PDFs contain additional content, such as bleed marks for printing and
cutting physical paper. If you're working with content different from this tutorial, you'll
need to read up on these options in the *API Reference* at http://apple.co/2v5LDlN.

Next, in **HomeViewController.swift**, replace `viewDidLoad()` with the following:

```
override func viewDidLoad() {
  super.viewDidLoad()
  preloadDocuments()
  loadDocumentThumbnails()
}
```

Finally, open **Main.storyboard**. In the **Wenderlich Beverages Scene**, change the background color of both **UIImageViews** to **default**.

Build and run, and you'll see beautiful thumbnails of your sales documents:

Annotations

You'll often run into PDF content that users can interact with. You may need to add some shapes to call attention to edits in a document, or have a user fill out a form. Regardless of the need, you'll find Apple has made it easy, yet again, to get the job done.

Build and run, and navigate to the **Contracts** tab. Tap on + in the top right. The app will show you a contract form, but it looks a little empty. Tapping on the lines doesn't bring up the keyboard, and there are no other elements to interact with.

To add your first interactive widget to the PDF, add the following extension to
DocumentViewController.swift:

```swift
extension DocumentViewController {

  func addContractAnnotations() {
    guard let page = document?.page(at: 0) else { return }
    let pageBounds = page.bounds(for: .cropBox)

    // Add Name Box
    let textFieldNameBounds = CGRect(
      x: 128,
      y: pageBounds.size.height - 142,
      width: 230,
      height: 23)
    let textFieldName = textWidget(
      bounds: textFieldNameBounds,
      fieldName: FieldNames.name.rawValue)
    page.addAnnotation(textFieldName)
  }

  func textWidget(bounds: CGRect, fieldName: String?)
    -> PDFAnnotation {

    let textWidget = PDFAnnotation(
      bounds: bounds,
      forType: .widget,
      withProperties: nil
```

```
    )
    textWidget.widgetFieldType = .text
    textWidget.font = UIFont.systemFont(ofSize: 18)
    textWidget.fieldName = fieldName
    return textWidget
  }
}
```

Here's what you added:

- `addContractAnnotations()` creates a `PDFAnnotation`, and adds it to the page, according to the `CGRect` provided

- `textWidget(bounds:fieldName:)` is a convenience method that can create `PDFAnnotations` with a widget type of `text`.

Inside `viewDidLoad()`, replace the comment `// This will come later` with the following:

```
addContractAnnotations()
```

Build and run, navigate to the new contract page, and tap in the area above the line next to **Full Name**. The keyboard will present itself, and you can now enter your name:

Add the rest of the text field annotations in `addContractAnnotations()`:

```
// Add Birthday Box
let textFieldDateBounds = CGRect(
  x: 198, y: pageBounds.size.height - 166,
  width: 160, height: 23)
let textFieldDate = textWidget(
  bounds: textFieldDateBounds,
  fieldName: nil
)
textFieldDate.maximumLength = 10
textFieldDate.hasComb = true
page.addAnnotation(textFieldDate)

// Add Price Boxes
let textFieldPriceColaBounds = CGRect(
  x: 182,
  y: pageBounds.size.height - 190,
  width: 176, height: 23)
let textFieldPriceCola = textWidget(
  bounds: textFieldPriceColaBounds,
  fieldName: FieldNames.colaPrice.rawValue)
page.addAnnotation(textFieldPriceCola)

let textFieldPriceRRBounds = CGRect(
  x: 200,
  y: pageBounds.size.height - 214,
  width: 158, height: 23)
let textFieldPriceRR = textWidget(
  bounds: textFieldPriceRRBounds,
  fieldName: FieldNames.rrPrice.rawValue)
page.addAnnotation(textFieldPriceRR)
```

In order to select a day of the week, you'll need a radio button annotation. First, add the following method below `textWidget(bounds:fieldName:)`:

```
func radioButton(fieldName: String, startingState: String,
                 bounds: CGRect) -> PDFAnnotation {

  let radioButton = PDFAnnotation(bounds: bounds,
                                  forType: .widget,
                                  withProperties: nil)
  radioButton.widgetFieldType = .button
  radioButton.widgetControlType = .radioButtonControl
  return radioButton
}
```

This method will generate another `PDFAnnotation` type of `button`. There are a few different subtypes of buttons, and in this case, you're using `radioButtonControl`.

In `addContractAnnotations()`, add the following radio button annotations after the text fields:

```swift
// Add radio buttons
let buttonSize = CGSize(width: 18, height: 18)
let buttonYOrigin = pageBounds.size.height - 285

let sundayButton = radioButton(
  fieldName: "WEEK",
  startingState: "Sun",
  bounds: CGRect(origin: CGPoint(x: 105, y: buttonYOrigin),
                 size: buttonSize))
page.addAnnotation(sundayButton)

let mondayButton = radioButton(
  fieldName: "WEEK",
  startingState: "Mon",
  bounds: CGRect(origin: CGPoint(x: 160, y: buttonYOrigin),
                 size: buttonSize))
page.addAnnotation(mondayButton)

let tuesdayButton = radioButton(
  fieldName: "WEEK",
  startingState: "Tue",
  bounds: CGRect(origin: CGPoint(x: 215, y: buttonYOrigin),
                 size: buttonSize))
page.addAnnotation(tuesdayButton)

let wednesdayButton = radioButton(
  fieldName: "WEEK",
  startingState: "Wed",
  bounds: CGRect(origin: CGPoint(x: 267, y: buttonYOrigin),
                 size: buttonSize))
page.addAnnotation(wednesdayButton)

let thursdayButton = radioButton(
  fieldName: "WEEK",
  startingState: "Thr",
  bounds: CGRect(origin: CGPoint(x: 320, y: buttonYOrigin),
                 size: buttonSize))
page.addAnnotation(thursdayButton)

let fridayButton = radioButton(
  fieldName: "WEEK",
  startingState: "Fri",
  bounds: CGRect(origin: CGPoint(x: 370, y: buttonYOrigin),
                 size: buttonSize))
page.addAnnotation(fridayButton)

let saturdayButton = radioButton(
  fieldName: "WEEK",
  startingState: "Sat",
```

```
      bounds: CGRect(origin: CGPoint(x: 420, y: buttonYOrigin),
                     size: buttonSize))
  page.addAnnotation(saturdayButton)
```

Build and run, and navigate to a new contract. You'll be able to interact with all of the annotations now. Try to select more than one of the radio buttons as well:

Something isn't quite right. You shouldn't be able to select multiple days of the week. To remedy this, add the following two lines before the `return` call in `radioButton(fieldName:startingState:bounds:)`:

```
  radioButton.fieldName = fieldName
  radioButton.buttonWidgetStateString = startingState
```

Each radio button provides the same title, which is assigned to `fieldName`. By doing this, you tell your `PDFDocument` which radio buttons are grouped together. When all buttons are grouped together with the same field name, the only way you can tell which one is selected is through the `buttonWidgetStateString`. You'll need to set this unique value anytime you group radio buttons.

Build and run, create a contract, and you'll see that you can only select one radio button at a time.

Next, add a check box widget below the radio buttons in `addContractAnnotations()` with the following code:

```
let checkBoxAgreeBounds = CGRect(
  x: 75,
  y: pageBounds.size.height - 375,
  width: 18,
  height: 18)
let checkBox = PDFAnnotation(
  bounds: checkBoxAgreeBounds,
  forType: .widget,
  withProperties: nil)
checkBox.widgetFieldType = .button
checkBox.widgetControlType = .checkBoxControl
page.addAnnotation(checkBox)
```

Performing custom actions

Finally, there may be situations where you want to perform some action when a button is pressed. In this case, you're going to add a button that will clear some fields in the form, while leaving others filled in.

Again in `addContractAnnotations()`, after the checkbox widget, add the following:

```
// 1.
let clearButtonBounds = CGRect(
  x: 75,
  y: pageBounds.size.height - 450,
  width: 106,
  height: 32)
let clearButton = PDFAnnotation(
  bounds: clearButtonBounds,
  forType: .widget,
  withProperties: nil)
clearButton.widgetFieldType = .button
clearButton.widgetControlType = .pushButtonControl
// 2.
clearButton.caption = "Clear"
clearButton.fieldName = FieldNames.clearButton.rawValue
page.addAnnotation(clearButton)

// 3.
let resetFormAction = PDFActionResetForm()
// 4.
resetFormAction.fields = [
  FieldNames.colaPrice.rawValue,
  FieldNames.rrPrice.rawValue
]
resetFormAction.fieldsIncludedAreCleared = false
// 5.
clearButton.action = resetFormAction
```

Breaking down what you added:

1. You create a new button widget with the type `pushButtonControl`

2. Next, you add a `caption`. This will set the text you see on the button.

3. Then you create a `PDFActionResetForm` action.

4. Adding an array of fields to the action indicates which the fields you do *not* want to be cleared. By setting `fieldsIncludedAreCleared` to `false`, the form will not reset the fields provided.

5. Finally, you attach the action to the `clearButton`'s `action` property.

Build and run, create a new contract, and fill out all the fields. Tap **Clear**, and all the fields except for the price fields reset.

Saving PDFs

Now that you can fill out a form, you'd probably like to save it somewhere. While saving a PDF isn't a difficult task, there are a few things to be aware of. For instance, any annotations you have created on a PDF page will also be saved to your document, and will be seen each time you open it thereafter. You can also set ownership levels for a document to prevent people from making changes to the original document, or to give them varying levels of capabilities within the document.

Open **DocumentViewController.swift** and replace `saveAnnotations(_:)` with the following code:

```
@IBAction func saveAnnotations(_ sender: Any) {
  guard let document = document,
    let page = document.page(at: 0) else { return }

  var contracteeName: String?
  for annotation in page.annotations {
    if annotation.fieldName == FieldNames.clearButton.rawValue {
      // 1
      page.removeAnnotation(annotation)
    } else if annotation.fieldName == FieldNames.name.rawValue {
      // 2
      contracteeName = annotation
        .value(forAnnotationKey: .widgetValue) as? String
    }
  }
  if let name = contracteeName {
    // 3
    var displayName = name
      .replacingOccurrences(of: " ", with: "_")
```

```
    displayName += ".pdf"
    let savePath = FileUtilities.contractsDirectory()
      .appending("/\(displayName)")
    // 4
    document.write(
      to: URL(fileURLWithPath: savePath),
      withOptions: [.ownerPasswordOption: "SoMuchSecurity"])
    delegate?.didSaveDocument()
    navigationController?.popViewController(animated: true)
  }
}
```

This is quite straightforward code:

1. You'll need to loop through each annotation to find the **Clear** button and remove it. This will ensure the saved document doesn't display this button in the future.

2. Get the text from the name field, which you will use for the document name.

3. Set the save path and document name.

4. Write the document to the save path, with an owner password option, and password.

There are two `PDFDocumentWriteOptions` available to users:

1. **ownerPasswordOption**: Designates the password to unlock all editable features of the document.

2. **userPasswordOption**: Indicates users will have limited access to change, save or print the PDF file.

You'll need to pick which options work best for your documents. You can find the *API Reference* documentation at http://apple.co/2tAUCHk.

Build and run, enter a new contract, and select Save. You'll now see your contract in the list. Select your document and open it, but when you try to alter the document, you'll find that it's locked.

> **Note:** There appears to be a bug in iOS 11.0 that prevents the annotations from actually being locked. At the moment, you *will* be given a keyboard and allowed to alter the fields. The way the app is structured, however, you will not be able to save any changes. Thus, the document is more "locked-ish".

Finally, there may be times you would like to change the way the document is presented on the page. By subclassing `PDFPage`, you can do nearly anything you like.

Still in **DocumentViewController.swift**, add the following to `viewDidLoad()` just before setting the document's `displayMode`:

```
// 1
if document.isEncrypted || document.isLocked {
  // 2
  document.delegate = self
  if let page = document.page(at: 0) {
    for annotation in page.annotations {
      // 3
      annotation.isReadOnly = true
    }
  }
}
```

Then add the following extension to the file:

```
extension DocumentViewController: PDFDocumentDelegate {
  func classForPage() -> AnyClass {
    // 4
    return LockedMark.self
  }
}
```

Taking each commented section in turn:

1. Check if the document is encrypted or locked. You should always check your document for these fields, so you can properly handle if the user can edit, view or print the PDF.

2. Set the document's delegate. This will come in handy in step 4 below.

3. Set the annotations in the document to read only. This will prevent users from modifying the document.

4. Indicate that you want the `LockedMark` class to take control of drawing the pages of the document.

LockedMark.swift has been provided as part of the starter project. Here's how it works:

```
override func draw(with box: PDFDisplayBox,
                   to context: CGContext) {
  // 1
  super.draw(with: box, to: context)
  // 2
  UIGraphicsPushContext(context)
  context.saveGState()
  let pageBounds = self.bounds(for: box)
  context.translateBy(x: 0.0, y: pageBounds.size.height)
  context.scaleBy(x: 1.0, y: -1.0)
```

```
    // 3
    let string: NSString = "SIGNED"
    let attributes: [NSAttributedStringKey: Any] = [
      NSAttributedStringKey.foregroundColor:
          #colorLiteral(red: 0.5,
                        green: 0.5,
                        blue: 0.5,
                        alpha: 0.5),
      NSAttributedStringKey.font:
          UIFont.boldSystemFont(ofSize: 30)
    ]
    // 4
    string.draw(at: CGPoint(x:250, y:40),
                withAttributes: attributes)
    context.restoreGState()
  UIGraphicsPopContext()
}
```

1. When performing custom drawing of your page, you can choose whether you want
    your document to be drawn *before* or *after* your custom code. In this case, you want
    your content drawn *over* the document's content, so you call
    `super.draw(with:to:)` first. If you want your content drawn *below* the document's
    content, call it at the end of the method.

2. This code gathers the information about the drawing context of the page in order to
    understand the size and location your custom drawing.

3. This code draws the word **SIGNED** at the top of any saved contract. Then it sets up
    the attributes of the text, like size and color.

4. Finally, the string is drawn on the page, based on the coordinates provided.

Build and run the app. You'll now see the word **SIGNED** appear at the top.

Where to go from here?

In this chapter, you learned how simple and powerful PDFKit can be. It isn't difficult to get up and running, and doing some powerful things with the framework is quite easy. Apple has removed a lot of the guesswork and pain that used to be involved working with PDFs, which means your users are sure to have a better experience themselves.

For more information, checkout **Apple's PDFKit Documentation**. https://developer.apple.com/documentation/pdfkit

You can also learn more from the WWDC 2017 video covering the topic:

• Introducing PDFKit on iOS (Session 241) - https://developer.apple.com/videos/play/wwdc2017/241/

Chapter 13: MusicKit

By Jerry Beers

You could say music is at the heart of the iPhone. Before we even had the iPhone, the iPod revolutionized the music player industry by putting 10,000 songs in your pocket! Of course, now that the iPhone has made having the whole internet in your pocket commonplace, it's possible to have every song in your pocket through the miracle of streaming.

MusicKit makes all the songs from Apple Music and the user's own iTunes library available for your app to play.

Getting started

You're getting a two-for-one deal in this chapter! The sample app for this chapter will use an iMessage app with live views, which is new to iOS 11. Because this chapter is about MusicKit, it won't explain much about iMessage live views, but the starter project has a working iMessage application that lets you send guess-that-song music quizzes back and forth with your friends, using Apple Music library!

Developer token

The MusicKit API is a little different than most other iOS APIs. Because all the information is on Apple's servers, you'll be making web service calls instead of calling methods in a framework. Each call you make will include an authorization header. Since only trusted developers and members of Apple's Developer Program are allowed to use the service, your authorization header will include information that uniquely identifies you to Apple. First you'll see how to create the token, then you'll learn how to keep it secure.

Creating a MusicKit private key

The first step in creating a developer token is to create a key. This key is how Apple knows that the token is from you. The key doesn't expire, but you can revoke it if your key or token is ever compromised.

First, go to the **Certificates, Identifiers, and Profiles** section of your developer account at http://apple.co/2vsfGmP. Under **Identifiers**, select **Music IDs** and click the Plus button (+) in the upper-right corner to create a new Music ID.

Enter a description. This will be the name of the product shown to users when asking for their permission to let your app access their music accounts. Enter an identifier; it must start with "music", but should then be followed with a reverse domain name style, similar to your bundle identifier (e.g. `music.com.<your-org>.Name-That-Tune`). Click **Continue**, then **Register**, then **Done**.

Now that you have an identifier, you can create a key. Under **Keys**, select **All**, then click the Plus button (+) in the upper-right corner to create a new key. Enter a unique description for the key, and check the **MusicKit** checkbox under **Key Services**.

> **Note:** If you only have one Music ID, it will be selected for you automatically, but if you have more than one, you'll have to specify which Music ID should be associated with this key. To do that, click **Configure**, select the appropriate ID, and click **Continue**.

Click **Continue**, review the information, and click **Confirm**. Click **Download**, and then **Done**.

The key will be downloaded as a file with a **.p8** extension. You can open this file in any text editor to see your private key. But before you leave the site, make note of the **Key ID** and your **Team ID**, as you'll be using those in a minute.

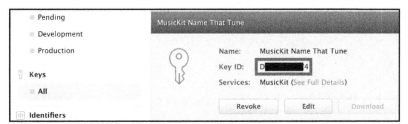

To get your Team ID, click **Account** at the top of the page, then **Membership**. Your Team ID will be listed there.

Creating a developer token

The developer token uses the JWT (JSON Web Token) standard. If you want to read more about JWT, you can find information at jwt.io. There, you can find quite a few different ways to create tokens in a variety of programming languages, but in this case you're going to use Python and the command line to create yours.

> **Note:** Thanks to Darren Baptiste for his post on GitHub where he shared how to create this token using Python: http://bit.ly/2vsHjw5.

First, you're going to need the Python package manager, so go to https://pip.pypa.io/en/stable/installing/ and download the **get-pip.py** file. While you may already have a version of pip installed, you need to perform this step to ensure it is current. Run Terminal and change to the directory where you downloaded the file: `cd ~/Downloads`.

Run the file you downloaded: `sudo python get-pip.py`. Enter your macOS password when prompted. Use the package manager to install the Python JWT library: `sudo pip install pyjwt`. Install the Cryptography package: `sudo pip install cryptography`.

In the downloadable content for this chapter, there is a **scripts** folder that contains a file named **music_token.py**. Open that file with a text editor. Open the **.p8** file you downloaded when you created your MusicKit Private Key. Copy the text between the "begin" and "end" tags and paste it into the **music_token.py** file between the tags.

```
secret = """-----BEGIN PRIVATE KEY-----
    Paste your key here
-----END PRIVATE KEY-----"""
```

Copy in the Key ID and Team ID you made note of earlier:

```
keyId = "9876543210"
teamId = "0123456789"
```

Your *key* does not expire, but your *token* will have an expiration built in. The expiration must not be longer than 6 months. The **music_token.py** script will take care of setting the "issued at" time and the "expiration time". Now you're ready to run the script and get your precious developer token!

Back in Terminal, in the directory where the **music_token.py** file is located, type `python music_token.py`. This will run the encryption step and print out your token and an example `curl` statement you can use to test it out. If you want to skip testing with `curl`, feel free; you'll be using the token in your own project very soon!

Securing your developer token

Because your developer token is like a secret key that you use to unlock access to the Apple servers, you want to keep it protected. You may also want the ability to revoke your key and issue a new one without waiting for a new version of your app to be approved. The best way to accomplish both of these is to host your key on a secure server and download it in your app.

Asking for permission

Open the starter project for this chapter, and set your team in the signing settings for both the main app and the MessagesExtension targets. To start, you can run on the simulator, but the project will work better on a device, and actual music playback will require a physical device.

Like other frameworks that allow you to access the user's data, MusicKit requires you to ask the user for permission. You're going to add an authorization manager class that will handle all the permissions aspects of the MusicKit API.

Open **AuthorizationManager.swift**, and add the following code:

```swift
import StoreKit

class AuthorizationManager {
  // 1
  static func authorize(
    completionIfAuthorized
      authorizedCompletion: @escaping () -> Void,
    ifUnauthorized
      unauthorizedCompletion: @escaping () -> Void) {
    // 2
    SKCloudServiceController.requestAuthorization {
      authorizationStatus in
      switch authorizationStatus {
      case .authorized:
        // 3
        DispatchQueue.main.async {
          authorizedCompletion()
        }
      case .restricted, .denied:
        // 4
        DispatchQueue.main.async {
          unauthorizedCompletion()
        }
      default:
        break
      }
    }
  }
}
```

Here's what this does:

1. This adds a static `authorize` method to the `AuthorizationManager` class. The method takes two closures: one for successful authorization, and one for an unsuccessful authorization attempt.

2. The `SKCloudServiceController` class in `StoreKit` has a
    `requestAuthorization` method. This method takes care of all the details for you.
    If the user has not previously been prompted, it will prompt the user and return the
    result to you. If the user has previously responded to the prompt, this will return
    immediately with the results.

3. If permission is `authorized`, this calls the completion closure on the main thread.

4. If the permission is `denied` (the user didn't give permission) or `restricted` (the
    device is restricting access to the music library), this calls the other closure on the
    main thread.

This method requires an entry in your Info.plist file to explain why you're asking for this
permission. Open the Info.plist file *for the application, not the extension*, and add a new
entry. Set the key to **Privacy - Media Library Usage Description** and enter a value, such
as "This allows you to listen to the selected song so you can guess which one it is". When
the system asks the user for permission, the prompt will show this description so your
user knows why you're asking for access.

In **MessagesViewController.swift**, at the top of the class in
`willBecomeActive(with:)`, replace this line:

```
presentViewController(for: conversation,
                      with: presentationStyle)
```

...with this code:

```
AuthorizationManager.authorize(
  completionIfAuthorized:
    { self.presentViewController(for: conversation,
                                 with: self.presentationStyle)
    },
  ifUnauthorized:
    { self.addController(self.authErrorViewController) }
)
```

This uses the `authorize` method you wrote above and shows your
`authErrorViewController` if the user denies authorization.

Getting a list of songs

If you run the app as it is now, you'll notice that there aren't any real song titles listed.
The first thing you want to do is to add a method to the `Song` class that will pull the top
40 songs from Apple Music. But there are two pieces of information that you'll need to
do this: the developer token and the storefront country code.

Getting the developer token

The best way to get the developer token is to download it from a server, instead of hardcoding it in the app. You're not going to set up a real server for this example, but I want to emphasize that you should download this value from somewhere. So like all good developers, you're going to fake it. The starter project has a class in **AuthorizationManager.swift** named MockURLProtocol.

Find this line:

```
static var fakeResponse = "" // Your developer token here
```

Place the developer token you generated earlier inside the quotes.

When your code asks the server for the token, instead of going to a real server, this class will intercept the request and serve up a response. Of course, you wouldn't ship this code with an app, but it is useful for testing or for simulating an API before it's finished.

Next, you'll add an AsyncOperation subclass to handle downloading the developer token. AsyncOperation is an Operation subclass that was included in the starter project. It's used to manage dependencies for asynchronous operations. For more on this topic, check out the video series "iOS Concurrency with GCD and Operations" http://bit.ly/2uzqoFf, available on raywenderlich.com.

Underneath the MockURLProtocol class in **AuthorizationManager.swift**, add this code:

```swift
class DownloadDeveloperTokenOperation: AsyncOperation {
  // 1
  var developerToken: String?
  override func main() {
    // 2
    URLProtocol.registerClass(MockURLProtocol.self)
    // 3
    let task = URLSession.shared
      .dataTask(with: developerTokenServerUrl) {
        data, response, error in
        guard let data = data else {
          self.state = .finished
          return
        }
        // 4
        self.developerToken =
          String(data: data, encoding: .utf8)
        // 5
        self.state = .finished
      }
    task.resume()
  }
}
```

Here's what this does:

1. You need a place to store the token after you download it. Think of this as the "output" of the operation.

2. Here is where you're telling the system to use your MockURLProtocol when loading network requests.

3. Then you create a normal dataTask, passing in the URL of your "server".

4. Once you get data back, store the downloaded token for later use.

5. The AsyncOperation doesn't finish until you tell it to. This is useful for running an async task inside the Operation. Since your dataTask is now done, set the state to .finished so any other operations that are waiting on this one can begin.

Getting the storefront country code

You faked the download of the developer token, but you'll download the storefront country code for real. A storefront is a country-specific view into the iTunes store. When the user is logged in, they have a default storefront set. You need to get the country code for that storefront as you'll use it to compose the URL to Apple's servers.

Fortunately, the StoreKit framework has a method you can use. Add this class right under the DownloadDeveloperTokenOperation you just added in **AuthorizationManager.swift**:

```
// 1
class RequestCountryCodeOperation: AsyncOperation {
  // 2
  var countryCode: String?
  override func main() {
    // 3
    SKCloudServiceController().requestStorefrontCountryCode {
      result, error in
      self.countryCode = result
      self.state = .finished
    }
  }
}
```

Taking each commented line in turn:

1. Just as before, you create a subclass of AsyncOperation to do this piece of work.

2. Again, you need a place to store the data you're requesting, so you add a variable for it here.

3. The StoreKit framework has a class, SKCloudServiceController, with a method requestStorefrontCountryCode(completionHander:) that will get the country code for the user. There are other MusicKit endpoints to get more information about different storefronts. They're outside the scope of this chapter, but if you need more information, see the Apple Music API Reference at http://apple.co/2vshzjh.

Controlling access

Now that you have a way to download the data, you need something to coordinate access to it. You don't want any callers to try to access the MusicKit API until both pieces of data are available. Operation objects are really good for that.

Add the following code at the bottom of the AuthorizationManager class:

```
// 1
fileprivate static let downloadDeveloperTokenOperation =
  DownloadDeveloperTokenOperation()
private static let requestCountryCodeOperation =
  RequestCountryCodeOperation()
// 2
private static let musicAPIQueue: OperationQueue = {
  let queue = OperationQueue()
  // 3
  queue.addOperation(downloadDeveloperTokenOperation)
  queue.addOperation(requestCountryCodeOperation)
  return queue
}()
// 4
static func withAPIData(
  completion: @escaping (String, String) -> Void) {
  // 5
  let operation = BlockOperation {
    // 6
    guard let developerToken =
      downloadDeveloperTokenOperation.developerToken,
      let countryCode = requestCountryCodeOperation.countryCode
    else { return }
    // 7
    completion(developerToken, countryCode)
  }
  // 8
  operation.addDependency(downloadDeveloperTokenOperation)
  operation.addDependency(requestCountryCodeOperation)
  // 9
  musicAPIQueue.addOperation(operation)
}
```

Let's take this line-by-line:

1. First, you create instances of the operations to download the developer token and country code.

2. `Operation` objects are controlled by an `OperationQueue`, so create one here.

3. Add your two operations to the queue.

4. The objects you've created so far are private. To allow callers to access the data, create a method with a completion closure.

5. Create a new type of `Operation` — a `BlockOperation` — to call the closure that was passed in.

6. Double check that the information you need has been downloaded.

7. Call the completion closure with the data.

8. But, before you let the `BlockOperation` run, you add the download operations as dependencies. This will ensure that the download tasks finish (or have previously finished) before running the `BlockOperation`.

9. Finally, you add the `BlockOperation` to the queue.

This makes sure that if any of your code requests to use the API before the developer token and country code have finished downloading, it will wait in the queue until that data is available, and then proceed.

The actual data

After all that build-up, you're finally to the point you've been waiting for: getting some actual songs from Apple! You're going to add a method to the `Song` class to get the top 40 songs, but that method is going to pass back some errors. To start, add this code to the top of **Song.swift**:

```
enum MusicError: Error {
    case invalidUrl
    case noData
    case jsonDecoding
    case networkError(innerError: Error?)
}
```

This is just an error type to specify what happened if something goes wrong.

Create an extension to `Song` at the bottom of the file:

```
extension Song {
}
```

Now, add this code to that extension:

```
// 1
static func top40Songs(
  completion: @escaping ([Song]?, Error?) -> Void) {
  // 2
  AuthorizationManager.withAPIData {
    developerToken, countryCode in
    // 3
    let urlString = """
      https://api.music.apple.com/\
      v1/catalog/\(countryCode)/charts?types=songs&\
      chart=most-played&limit=40
      """
    guard let url = URL(string: urlString) else {
      completion(nil, MusicError.invalidUrl)
      return
    }
    var request = URLRequest(url: url)
    // 4
    request.setValue("Bearer \(developerToken)",
      forHTTPHeaderField: "Authorization")
    // 5
  }
}
```

This is just a part of the method, but here is what you have so far:

1. This adds a new static method to the `Song` class to get top 40 songs.

2. This code is going to need to access the developer token and country code information, so you use the method on `AuthorizationManager` that you created to coordinate this access.

3. This URL has several parts. `https://api.music.apple.com/` is the server where you access the data. `v1/catalog/{country code}/` is how most requests that aren't asking for user-specific information begin. The country code is the one you just downloaded. `charts` tells the server you're interested in "top" songs, while `types=songs` specifies that you're only interested in songs, not albums or music videos. `chart=most-played` specifies the name of the chart you want to get data for. `limit=40` specifies that you want 40 results. Note that different calls have different values for `default` and `max` for this parameter, so check the documentation for more details on that. http://apple.co/2vW3MCt

4. Each request to the server has to include the `Authorization` header with your developer token, so set that here.

Add this code under step // 5:

```swift
let task = URLSession.shared.dataTask(with: request) {
  data, _, error in
  // 6
  let completeOnMain: ([Song]?, Error?) -> Void = {
    songs, error in
    DispatchQueue.main.async {
      completion(songs, error)
    }
  }
  // 7
  if let error = error {
    completeOnMain(nil,
                   MusicError.networkError(innerError: error))
    return
  }
  // 8
  guard let data = data else {
    completeOnMain(nil, MusicError.noData)
    return
  }
  // 9
}
task.resume()
```

Breaking this down:

5. In the code above, you built your request. Here, you're creating a `dataTask` to execute it.

6. This block performs a little trick to clean up the code. Several places in the code that follows will call back to the completion closure. But you always want to make sure that you call it on the main thread. Instead of repeating the Dispatch boilerplate, you create this wrapper closure that does that work and call it instead.

7. If the download resulted in an error, pass that back to the completion handler.

8. If there is no error, there should be data. To be safe, check for that condition as well and pass an error back if no data was found.

Next, you'll take a look at how to parse the response from the server.

JSON parsing

Here is what the structure of the data returned for this call looks like:

```json
{
  "results": {
    "songs": [
```

```json
{
  "chart": "most-played",
  "data": [
    {
      "attributes": {
        "artistName": "LINKIN PARK",
        "artwork": {
          ...
          "url": ".../{w}x{h}bb.jpg",
        },
        ...
        "name": "Iridescent",
        "url": "https:...?i=528969719"
      },
      "href": "/v1/.../528969719",
      "id": "528969719",
      "type": "songs"
    },
    { ... },
    { ... }
  ],
  "href": "/v1/...chart=most-played&limit=40",
  "name": "Most Played Songs on Apple Music",
  "next": "/v1/...chart=most-played&offset=40"
}
]
}
}
```

You want to use the new `Decodable` protocol to deserialize the data from JSON into your objects, but most of the data you want is a little buried in there. You could mirror the beginning part of that hierarchy in dummy structures, but there's another way.

First, you use `JSONSerialization` to convert from the JSON string to a dictionary. Then you drill down in that dictionary a bit to get to the piece that you want (the array of songs under the `data` key). You serialize that part of the structure back to JSON and then use the `JSONDecoder` to parse it. But, before you can parse it, you need to fix your `Decodable` conformance to handle this structure.

Remove the `Decodable` protocol from the `Song` struct at the top of this file and add this extension at the bottom:

```swift
extension Song: Decodable {
  enum CodingKeys: String, CodingKey {
    case id
    case attributes
  }

  enum AttributesKeys: String, CodingKey {
    case title = "name"
```

```
    case artist = "artistName"
    case artwork
  }

  enum ArtworkKeys: String, CodingKey {
    case url
  }

}
```

You now have a lot of compilation errors. Don't worry; you'll fix them shortly.

To help visualize this, take a look at the part of JSON that you're parsing:

```
{
  "attributes": { ... },
  "href": "/v1/catalog/us/songs/528969719",
  "id": "528969719",
  "type": "songs"
},
{ ... }
```

The pieces of this that you'll need are the values inside `attributes` and the `id`, so the `CodingKeys` enum contains those two keys. Here's what the `attributes` piece looks like broken out:

```
"attributes": {
  "artistName": "LINKIN PARK",
  "artwork": {
    ...
    "url": "https://example.mzstatic.com/.../{w}x{h}bb.jpg",
  },
  "discNumber": 1,
  "durationInMillis": 296575,
  "genreNames": [ ... ],
  "name": "Iridescent",
  "playParams": { ... },
  "releaseDate": "2010-09-08",
  "trackNumber": 12,
  "url": "https://itunes.apple.com/us/album/iridescent/
id528969611?i=528969719"
},
```

Out of that, you're going to use `name`, `artistName`, and `url` under the `artwork` structure. So, you construct your `CodingKey` enums to handle that structure.

Since you changed the structure of `CodingKeys`, you're probably seeing errors in the `init` and `queryItems` code at the top of the class. Fix those by replacing `CodingKeys` with `AttributesKeys` for the `title`, `artist`, and `artworkUrl` lines and change `artworkUrl` to simply `artwork`.

Then, replace the method `init(title:)` with this implementation:

```
init(id: String, title: String,
      artist: String, artworkUrl: URL) {
  self.title = title
  self.artist = artist
  self.id = id
  self.artworkUrl = artworkUrl
}
```

Finally, in the `Decodable` extension, add the following `init` method:

```
init(from decoder: Decoder) throws {
  let topContainer =
    try decoder.container(keyedBy: CodingKeys.self)
  let id = try topContainer.decode(String.self, forKey: .id)

  let attributes =
    try topContainer.nestedContainer(keyedBy:
    AttributesKeys.self, forKey: .attributes)
  let title =
    try attributes.decode(String.self, forKey: .title)
  let artist =
    try attributes.decode(String.self, forKey: .artist)

  let artwork =
    try attributes.nestedContainer(keyedBy:
    ArtworkKeys.self, forKey: .artwork)
  let artworkUrlTemplate =
    try artwork.decode(String.self, forKey: .url)
  let urlString =
    artworkUrlTemplate
      .replacingOccurrences(of: "{w}", with: "150")
      .replacingOccurrences(of: "{h}", with: "150")
  guard let url = URL(string: urlString) else {
    throw DecodingError.dataCorrupted(
      DecodingError.Context(
        codingPath: [ArtworkKeys.url],
        debugDescription: "Artwork URL not in URL format"))
  }

  self.init(id: id, title: title, artist: artist,
            artworkUrl: url)
}
```

This method goes through the JSON structure and pulls out the data for your struct. Notice that the URL for the album artwork isn't really a valid URL, but more like a URL template that allows you to specify the size of the image you want. You take the template and replace the width and height tokens with a fixed value of 150. Then you take the string and turn it into a URL.

Now that the Song struct is capable of handling our JSON data, you can finish the top40Songs method.

Add this code under step // 9 of top40Songs:

```
guard let jsonData =
  // 10
  try? JSONSerialization.jsonObject(with: data),
  let dataDictionary = jsonData as? [String: Any],
  let results = dataDictionary["results"] as? [String:Any],
  let songsArray = results["songs"] as? [[String: Any]],
  let songsItem = songsArray.first,
  let songsDictionary = songsItem["data"],
  // 11
  let songsData = try? JSONSerialization.data(
    withJSONObject: songsDictionary),
  // 12
  let songs = try? JSONDecoder().decode([Song].self,
                                      from: songsData) else {
    completeOnMain(nil, MusicError.jsonDecoding)
    return
  }
completeOnMain(songs, nil)
```

Here's what this code is doing:

10. First, you create a dictionary with the JSON data, parsing through the "results", "songs", and "data" hierarchy.

11. Then, you take the subset that you want to look at, and turn it back into JSON data.

12. Finally, you use the JSONDecoder, along with the code you wrote above, to turn your JSON data into an array of Song instances and pass that array back to the completion closure.

Now that the top40Songs method is finished, you can call it and use the data it returns instead of your hard-coded and unimaginative song titles.

In SongListViewController, replace the whole declaration of private var songs with:

```
private var songs: [Song] = [] {
  didSet {
    tableView.reloadData()
  }
}

override func viewDidLoad() {
  super.viewDidLoad()

  Song.top40Songs { songs, error in
```

```
    if let songs = songs {
      self.songs = songs
    }
  }
}
```

This starts with an empty `songs` array, asks `top40Songs` for the songs, and reloads the table when they've finished downloading.

Build and run, and you'll see the Messages app launch with a list of the songs:

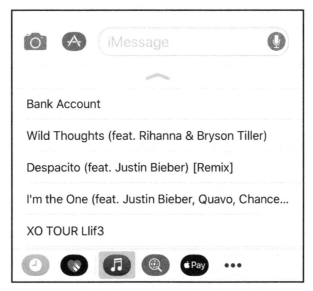

Note: If you have run the app before in the simulator, you may get a crash due to an unhandled exception in `UICollectionView`. If this happens, select **Hardward\Erase All Content and Settings...** from the **Simulator** menu.

Select one of the songs, and the app will create a quiz with that song and three others (chosen at random from the list) to send as a message. Your recipient of the message will play the song and then tap on the button for the correct title.

The iMessage app sends the data by transforming it into a URL. Both the `Quiz` class and the `Song` class have methods to convert their instances to and from an array of query items. The `MessagesViewController` class uses those methods to construct a URL, adds it to a new message, and inserts that message into the conversation. Then the app on the recipient's phone will take the URL of the message and turn it back into instances of `Quiz` and `Song`. Your next step will be to get the play button to start playing the song that was sent.

274 iOS 11 by Tutorials

Music playback

There are two ways to play music once you have a song: using the system player and using an application player.

If you use the system music player, your app acts like a remote control for the Music app, setting items on the playback queue and starting or stopping playback. Anything you do with the system player impacts what the user will see in Control Center and in the Music app.

If you use an application player, the system will stop playing (if currently playing) and your application will play, but changes you make won't have any impact on the playback queue of the Music app.

Capabilities

Before you try to play music or add anything to the user's music library, you need to find out what capabilities you have. Back in the **AuthorizationManager.swift**, you'll add a new operation and queue to manage this information.

Add this class above the `DownloadDeveloperTokenOperation` class:

```
class RequestCapabilitiesOperation: AsyncOperation {
  var capabilities: SKCloudServiceCapability?
  override func main() {
    SKCloudServiceController()
      .requestCapabilities { result, error in
        self.capabilities = result
        self.state = .finished
    }
  }
}
```

Then, under `authorize` in the `AuthorizationManager` class, add this code:

```
private static let capabilitiesOperation =
  RequestCapabilitiesOperation()
private static let capabilitesQueue: OperationQueue = {
  let queue = OperationQueue()
  queue.addOperation(capabilitiesOperation)
  // TODO: Add subscription operation
  return queue
}()
static func withCapabilities(completion:
  @escaping (SKCloudServiceCapability) -> Void) {
  let operation = BlockOperation {
    guard let capabilities =
    capabilitiesOperation.capabilities else { return }
```

```
        completion(capabilities)
    }
    operation.addDependency(capabilitiesOperation)
    capabilitesQueue.addOperation(operation)
}
```

This is very similar to the code you added before, but with a new queue to coordinate access to a new piece of information. The capabilities returned will indicate if you can play back music for the user, and if not, if they're eligible for a subscription.

Subscribing

As of this writing, Apple Music has "well past 20 million" subscribers, maybe as high as 40 million, or more. Whatever the number, there are a lot! But not every user of your app will be an Apple Music subscriber. For your MusicKit-enabled app, you'll want to offer your users an easy way to sign up. Plus, if you participate in Apple's affiliate program (https://www.apple.com/itunes/affiliates/), you can make some money when users sign up.

You'll check for this state and show a system subscription view. In `capabilitiesQueue`, replace the `TODO` with the following:

```
// 1
let subscribeOperation = BlockOperation {
  guard let capabilities =
    capabilitiesOperation.capabilities else { return }
  // 2
  if capabilities.contains(.musicCatalogPlayback) == false,
    capabilities.contains(.musicCatalogSubscriptionEligible) {
    // 3
    DispatchQueue.main.async {
      // 4
      let signupController = SKCloudServiceSetupViewController()
      // 5
      signupController.load(options:
      [.action: SKCloudServiceSetupAction.subscribe]) {
        isLoaded, error in
        guard error == nil else {
          print("Error loading subscription view:" +
            " \(error!.localizedDescription)")
          return
        }
        // 6
        if isLoaded {
          signupController.show(true)
        }
      }
    }
  }
}
```

```
}
// 7
subscribeOperation.addDependency(capabilitiesOperation)
queue.addOperation(subscribeOperation)
```

Taking it line-by-line:

1. You create a new block operation to perform this check.

2. You present the subscription view if `capabilities` *does not* contain the `musicCatalogPlayback` capability, but *does* contain the `musicCatalogSubscriptionEligible` capability.

3. Because you're about to present a view controller, you'll do this next part on the main queue.

4. The system view controller to use is `SKCloudServiceSetupViewController`.

5. First call `load`. You can specify some options, such as to show a specific song in the subscription view.

6. Once the view controller is loaded, you can present it like any other view controller. Because this class (`AuthorizationManager`) is not a view controller, I've included an extension in the project that will let you show it from here in a new `UIWindow`. Take a look at the extension in **UIViewController+extensions.swift** if you want to see how it's done.

7. You don't want this block operation to run until the `capabilitiesOperation` has finished, so you add the dependency here and then add this operation to the queue.

Adding the player

Next, you'll add playback and manage the state of the play/pause button. The play button is connected to the `playPauseButton` outlet. Open **SongSelectionViewController.swift** and add this import line:

```
import MediaPlayer
```

Then, add the following under the `bottomMargin` declaration:

```
private let musicPlayerController: MPMusicPlayerController
  = MPMusicPlayerController.systemMusicPlayer
```

You'll use the system player to playback music.

At the end of `viewDidLoad`, add this code:

```
// 1
musicPlayerController.setQueue(with: [quiz.song.id])
// 2
musicPlayerController.prepareToPlay()
// 3
musicPlayerController.beginGeneratingPlaybackNotifications()
// 4
NotificationCenter.default.addObserver(
  forName: .MPMusicPlayerControllerPlaybackStateDidChange,
  object: musicPlayerController, queue: OperationQueue.main) {
    [weak self] (_) in
    guard let `self` = self else { return }

    // 5
    self.playPauseButton.isEnabled = true
    switch self.musicPlayerController.playbackState {
    case .playing:
      self.playPauseButton.setImage(
        #imageLiteral(resourceName: "Pause"), for: .normal)
    default:
      self.playPauseButton.setImage(
        #imageLiteral(resourceName: "Play"), for: .normal)
    }
}

// 6
AuthorizationManager.withCapabilities {
  [weak self] (capabilities) in
  guard let `self` = self else { return }
  // 7
  self.playPauseButton.isEnabled =
    capabilities.contains(.musicCatalogPlayback)
}
```

Here's what you added:

1. This will overwrite the current playback queue with the correct song for the quiz. Note that you use the ID of the song to tell the player what to play.

2. It can take a little time once you request playback to start before the player actually starts playing. To help reduce that time, you tell the player to get ready, so by the time the user taps the play button, it might be ready to play.

3. You want to be notified when the playback state changes. To get those, you have to tell the player to start generating notifications.

4. Add an observer for the state change notification.

5. When the state changes, you set the image of the button to play or pause to reflect the current state.

6. Here, you use the capabilities method you added earlier to gain access to that setting.

7. You only enable the play button if the capabilities shows you that you can play back music.

The call to beginGeneratingPlaybackNotifications should be balanced, so below viewDidLoad, add this deinit code:

```
deinit {
    musicPlayerController.endGeneratingPlaybackNotifications()
}
```

The last step in getting the player to play is to replace the TODO in playPauseTapped with this:

```
playPauseButton.isEnabled = false
if musicPlayerController.playbackState == .playing {
    musicPlayerController.pause()
} else {
    musicPlayerController.play()
}
```

In the time between the first tap on the button and the change to the playback state, you don't want the user to be able to tap the button again. Therefore, the first thing you do is disable the button. Then, if the player is playing, you pause it, and if it's not playing, you tell it to play.

Build and run; select a song and you should be able to tap the play button to hear it.

> **Note:** If you're running on the simulator, this is where things will start to break down for you. The code to get a list of songs should work fine, but there is no Music app on the simulator, so playback will not work.

Handling errors

Note that there are two possible sources of information about errors: the HTTP status code, and an errors array in the body of the response. There may also be situations that you might think of as an error that don't indicate an error in either of those.

For example, if you request multiple resources by ID that aren't found, you may get a status code of 200 (OK) and an empty data array. For robust error handling, you'll need to check for all of these conditions.

For more information, see the documentation here: http://apple.co/2hUlyjL.

Where to go from here?

The WWDC session "Introducing MusicKit" at https://developer.apple.com/videos/play/wwdc2017/502/ covers the basics of MusicKit playback — basically what you already covered in this chapter.

Now you have all the data you need to add more information to the app. You can show how much time it took for the user to pick their answer (using `musicPlayerController.currentPlaybackTime`), download the album artwork to show in the `SongAnswerViewController`, limit the list of top 40 songs by genre, change the list from using charts to searching the whole catalog (https://api.music.apple.com/v1/catalog/{storefront}/search), or even search the user's heavy rotation (https://api.music.apple.com/v1/me/history/heavy-rotation) for music. For that last one, you'll need the user token. To see some of these in action, check out the finished project for this chapter.

The Apple Music API Reference has information about all the endpoints you can call and each of the parameters you can use for them. You can find that at https://developer.apple.com/library/content/documentation/NetworkingInternetWeb/Conceptual/AppleMusicWebServicesReference/index.html.

Chapter 14: Password AutoFill

By Andy Pereira

Friction is the resistance that one surface encounters when moving against another surface. Without it, you wouldn't be able to drive, run, or even hold your phone.

However, if you're a developer, friction is bad. One source of friction your users encounter regularly is the dreaded login screen. Maybe it's an app for a website you just signed up for, or perhaps you were just logged out from a frequently used app. It really doesn't matter, though — these all are a source of pain for users.

New in iOS 11 is Password AutoFill. With a few small additions to your login screen, you can provide a login experience with the least amount of friction possible.

In this chapter, you'll learn how to use iOS 11's two new `UITextContentType` attributes to enable Password AutoFill, and use Associated Domains to link your website's saved credentials with your native iOS application.

Getting started

Open the **AppManager** starter project found in the **iOS** directory of the starter project folder for this chapter. Build and run.

App Manager is your next big idea for an app that will safely store all of your top secret project ideas. Therefore, you'll need users to log in. The app already has a login screen, but it doesn't have any validation checks and lets you log in without any username or password.

To fix this, open **LoginViewController.swift**, and add the following two methods to `LoginViewController`:

```
// 1
private func validate(username: String?, password: String?)
  -> Bool {
  guard let username = username,
    let password = password,
    username.count >= 5,
    password.count >= 5 else {
      return false
  }
  return true
}
// 2
private func enableLoginButton(_ enable: Bool) {
  loginButton.isEnabled = enable
  loginButton.alpha = enable ? 1.0 : 0.5
}
```

Here's what you added:

1. `validate(username:password:)` does a simple check to ensure that the username and password fields have enough characters to be valid. In this case, the rule is that both fields must have at least five characters.

2. `enableLoginButton(_:)` is a convenience method to disable and gray out the login button if the fields are invalid.

Next, update `viewDidLoad()` by adding the following line after call to `super`:

```
enableLoginButton(false)
```

The app will disable the login button but won't re-enable it, even if the validation requirements are met. To fix that, you'll add two `UITextFieldDelegate` methods:

- `textField(_:shouldChangeCharactersIn:replacementString:)`

- `textFieldShouldReturn(_:)`

Start by adding `textField(_:shouldChangeCharactersIn:replacementString:)` to **LoginViewController.swift**:

```swift
// 1
extension LoginViewController: UITextFieldDelegate {
  // 2
  func textField(_ textField: UITextField,
    shouldChangeCharactersIn range: NSRange,
    replacementString string: String) -> Bool {

    var usernameText = username.text
    var passwordText = password.text
    if let text = textField.text {
      // 3
      let proposed = (text as NSString)
        .replacingCharacters(in: range, with: string)
      if textField == username {
        usernameText = proposed
      } else {
        passwordText = proposed
      }
    }
    // 4
    let isValid = validate(username: usernameText,
                           password: passwordText)
    enableLoginButton(isValid)
    return true
  }

  // More to come next
}
```

Taking this step-by-step:

1. To keep things organized, add an extension to `LoginViewController` and make it conform to `UITextFieldDelegate`.

2. Implement `textField(_:shouldChangeCharactersIn:replacementString:)`.

3. Get the value of the text the user is trying to enter, not what is displayed on the screen at this moment. This lets the next step work in real-time as the user types.

4. Validate that the text entered is a valid username/password combination, and enable the login button if it is. This means the login button will become enabled the moment the validation rules are met.

Finally, add `textFieldShouldReturn(_:)` to the extension after `// More to come` next:

```
func textFieldShouldReturn(_ textField: UITextField) -> Bool {
  if textField == username {
    password.becomeFirstResponder()
  } else {
    password.resignFirstResponder()
    if validate(username: username.text,
      password: password.text) {
      login(loginButton)
    }
  }
  return false
}
```

If the validation rules are met, the app will automatically log in when the user taps **Done** on the keyboard. This will provide a smooth experience for your user.

Build and run, and try out the new validation behavior. You're still able to enter any combination of words, so long as both contain at least five characters.

Now that the foundation of your login screen has been laid, it's time to add Password AutoFill.

Basic autofill

Autofill has two distinct modes in which it can work.

The first mode provides users a link to their saved passwords from the device/iCloud Keychain. By doing this, your app will automatically show a QuickType bar with a lock button.

The second way Password AutoFill can work is by prompting the user with a username and password in the QuickType bar without having to select the lock button. At the moment, it will suggest up to two usernames that can be auto populated. This makes logging in even easier than the previous step.

You'll start by implementing the first mode: providing a link to the user's passwords.

To add this, open **Main.Storyboard**, and select the **Username** field in the **Login View Controller** scene. Select the **Attributes inspector**, and under **Text Input Traits**, change **Content Type** to **Username**.

Repeat the same thing for the password field, but choose **Passsword** for the **Content Type**. With these two changes, your app is now ready to autofill passwords!

> **Note:** In this app, usernames are simply strings that contain five or more characters. However, your app may be using email addresses as the username. While there is a **Content Type** for email, you'll need to set it to **Username** in order for Password AutoFill to work. To make emails work properly as a username, all you need to do is set the **Keyboard Type** to **E-mail Address**.

Before you can test this, you'll need to have a saved password on your device. If you don't have one, iOS won't display the QuickType bar.

If you're using the simulator, navigate to **Settings/Safari/Autofill** and turn on **Names and Passwords**.

Still in the simulator, open **Safari** and navigate to https://appmanager-rw.herokuapp.com. This is a sample website that was created specifically for this tutorial and *it does not record or save your input in any way*. For now, enter any username and password combo that you would like, and select **Login**. Be sure to save the password when prompted.

Now, build and run your app, and select the username or password field. You'll see that you have the QuickType bar with the lock button.

If you select the lock button on the Simulator, you'll be prompted with a password screen. The password is your *device's* password. On a Touch ID enabled device, you will be prompted to authenticate with your fingerprint. You'll then see a screen with all your saved passwords.

> **Note**: If you're running on the Simulator and did not set a passcode, just enter a single space when prompted for the passcode.

When you select any of the saved passwords, the modal dialog will dismiss, your app's username and password fields will be filled in, and you can continue logging in.

That takes care of the first way to implement Password Autofill. Next, you'll implement the second method by associating your website and using the user's login info for your site.

Associating your website

Instead of coding in this section, you're going to use the sample Vapor project included in the **Server** directory of the starter project. You're going to deploy a website to Heroku, which has SSL/HTTPS configured. Having an SSL-configured website is required for this next section to work.

In order to continue, there are a few requirements:

1. Use a physical device. The Simulator does not currently work with this feature.

2. Have a developer account with Apple.

3. Sign up for a free Heroku account at http://heroku.com. There is no need to configure any site, as you'll do this later. Just remember your username and password.

4. Have some familiarity with the command-line.

5. Have your Apple developer **Team ID**. This is not the ID found in an Xcode project settings, but the one on developer.apple.com, under your account's **Membership** page.

In the **Server** directory of this chapter's starter files, unzip **AppManager-server.zip**. In Terminal, navigate into the **AppManager-server** directory of this chapter's starter project directory:

```
cd Path/To/Starter/Server/AppManager-server
```

Verify that you have Homebrew installed on your machine by entering the following command in Terminal:

```
brew help
```

Note: If you get an error message that brew is not a command, follow the steps to install it at https://brew.sh.

Next, you'll need to install Vapor to build the project and deploy it to Heroku. Run the following commands to install Vapor:

```
brew tap vapor/homebrew-tap
brew update
brew install vapor
```

Note: If you get an error that Vapor cannot be built, and that you need to install GCC compiler, run `brew install gcc` command in Terminal. You may also see brew complaining about `xcrun`. If that happens, you need to set the Command Line Tools via Xcode preferences. Go to **Xcode/Preferences/Locations** and set **Command Line Tools** by selecting the appropriate version of Xcode from the drop-down menu.

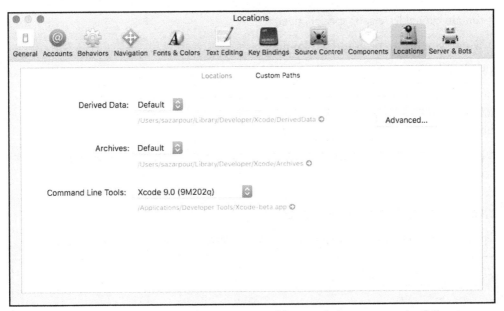

Finally, you need to install the Heroku command line tools by running the following:

```
brew install heroku
```

When finished, login to Heroku with the following command:

```
heroku login
```

You're almost there. There's only a few more steps left!

Next, enter your Heroku credentials. To finish the setup process, initialize a git repo for the project:

```
git init
git add .
git commit -m "Initial Commit"
```

This will prepare your project to be deployed to Heroku.

Next, deploy your project to Heroku by running the following:

```
vapor heroku init
```

This will prompt you with several questions. Answer the questions with the following:

- **Would you like to provide a custome Heroku app name?** y

- **Custom app name:** Name this something simple and relevant, so long as it does not contain capital letters, or special characters.

- **Would you like to push to Heroku now?** y

All other answers can be **n**.

This process will take several minutes to complete. At this point, your project code is uploading to Heroku and installing the Swift tools necessary to build on the server. Once this is complete, pushing your code will be much quicker.

While the code is being uploaded to Heroku, you can set up the associated domains in Xcode.

Enabling associated domains

Open the **AppManager** Xcode project and select **AppManager** in the Project navigator.

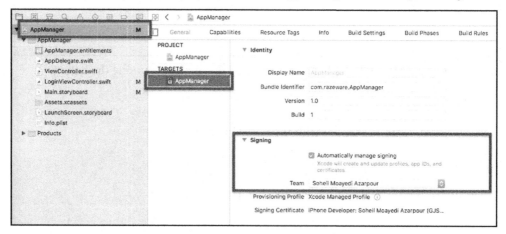

Select **AppManager** target in the Editor pane, and make sure the **General** tab is selected. Under **Signing**, verify **Automatically manage signing** is checked, and select your Team from the dropdown.

While you're still on that page, change the **Bundle ID** to be something unique for you. Remember to keep the standard reverse domain name pattern:

```
com.<yourdomain>.AppManager
```

Now, switch to **Capabilities**, and enable **Associated Domains**.

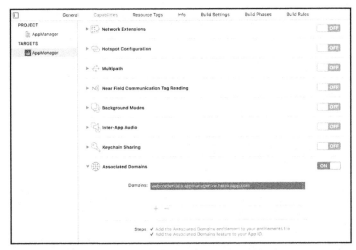

Select the + under the table. Now you will see an entry with the text `webcredentials:example.com`. This is a key for Apple to know which website's credentials will be associated with this application. In the text field, after `webcredentials:`, replace `example.com` with the Heroku custom name you set up in the previous step, plus the Heroku app domain, like the following:

```
webcredentials:<yourcustomname>.herokuapp.com
```

> **Note:** Do not put `https://` in this entry. Apple will take care of handling this check for you, so keep it restricted to domain names.

Finishing up

Go back to Terminal and verify the Heroku deploy is finished. Then open the server project in Xcode with the following command:

```
vapor xcode
```

When prompted, enter **y** to open the Xcode project. Open **Public/.well-known/apple-app-site-association**, and replace the tokens in the file with your **Team ID** and your app's **Bundle ID**. **apple-app-site-association** is a file, which lives on your domain, that Apple will look for if you enable the Associated Domains capability in your app.

Apple recommends you put the file in a directory named **.well-known**, but it can live at the root of your domain as well. Password AutoFill will check that your Team ID combined with the Bundle ID are found under the **apps** node of the file. This ensures a secure link between your app and your website without having to do any security on your end.

Go back to Terminal, commit your changes and deploy them to Heroku by entering the following commands:

```
git add .
git commit -m "Added webcredentials"
vapor heroku push
```

> **Note:** The push to Heroku may take a few minutes.

You can test that the changes worked by going to Safari on your iOS device and navigating to https://yourherokudomain.herokuapp.com/ and log in. When prompted, save your password.

Finally, go back to the AppManager Xcode project. Build and run, and select the username or password field.

You'll now see a suggested username in the QuickType bar. Selecting it will fill in your credentials, thus eliminating nearly all friction your users would have faced otherwise.

Notice that you don't have to write *any* code to make this feature work. Simply setting the Content Type of your username and password fields will automatically enable this feature if a properly-configured **apple-app-site-association** file is found on your domain.

Where to go from here?

In this chapter, you learned how to enable Password AutoFill in your application, and how to associate your app and your SSL-configured website that has login capabilities. It's clear that Apple is doing everything possible to make it easy for developers to enable this feature, so that it's even easier for your users to log in!

You can learn more from the WWDC 2017 video covering the topic, "WWDC17 Session 206 - Introducing Password AutoFill for Apps": http://apple.co/2vV8ekS.

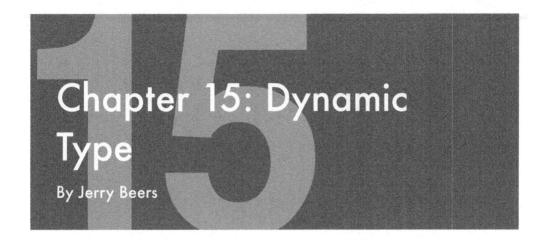

Chapter 15: Dynamic Type

By Jerry Beers

Have you ever looked at someone else's iPhone or iPad and noticed that their text size is different from what you're used to? Maybe they have the size turned up to make it easier for them to see. Or maybe they have smaller text to fit more content on the screen.

This is a really thoughtful feature from Apple to allow users to customize their device to the text size that suits them best. But if your app doesn't play along, your users won't get the benefit of this setting.

It's handy for a user to be able to specify if they want smaller text, but this feature is more important than that. The sample app for this chapter, MedJournal, is an example of the important information people have come to rely on their iPhones for.

Open the starter project, build and run, and you'll see the main interface of the app. From anywhere in the app, if you triple tap, the app will show a blurred snapshot of the interface (the blurring process may take several seconds).

> **Note:** On the Simulator, the blurring process can take as long as 60 seconds. Be patient or use a device to test this.

Do not adjust your television...

You can then single tap to get back to the normal interactive app. This "feature" illustrates what the app might look like to someone with low visual acuity. As you can see, you can't really read any of the text.

Dynamic type is important for the millions of people without perfect vision to be able to actually see and use your app.

A brief review

While the basic support for dynamic type has been available since iOS 7, iOS 11 introduces a number of new features to make it easier to adopt in your app. When you create a view with text, like a label, one of the properties you can set is the font. You can specify a system font, a custom font, or a font style.

If you specify a style, the system will assign the actual font based on the user's preferred content size. There are several styles available, such as "body", "headline" and "footnote". You can use these different styles to create text elements of different sizes that respond to the user's settings.

You don't have to make every text element respond to changes. Usually, you only have to worry about the ones focused on content. You can set the font style in Interface Builder or in code, using `UIFont.preferredFont(forTextStyle:)`.

In the Settings app, under **Display & Brightness**, you'll find a **Text Size** setting. This setting lets you choose between seven different font sizes. Under **General\Accessibility\Larger Text**, the user can turn on a switch that makes five larger sizes available.

Beginning with iOS 10, your code can read the value of the user's setting using the `preferredContentSizeCategory` property on `UIApplication`, or on objects conforming to the `UITraitCollection` protocol. You can also be notified when the user changes this setting while your app is running, using the `UIContentSizeCategoryDidChange` notification, or through `traitCollectionDidChange`.

How dynamic type impacts layout

There are several layout scenarios where you should consider the length of text: displaying user-supplied content, translating text into different languages, and dynamic type.

For example, when you're designing your user interface, you may think that there is plenty of room on the screen to display all of your text on one line. But if the user chooses a very large font, that may no longer be true. This means that you need to think about more constraints than you may be used to.

If you're already in the habit of adding trailing constraints to your labels, congratulations! You're ready to support dynamic type. But if you're not in that habit yet, there's good news: Xcode 9 will help you get in the habit.

In fact, open **Main.storyboard** in the sample project and you'll see a new warning right away: Trailing constraints are missing on some of the views.

Select the Doctor Scene and add trailing constraints >= **0** to the superview margin for the **Name**, **Phone**, **Address**, **City/State/ZIP** (CSZ) and **Notes** labels. You should now see all the warnings have cleared.

You may also want to think differently about the number of lines for your label. If your label has number of lines set to 1 and line break set to "truncate tail" (the default settings), two things will happen:

1. Your new trailing constraints will keep the label from running off the right of the screen.

2. The right side will start to truncate the text grows.

That may be what you want, but if you need the text to wrap, then you'll have to set number of lines to **0** and line break to **word wrap**.

If the setting for text size is very large, it may make sense to adopt a different layout entirely. For example, rather than having text side-by-side, it may make more sense to stack the text vertically. You'll see an example of that later in this chapter.

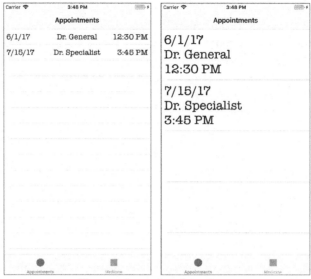

Changing layout based on text size

Getting started

Let's convert the starter project to use dynamic type. The first thing you need to do is set a style for each label you want to be dynamic.

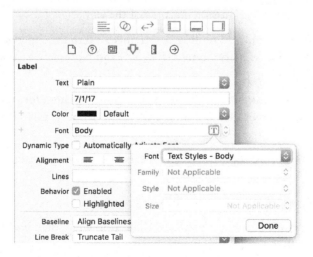

In **Main.storyboard**, select the **Appointments Scene** and click on the **Date Label**. In the Attributes inspector, change the font to the **Body** text style.

In Xcode 9, you can instruct the system to adjust the font size automatically when the user changes their preferred size. Just below the Font setting, check the **Automatically Adjusts Font** checkbox:

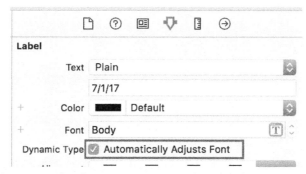

Repeat both of these steps for the **Doctor Name Label** and the **Time Label**.

Then select the **Medicine Scene** and repeat for the **Title** and **Detail** labels.

Now, select the **Doctor Scene** and change the following:

- Name Label style to **Headline**
- Phone, Address, and CSZ Labels to **Footnote**
- Notes Label to **Body**.

Make sure the **Automatically Adjusts Font** checkbox is checked for all of the labels.

Using the Accessibility Inspector

Build and run the app in the simulator. To change the text size and see your labels adjust, you could background the app, go to the Settings app, navigate to **General\Accessibility\Larger Text**, set a new setting, then switch back to your app — but that's a very tedious way to change the font size!

There's a much better way. From Xcode, click on the **Xcode** menu, then **Open Developer Tool\Accessibility Inspector**. This will bring up a window that lets you view and modify the settings for the simulator.

Make sure the simulator is selected and then click on the **Settings** button. From there, you can drag the Font size slider around. When you let go, the size of the text in your app will automatically adjust to the new setting! Try setting the value to one of the larger sizes and then triple-tapping the interface to show the blurry version.

> **Note:** If you're having trouble seeing the font size change in your app, first make sure you're letting go of the slider, as the size won't change as you drag the slider around until you let go. Second, the connection between the simulator and the Accessibility Inspector can sometimes be fragile, so try rebuilding your app after you've opened the Accessibility Inspector. Third, make sure the right instance of the simulator is selected.

If you tap on a doctor to see the doctor detail view and set the font size to one of the four largest sizes, you'll notice that you have a problem — things start to overlap.

At design time, there is no overlap of the labels, and the Notes label has a constraint to position it below the profile image view. But when the user chooses a font that is large enough, you can see that you'll need some more constraints, specifically between the Notes Label and the CSZ Label.

Baseline to baseline

When creating constraints between labels in a vertical direction, you might create a standard spacing constraint between the bottom of the first label and the top of the second.

Dr. General
555-123-4321
123 Main St, Suite 250
Frisco, TX 75034

This constraint will work, but there is a better way to create constraints between two text elements with standard spacing baseline-to-baseline constraints, like this:

Dr. General
555-123-4321
123 Main St, Suite 250
Frisco, TX 75034

The spacing that looks best between text that is very small, is not the same spacing that will look best between text that is very large. When you create a baseline-to-baseline constraint with standard spacing, the system will take text size into account when determining what that standard spacing should be.

So, before you add your new constraints between the Notes Label and CSZ Label, change the existing top–bottom constraints into baseline–baseline constraints. In the Doctor Scene:

1. Select the **Name Label** and double click on the **Bottom Space to Phone Label** constraint in the Size inspector.

2. Change the **First Item** to **Phone Label.First Baseline**.

3. Change the **Second Item** to **Name Label.Last Baseline**.

If the text spans multiple lines, the constraint will go from the baseline of the last line of text in the Name Label to the baseline of the first line of text in the Phone Label.

Because the Constant of the constraint is already set to Standard, you don't need to to anything more to get the system to position the labels using the best vertical spacing between them. Repeat for the **Phone–Address** and **Address–CSZ** spacing.

You have a somewhat complicated relationship between the Notes label, the Profile Image View, and the CSZ Label. You want the Notes label to be below the Profile Image View, but if the text above it gets too tall, you also want it to always stay below the CSZ label.

Here's how you accomplish that:

1. Add a baseline–baseline constraint between the **CSZ label** and the **Notes label** that is >= the Standard value.

2. Change the existing **Notes Top Space to Profile Image View** constraint priority to **Low** (250).

3. Add another **Notes Top Space to Profile Image View** constraint, but >= the Standard value.

This will keep the Notes label from overlapping the image view, and try to keep it a standard space below it, but allow the notes to move down, if necessary.

There are only a few touch-ups left to do:

1. Increase the **horizontal compression resistance priority** of the **Profile image view** to **751**, to keep it from getting compressed as text gets larger.

2. Change the **Lines** of the **Address** and CSZ labels to **0**.

3. Change the **Line Break** of the **Address** and CSZ labels to **Word Wrap**.

Notice that you didn't change the Lines and Line Break properties of the Name and Phone Number labels.

Build and run, and you can see how the Phone Number label and the Address label behave differently. Large text will clip at the edge for the phone number, but wrap to multiple lines for the address. Use whichever behavior you need in a particular situation.

UIFontMetrics

When you choose a font style, you no longer have control over the font used in your app, since the system will choose the font for you. So, if your design calls for a different font, will you find yourself left out of all the Dynamic Type goodness?

Nope! `UIFontMetrics` is a new class that helps scale your custom fonts based on the user's preferred size.

That's not all — `UIFontMetrics` has a couple of other tricks up its sleeve. You can use it to scale numbers, which is useful if you want to adjust the constant of a constraint based on the text size. And you can scale a font while specifying a maximum point size, for cases when your user interface cannot handle text larger than a certain size.

Custom fonts

You'll now change the font of your app to use a custom font. Select the labels in the **Appointments Scene** and change their font to a custom font, such as **American Typewriter 17.0**. At this point, you may notice a new warning:

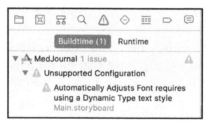

The Interface Builder checkbox **Automatically Adjusts Font** corresponds to the property `adjustFontForContentSizeCategory`. It's only appropriate to set this value to `true` when using a font style, or when using `UIFontMetrics.scaledFont(for:)`.

Since Interface Builder doesn't know what you're doing with these labels in code, it warns you that you should not set that checkbox to `true` if you're not using a font style. Clear the checkbox for all three labels.

Repeat this process for the labels in the **Medicine Scene**, setting the font to **American Typewriter 17.0** and clearing the **Automatically Adjusts Font** checkbox.

For the **Doctor Scene**, you're going to use a couple of different fonts:

• Set the **Name** label to **American Typewriter Semibold 17.0**.

• Set the **Notes** label to **American Typewriter 20.0**.

• Set the other three to **American Typewriter 13.0**.

Be sure to clear the checkbox on all of those views.

Now that the custom font is set, you'll add the code to make it adjust to the user's preferred size. Open **AppointmentCell.swift** and add the following code before `setupConstraints()`:

```
override func awakeFromNib() {
  super.awakeFromNib()
  // 1
  let metrics = UIFontMetrics(forTextStyle: .body)
  // 2
  dateLabel.font = metrics.scaledFont(for: dateLabel.font)
  doctorNameLabel.font =
    metrics.scaledFont(for: doctorNameLabel.font)
  timeLabel.font = metrics.scaledFont(for: timeLabel.font)

  // 3
  dateLabel.adjustsFontForContentSizeCategory = true
  doctorNameLabel.adjustsFontForContentSizeCategory = true
  timeLabel.adjustsFontForContentSizeCategory = true
}
```

Here's what this is doing:

1. In this case, you can use the same `UIFontMetrics` instance for all the labels, so you create one with the `.body` style.

2. Then you tell each label to use a scaled font using the `UIFontMetrics` instance. You pass the font that was set in the storyboard as the font to scale.

3. Setting this property is the same as setting the checkbox in Interface Builder.

Now, open **DoctorViewController.swift** and add this code:

```
override func awakeFromNib() {
  super.awakeFromNib()
  loadViewIfNeeded()
  nameLabel.font = UIFontMetrics(forTextStyle: .headline)
    .scaledFont(for: nameLabel.font)
  phoneLabel.font = UIFontMetrics(forTextStyle: .footnote)
    .scaledFont(for: phoneLabel.font)
  addressLabel.font = UIFontMetrics(forTextStyle: .footnote)
    .scaledFont(for: addressLabel.font)
  cityStateZipLabel.font =
    UIFontMetrics(forTextStyle: .footnote)
    .scaledFont(for: cityStateZipLabel.font)
  notesLabel.font = UIFontMetrics(forTextStyle: .body)
    .scaledFont(for: notesLabel.font)

  nameLabel.adjustsFontForContentSizeCategory = true
  phoneLabel.adjustsFontForContentSizeCategory = true
```

```
   addressLabel.adjustsFontForContentSizeCategory = true
   cityStateZipLabel.adjustsFontForContentSizeCategory = true
   notesLabel.adjustsFontForContentSizeCategory = true
}
```

No surprises here; this is simply doing the same thing, and using the right style for each label.

Finally, open **MedicineViewController.swift** and replace these lines in `tableView(_:cellForRowAt:)`:

```
cell.textLabel?.text = medicine.name
cell.detailTextLabel?.text = medicine.dose
```

With these:

```
if let textLabel = cell.textLabel {
  textLabel.text = medicine.name
  textLabel.font = UIFontMetrics(forTextStyle: .body)
    .scaledFont(for: textLabel.font)
  textLabel.adjustsFontForContentSizeCategory = true
}

if let detailLabel = cell.detailTextLabel {
  detailLabel.text = medicine.dose
  detailLabel.font = UIFontMetrics(forTextStyle: .body)
    .scaledFont(for: detailLabel.font)
  detailLabel.adjustsFontForContentSizeCategory = true
}
```

Build and run, and you'll see the interface using your custom font, dynamically adjusted to the correct size.

Scaling sizes

Your little app doesn't have any size values in code, but you can simulate that situation.

Start by opening **Main.storyboard**, selecting the Doctor Scene, and creating an outlet for the width constraint on the Profile Image View. Name the outlet `profileImageSizeConstraint`. Add this constant below the `IBOutlet`:

```
private let defaultImageSize: CGFloat = 128
```

And add this code to the bottom of the class:

```
override func traitCollectionDidChange(
  _ previousTraitCollection: UITraitCollection?) {
```

```
// 1
let preferredSize =
  traitCollection.preferredContentSizeCategory

if preferredSize !=
  previousTraitCollection?.preferredContentSizeCategory {

  // 2
  setImageSize()
  }
}

private func setImageSize() {
  // 3
  profileImageSizeConstraint.constant =
    UIFontMetrics.default.scaledValue(for: defaultImageSize)
}
```

Here's what this does:

1. The system calls the view controller's `traitCollectionDidChange` method when the preferred content size category changes. There are several other traits that can change, so you first check that it was this setting that changed.

2. Then you call your `setImageSize` method...

3. ...which sets the constant on the constraint to a scaled value, passing the original value to scale. Notice that this uses the `default` instance of `UIFontMetrics`, which simply uses the `.body` font style.

There are two constraint changes you have to make to avoid some constraint errors in the console when running on smaller devices (5s/6/6s/7) and at the largest text settings:

1. Change the priority of the width constraint on the profile image view to 999.

2. Add a trailing space constraint on the profile image view >= 16 to the safe area.

If you build and run, you'll see the size of the profile image view grow as the `UIFontMetrics` class scales the constant for its constraint.

Images

If you want to evenly scale your image based on the text size, you can use the `scaledValue` method on `UIFontMetrics` and a size constraint, as you've just done in the previous section. However, there is an easier way to adjust image sizes for accessibility.

In fact, if you just want your image to be visible for people using the accessibility text size categories, there is a property you can set that will handle the resizing for you.

`UIImageView`'s `adjustsImageSizeForAccessibilityContentSizeCategory` property, when set to `true`, will cause your image size to remain the same for all seven text sizes. But if the user chooses one of the five additional accessibility text sizes, your image will be scaled up to ensure your users can see it.

You can also set this value in Interface Builder, using the **Accessibility\Adjusts Image Size** checkbox in the Attributes inspector for an image view. Try it out:

1. Remove the `traitCollectionDidChange` and `setImageSize` methods from **DoctorViewController.swift**.

2. Open **Main.storyboard** and remove the image view width constraint.

3. Check the **Adjusts Image Size** checkbox

Build and run and change the text size using the Accessibility Inspector to several different values. You should notice the following:

• The image remains the same using any of the smaller text sizes.

• The image is scaled up for the five largest text sizes.

Modifying the layout

It may make sense to adjust the structure of the layout when the user's preferred font size is very large. In fact, you may have already noticed that table cells with a system style will do this for you!

Build and run and view the Medicine tab. Change the font to one of the five largest accessibility sizes and you'll notice that the cell goes from a side-by-side layout to a top-to-bottom layout.

There are a couple of checks that you can do in code to decide whether to adjust the layout:

1. You can check the `preferredContentSizeCategory.isAccessibilityCategory` property of `traitCollection`. This will return `true` if the user has selected one of the five larger accessibility text sizes.

2. You can use comparison operators; `UIContentSizeCategory` implements operators for comparison. For example, you could adjust your layout if `traitCollection.preferredContentSizeCategory > .extraLarge`.

You'll modify the appointment cell to adjust its layout.

Because you're going to set the constraints in code, you'll need to remove them from the storyboard. Open **Main.storyboard**, select one of the labels in the Appointments Scene, and clear all the constraints. To do this, click the triangle in the lower right and choose **Clear Constraints** under **All Views in Appointment Cell**.

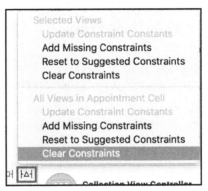

You have a `setupConstraints` method in **AppointmentCell.swift** from the starter project, but nothing is calling it. Add this code to `awakeFromNib`:

```
override func awakeFromNib() {
  ...
  setupConstraints()
  updateConstraints()
}
```

`setupConstraints` creates three arrays of constraints: one common to both layouts, one for the regular layout, and one for the layout when larger text is selected.

`updateConstraints` is a `UIView` method that you need to override to activate the correct constraints, so add that now:

```
override func updateConstraints() {
  NSLayoutConstraint.activate(commonConstraints)

  if traitCollection.preferredContentSizeCategory
    .isAccessibilityCategory {

    NSLayoutConstraint.deactivate(regularConstraints)
    NSLayoutConstraint.activate(largeTextConstraints)
  } else {
    NSLayoutConstraint.deactivate(largeTextConstraints)
    NSLayoutConstraint.activate(regularConstraints)
  }

    super.updateConstraints()
}
```

This uses the `isAccessibilityCategory` property to decide which constraints to activate, but you could use comparison operators here instead if you wanted.

Although this will set up the constraints properly when the view is first shown, you also need to check when the preferred size changes. Add the following override to the class:

```
override func traitCollectionDidChange(
  _ previousTraitCollection: UITraitCollection?) {

  let isAccessibilityCategory = traitCollection
    .preferredContentSizeCategory.isAccessibilityCategory

  if isAccessibilityCategory != previousTraitCollection?
    .preferredContentSizeCategory.isAccessibilityCategory {

    setNeedsUpdateConstraints()
  }
}
```

This is similar to what you did before in `traitCollectionDidChange`, but this time you're checking if the `isAccessibilityCategory` value is different and then calling `setNeedsUpdateConstraints`, which will trigger another call to `updateConstraints`.

Build and run, and you'll see the layout change when you pick one of the five larger text sizes.

Where to go from here?

There are a couple of sessions from WWDC 2017 that are helpful for this topic, including one that is a bit of a surprise!

- **Building Apps with Dynamic Type**: You would expect this sesstion to be loaded with good information on this topic, and you won't be disappointed. apple.co/2uSN6qX

- **Localizing with Xcode 9**: There's a little nugget here that shows you how to use a strings dictionary (`stringsdict` file) to create adaptive strings using `NSStringVariableWidthRuleType` and `variantFittingPresentationWidth` to present a completely different string based on the available space. This could be handy for a variety of situations! apple.co/2vuvUvF

Although you've covered quite a lot of territory in this chapter, if you're already using Auto Layout, adding support for dynamic type is really rather simple — and helpful for millions of users!

Conclusion

We hope this book has helped you get up to speed with the new changes in Xcode 9 and iOS 11.

If you have any questions or comments as you continue to develop for iOS 11, please stop by our forums at http://forums.raywenderlich.com.

Thank you again for purchasing this book. Your continued support is what makes the tutorials, books, videos, conferences and other things we do at raywenderlich.com possible — we truly appreciate it!

Wishing you all the best in your continued iOS 11 adventures,

– The *iOS 11 by Tutorials* team

Made in the USA
Columbia, SC
05 August 2019